Second Edition

COMPARATIVE ECONOMIC S·Y·S·T·E·M·S

Second Edition

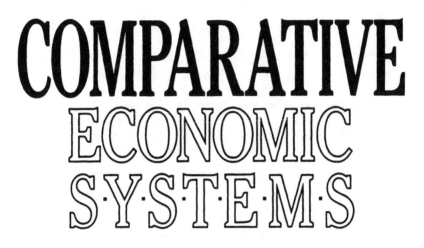

COMPARATIVE ECONOMIC S·Y·S·T·E·M·S

VOLUME I · MARKET AND STATE IN ECONOMIC SYSTEMS

Richard L. Carson

Routledge
Taylor & Francis Group

LONDON AND NEW YORK

First published 1997 by M.E. Sharpe

Published 2015 by Routledge
2 Park Square, Milton Park, Abingdon, Oxon OX14 4RN
711 Third Avenue, New York, NY 10017, USA

Routledge is an imprint of the Taylor & Francis Group, an informa business

Library of Congress Cataloging-in-Publication Data

Carson, Richard L.
Comparative economic systems / Richard L. Carson. — 2nd ed.
p.   cm.
Includes bibliographical references and index.
Contents: 1. Market and state in economic systems
ISBN 1-56324-920-0 (v. 1)
1. Comparative economics.
I. Title.
HB90.C37   1996
330—dc20
96-20587
CIP

ISBN 13: 9781563249204 (pbk)

Contents

List of Tables and Figures

Tables

Figures

Preface

Like its predecessor, the second edition of this volume represents an effort to analyze and understand economic systems by using the standard principles of supply, demand, and cost analysis, along with property rights. The basic framework is developed in chapter 1 and extended in the following four chapters. The political dimension of an economic system is also developed, and there is a brief examination of the compatibility of different economic and political organizations. Since the first edition appeared in 1990, much of the world has been engaged in one of history's great economic upheavals, in which state-managed economies of the Soviet type are transforming themselves into market-based systems. Nearly one-third of the world's population lives in these "transition" economies, and most of these people did not expect the experience to be as painful or as drawn out as it has proved to be. Most transitions have nevertheless been peaceful, and a diversity of experience is now available to study. Therefore, the coverage of transition is the biggest single change between the first and second editions.

As in the first edition, we begin with a discussion of property rights, which allows us to distinguish between different kinds of economic systems. A newly added appendix to chapter 1 develops the notion of common property (communal property rights) more thoroughly than before and uses this concept to analyze problems of resource depletion and environmental degradation. Chapter 2 deals with the traditional Soviet-type economy. Many observers now consider this to be an economic system of the past and indeed one of history's great failures in terms of increasing living standards, allocating resources efficiently, and producing in an environmentally friendly way. I basically agree with these views, but unless we achieve a basic understanding of this system, our efforts to comprehend the problems faced by transition economies are likely to fail.

Chapter 3 deals with the role of government in a market economy; chapter 4 analyzes historical systems; and chapter 5 explores theories of capitalist development, with capitalism viewed as a "pressure" economy. Following Janos Kornai, the latter refers to a kind of symmetry between a Soviet-type economy, which is based in part on shortage or "suction," and a capitalist market economy, which is based in part on pressure or nonprice competition among suppliers. The result is a quite different perspective on capitalism than that usually found in the economics literature. Chapter 5 also deals with the theories of Marx and Schumpeter, including the concept of "creative destruction."

Chapter 6 analyzes varieties of socialism, along with pretransition efforts to reform Soviet-type economies. Chapter 7 closes volume I with an exploration of transition problems. Included is an extended discussion of the nature of these difficulties, as well as the sequencing of reforms, the different types of reform, and an analysis of what has come to be known, rightly or wrongly, as the "Big Bang" approach to transition versus gradualism. Examples are drawn from several transition economies, mainly in Europe and with a focus on Russia, since volume II will deal in some depth with the Chinese economy and with other transition experiences. Chapter 7 also considers common denominators of these experiences and reasons for success or failure, in the sense of combining transition with economic growth. It is quite possible to jump from chapter 2 to chapter 6 and/or chapter 7, and then return to pick up some or all of chapters 3 through 5. The order of presentation in the book follows my own course at Carleton University, but I would not pretend that it is the only logical sequencing of these topics. I have tried to make the book flexible in this regard.

I intend this work to appeal to a variety of readers in terms of their backgrounds and interests. It should be accessible to anyone who has completed a standard one-year course in the principles of economics, but I have also found this material to be interesting to graduate students (not only those in economics) and believe it will be useful and interesting as well to specialists and businessmen dealing with one or more of the countries covered here.

Special thanks are due to Guylaine Malo, who did most of the word processing. She worked under a very tight schedule and was indispensable, despite the fact that English is not her first language. Also assisting in the word processing and doing excellent work were Nonie Shickle, Diane Berezowski, Charlotte Burba, and Lalita Figueredo. Finally, I would also like to thank the students and colleagues who have given me moral support. I have always found my students' enthusiasm for this subject to be a source of strength.

Second Edition

COMPARATIVE
ECONOMIC
S·Y·S·T·E·M·S

Chapter 1

Property Rights

Under capitalism, man exploits man. Under socialism, it's just
the reverse.
—Anonymous

Introduction to Property Rights

In every society, economic activity is organized via a network of institutions that
makes it possible to specialize and to cooperate in production and exchange, and
thus to solve the economic problem of allocating scarce resources among competing needs. This problem has an efficiency dimension concerned with stretch-
ing resources as far as possible and a social priorities dimension concerned with
deciding what mix of goods to produce and how to distribute them. In all cases,
there are many more potential needs for a nation's resources than they can
possibly be made to serve. Therefore, choices are necessary, and the nature of a
society's institutions plays a major role in determining how these choices are
made.

In recent history, economic systems have been divided into two major categories. Capitalism implies private ownership and socialism public ownership of
most of the material means of production and distribution (capital and natural
resources). On this basis, Canada, Sweden, West Germany, the United Kingdom,
Japan, the United States, France, Brazil, Italy, and Australia have been examples
of capitalism, while the Union of Soviet Socialist Republics, China, Cuba, Poland, Czechoslovakia, Hungary, East Germany, North Korea, Vietnam, and Yugoslavia have been examples of socialism.[1] Except for Yugoslavia and possibly
Hungary, they were also examples of Soviet-type economies that featured state
management as well as state ownership of the means of production. Following
the revolutionary changes of 1989–90, most of these have become transition
economies in which the role of private property is increasing and that of the state
is receding. A major purpose of this volume is to explore the nature of these
changes.

To this end, we first note that differences in legal ownership are less important in determining how a nation solves its economic problems than are differ-

3

ences in *property rights*. These include rights of individuals, firms, and government bodies to use or to decide how to use goods and services and exclude others from using them, to receive the income generated by their use, and to transfer them to others. We shall call these *use rights, income rights,* and *transfer* or *exchange rights,* respectively. In every modern economy, property rights govern the use of goods and services, the nature of exchange, and the behavior of producers and consumers. Property rights also affect relations between individuals and find expression implicitly as customs, traditions, and mores and explicitly as rules and laws. For this reason, they are also often called *property relations.* Therefore, it has been said that "property rights are an instrument of society and derive their significance from the fact that they help a man to form those expectations which he can reasonably hold in his dealings with others."[2] Property rights always underlie the institutions through which a nation solves its economic problems.

Forms of legal ownership often mean one thing in one set of circumstances and something else in another. For example, the Togliatti factory producing Ladas in the Union of Soviet Socialist Republics and the Renault works in France were both publicly owned during the 1980s, and both made automobiles. But whereas the former was integrated into the Soviet planning network, the latter stressed its independence from the government. A Soviet collective farmer had no right to sell his "private" plot, nor was he allowed to work it with hired labor, although he could keep any income that he and his family were able to earn by growing produce on it, and he could leave it to an heir. To capture such distinctions, we must look at property rights. Finally, many firms in transition economies have become legally "private" but have continued to operate much as they did when they were state-owned. In part, this is because property rights have not changed as much in practice as they have in law.

Let us define the *state* or *government* to be the collection of all public executive, legislative, and administrative bodies. We also include organs of the dominant political party in a one-party state (and, thus, of the Communist Party in countries where it is in power), but we exclude public enterprises whose main task is production. Government may be defined as the only entity with power to create or destroy property rights that automatically apply to all citizens or residents of the territory under its jurisdiction. From the standpoint of property rights, we may then identify three basic categories of property, which in their pure forms are as follows:

Private property. A particular individual or group, called the owner, has the right to decide how a piece of private property will be used, as well as to exclude others from using it or from altering its physical nature in any way. The owner may also receive any income generated by its use, and he or she may transfer rights associated with the property via gift or sale, keeping the income from such a sale. (Private property may be used or sold for private gain.) In its pure form, private property encompasses all three kinds of rights—use, income, and transfer. However, the right to exclude implies that one owner may not use his or her property in a way that damages the property of others or interferes with their rights to use their property without their consent.

State property. The government controls the use of state or public property and the distribution of income from it, subject to accepted political procedures. Therefore, it may exclude anyone from using such property and decide who will manage it under what rules. Once again, the right to exclude implies that no one may damage state property or interfere with the use rights of state-appointed officials without government permission. In comparison to private property, state property has more restricted income and transfer rights. If we think of it as ultimately owned by the citizens of a nation, region, or community, then we see that an individual citizen cannot transfer his ownership share through gift or sale. Moreover, the current management of a public enterprise cannot transfer the use and income rights delegated to it without government permission. Such a transfer could threaten state control over these rights. Finally, state property may not be used or sold for private gain—a minimum requirement for property to be considered public rather than private in the property rights sense. This means that, except via social insurance, no individual may receive an income that derives solely from the use or exchange of state property, in the sense that such income is independent of his or her labor input (into the production of useful goods or services).

Communal property. All individuals in a community have the right to freely use communal property as they wish and are able to do so, subject to their behavior as good citizens. The government does not exclude anyone from using it, nor may one group exclude another. The inability to exclude is the identifying feature of communal property, which has extensive use rights but no transfer rights, since the latter can exist only when there is exclusion. Because of free access, communal property also yields no income, as is shown in the appendix to this chapter.

We may similarly identify private, state, and communal property rights. Thus, a private property right is a right of a specific individual or group to use a specific piece of property in a particular way, to receive all or part of the income generated by it, to exclude others from using it, or to transfer one of these rights to someone else. The rights to consume a given good, to produce it in a specific way, or to decide how much of it to buy or to sell are private property rights, as is the right to enter into a specific type of contract. Often these rights will be split among two or more individuals. For example, a landlord may "own" an apartment or office building both in the legal sense and in the property rights sense of being able to claim the income generated by it. (He may also be able to sell the income rights.) However, the building may be rented to others to use, subject to terms in a rental contract. The tenants normally have some use rights for a restricted time period that they may be able to transfer to others by subletting.

A state property right is a right exercised by one or more organs of government or of the dominant political party in a one-party state. The rights of a government agency to make decisions about the use of property, to exclude others from using it in specific ways, to distribute all or part of the income generated by it, or to transfer these rights from one individual or organization to another are state property rights, as are the rights to tax and to enforce good citizenship. As a rule, transferability of state use and income rights is restricted or disallowed in an effort to ensure conformity with distribution, production, or other norms determined by society's political processes. While state property rights may result from collective initiative, their exercise usually imposes obligations or responsibilities on one or more households or firms—that is, constrains their income rights and their autonomy as individual decision makers. These include the responsibilities associated with good citizenship. Advocates of socialism have often used the labor theory of value to justify its basic constraint on income distribution. The belief that labor alone creates value makes it natural to argue that an individual's income should depend only on his or her labor input, although such a restriction is open to interpretation in practice. Finally, a communal property right is a right of all citizens to make a specific, unconstrained use of property—for example, to stroll through a public park, to fish without restriction, or to travel on a toll-free road.

In practice, pure forms of property are rarely found, if ever. Virtually every piece of property has different kinds of rights attached to it, and the way we classify it depends on the relative importance we assign to its private, state, and communal rights. For example, despite tax loopholes, private owners of capital must usually share the income generated by its use with the state. Even in societies with a strong tradition of private ownership, enterprise managers are constrained in their production choices by the criminal code, by labor laws, and by zoning ordinances. However, they may also be able to interfere with others' use rights to public or private property—for instance, by polluting air or water resources. By the same token, most managers are able to gain some freedom to produce as they like, even in the most highly centralized economies. State control over the use of capital or over the income from its use is never complete.

Property Rights and Ownership

Because the rights associated with a given asset are often split among different individuals, agencies, or groups, its "owners" (in the property rights sense) may be hard to identify. In particular, nearly all capital is both public and private in varying degrees, and these variations play a role in determining how an economy will function. For example, in a state-managed socialist economy, such as the former Soviet Union, central government agencies retain the power to make basic decisions about how capital is to be used, delegating less important choices to regional authorities and to enterprise directors. The latter are appointed by the state and play a decision-making role somewhere between that of a foreman and a divisional manager in a Western market economy. In the former Yugoslavia, representatives of the employees of each enterprise helped to choose its manager and to determine his or her salary. The state legally owned the capital of each firm but imposed fewer restrictions on the range of choices (use and transfer rights) exercised within the enterprise. The result was a more decentralized economy.

With this understanding, it is still useful to introduce a greater acid test of ownership in the property rights sense, as follows. Anyone with access to communal property may be said to "own" it. Otherwise, when an asset is not used mainly to generate an income, its owners will be those individuals or organizations that determine how it will be used. When an asset is used mainly to generate an income, its owners will be those with residual claims to this income stream. By this definition, the owners of capital may not have any formal rights to determine how it is used. This is, in particular, what is meant by the separation of ownership from control of a corporation, although we shall see that managers can take advantage of their use rights to establish or increase their income rights.

In practice, the separation between use and income rights is never complete. The owners of a firm, in the property rights sense, get whatever income remains after all contractual costs related to its operation plus tax liabilities not related to its profitability have been paid. Therefore, the owners' claims are residual in the sense that they come off the bottom of a firm's revenues while other obligations come off the top (must be paid first). By this definition, the state is part owner of legally private firms to the extent that it collects taxes tied to their profit residuals. An individual with the right to sell capital for private gain is also at least part owner, because the sales price of the asset will reflect its expected future income yield.

Property Rights and Exclusion

If we can decide whether private, state, or communal property rights vis-à-vis the material means of production predominate in a particular economy, then we can classify it as *capitalist, socialist,* or *communist* on this basis. However, while communal rights exist in every economic system, they hardly ever predominate. The reason is that communal goods and resources will be overused—unless they are not scarce—since there is no charge for or restriction on their use. Communal rights also reduce the incentive to produce goods or to invest in future production.

For example, the problem of pollution results largely from easy access to air and water resources for purposes of waste disposal. The depletion of natural resources has often resulted from an absence of well-defined or enforced state or private property rights to control their use. The incentive to invest in or to maintain common property is diluted by the need to share the resulting benefits with whoever wants them. If a farmer has no right to the crop he is planting, either to sell or to eat, he may well decide not to plant. If he has a right to the current crop but no right to future crops, he may be unwilling to invest in maintaining and improving the long-term productivity of the soil. Similarly, if one individual or group were to decline to hunt deer in a forest as a way of allowing the deer population to rise—and if there were no exclusion—someone else would probably come along and slay the deer. A hunting party would be unlikely to forgo its kill, even if the deer were close to extinction. An individual can preserve the deer population only in cooperation with the rest of the community. Such cooperation would have to be enforced through some form of exclusion.

Many organizations claiming to be communal in nature may have property whose legal ownership is common to all members. But on closer examination, access to this property may turn out to be restricted, so that its use is at least partly governed by the organization's rules and regulations. The rights to use such common property or to receive any income from it may be equally distributed among the membership, and/or the organization may democratically decide what rights will prevail. But when all property rights are communal, we have anarchy within a society or organization, and we may define *anarchy* in this way.

We often identify private property rights with markets and prices, because access to goods or resources being sold or leased through the marketplace is done so on the basis of price and ability to pay. A buyer acquires one or more rights attached to such a good solely by paying a price at which a supplier is willing to sell. Anyone who is unable or unwilling to pay such a price is excluded from acquiring rights to the good. In this way, private property rights are usually allocated or rationed out through the price mechanism. The simplest example occurs when the price comes to a level, such as $\overline{P}$ in Figure 1.1(b), that just balances supply and demand. When a good is public property, access to it may be granted on the same basis. For example, a government body could rent publicly owned apartments at market-clearing prices that just equate demand with supply. By implication, it would be seeking the maximum rents obtainable on whatever supply it offered.

According to our definition, however, state property cannot be sold for private gain. In this spirit, state property rights usually imply allocation of goods or resources at least partly on the basis of state authorizations or quotas. In the above example, rents on public apartments would be set below market-clearing levels, producing an excess demand for the good and requiring criteria besides ability to pay to determine who would gain access to it. Families would have to qualify for occupancy on the basis of "need," number of children, political reliability or influence, or some other standard. Even then, there might be more qualified families than apartments, resulting in a waiting list. Similarly, the state in most socialist countries did not sell raw materials or intermediate goods to state-owned enterprises on the basis of price and ability to pay. Instead, it authorized each firm to receive a maximum amount of each kind of input. A steel mill would get a coal shipment just by offering to pay for it. The mill also needed a quota—that is, a state permit for the quantity in question—which was generally not transferable. The lack of a quota could exclude a socialist firm from access to raw materials or intermediate goods, just as the need to pay the going price can exclude a private firm under capitalism.

Figure 1.1 Efficiency of Communal Rights When a Good Is Not Scarce

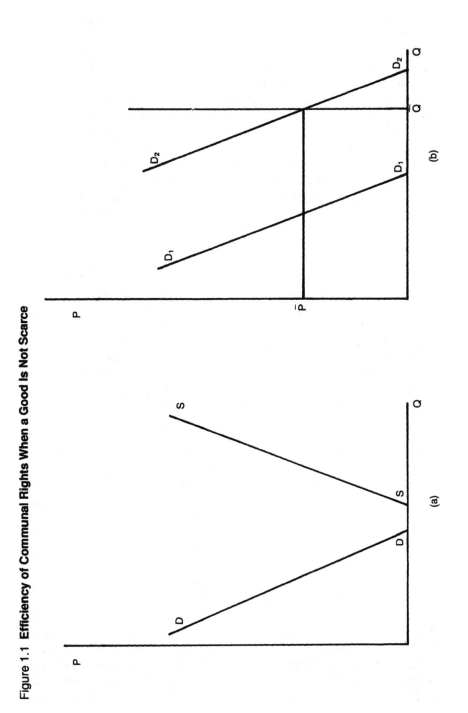

By contrast, we have identified communal property rights with the absence of exclusion. This interferes with efficiency, except when the goods in question are not scarce, meaning that they are in superabundant supply relative to demand. Figure 1.1(a) shows a good whose supply exceeds demand at every positive price. If this situation is expected to persist, there is no need to exclude anyone from using the good. Similarly, let $\bar{Q}$ be the stock of a resource in Figure 1.1(b). If demand for the resource is D_1D_1, and if this demand is expected to continue to be less than the stock at a zero price, communal property rights are consistent with efficiency. But if demand is higher, say at D_2D_2, use of the resource must be restricted or it will be overexploited. Through overuse, its value to society will be reduced to zero, a result that is shown in the appendix to this chapter. Therefore, communal property rights destroy the value of scarce resources. Nevertheless, in the short run free access will benefit many who are able to exploit a scarce resource without paying any rent or facing any quota restriction. In the long run, however, everyone may lose because of more rapid resource depletion.

Communal rights to a scarce good or resource also cause it to be in excess demand. As a result, there will be congestion among prospective users. That is, in using the good or in trying to gain access to it, some demanders will inflict costs on others (or on one another)—notably by making it harder for others to obtain or to use the good. This congestion shows up in a variety of ways, from queuing and additional search activity to excessive resource depletion and even physical conflict. As indicated above, there are two basic methods of restricting access, which are also the two basic ways of allocating goods and resources and of balancing supply and demand in such a way as to prevent or limit demand-side congestion.

First, market exclusion is based on willingness and ability to pay the price that the supplier requests. When a price is set that equates supply with demand—for instance, $\bar{P}$ in Figure 1.1(b)—access to a good or resource depends entirely on payment of this price. Second, it is possible to restrict access by means of quotas or authorizations, of which hunting and fishing permits are common examples. The two approaches may be combined by setting the price below equilibrium but requiring, in addition, a permit or authorization as a condition for access. The good then remains in excess demand, but quotas are used to pare down demand so it balances available supply.[3] In some cases, a black market with price rationing will also spring up to satisfy part of the remaining demand. (The good will then have two prices, with the black market price being higher.)

The use of quotas and below-equilibrium prices allows the government or other authority that sets the quotas to implement its own priorities in determining how the good or resource will be allocated. However, the use of quota allocation also reduces the information content of prices. When prices balance supply and demand, they measure the marginal values of goods to users as well as their marginal costs of supply—although the latter will not be done perfectly when sellers have market power or avoid some of their costs. When quotas are used, prices may bear little relation to marginal values or marginal costs, which are then likely to be unknown. As a result, the value of the firm supplying these products will also be unknown. Widespread use of price ceilings and quotas is therefore apt to lead to a widespread lack of information about values and costs.

Over time, growing scarcity has progressively reduced the sphere of communal property rights. For example, until 1977 no nation could legally claim exclusive jurisdiction over fishing in the oceans except within a narrow band of 12 miles around its coast. Because of free access, fish stocks were being depleted. A nation had no incentive to conserve this resource by restricting its own fishing, because other countries would expand theirs to make up the difference. In 1977, the band of exclusive jurisdiction was extended to 200 miles, within which many coastal nations began to use quotas to restrict foreign fishing vessels (and in some cases their own). Unfortunately, however, overfishing has increased—the quotas have not been very effective—and depletion of fish stocks has reached crisis proportions.

In earlier times, the population was smaller, incomes were lower, and fishing ships were smaller and less efficient. Therefore, the demand for fish, using Figure 1.1(b), was plausibly at D_1D_1 or below, and no need for exclusion arose. Similarly, as late as 25,000 years ago, the world's entire human population was tiny, and the technologies of hunting, food gathering, and fishing were primitive. This restrained effective demand for plants, animals, land, and other resources, which usually were not scarce in most places. Since there was limited exclusion and not much organization of production or distribution, wealth and socioeconomic class differences were minor by modern standards. But as the population grew and the technologies of hunting, fishing, and gathering improved, the demand for animal and plant resources grew as well, until these became scarce. Thus, the economic problem was born.

Subsequently, it became necessary for the human race to begin renewing and expanding the stocks of animals and plants on which it depended for survival. This required exclusion and led to the Neolithic Revolution, which turned people away from a nomadic existence as hunter-gatherers toward farming, herding, and breeding. The Neolithic Revolution was also the precursor of civilization. Tribes began to organize themselves politically to both lay claim to and exclude other tribes from resources, to introduce a more extensive internal division of labor, and to enforce the emerging property rights and internal socioeconomic class differentiation. The economic problem has been with us ever since, but the notion of communal property lives on in our dreams of a utopia in which scarcity again disappears. One example of such a utopia is Karl Marx's full communism, which is based partly on restriction of individual wants but mainly on high productivity levels made possible by advanced technology that leads to a superabundance of supply. In the words of Peter Wiles, "Leisure increases to almost intolerable proportions, money falls out of use, and we can all go and help ourselves in the shops."[4] Theft becomes meaningless, and all the savings, investment, or work effort that society could want is forthcoming with no material reward—generated out of an inner need to create, a desire to serve the community, as a means of self-expression, or last of all, to relieve the boredom of too much leisure. Unfortunately, this is utopia rather than reality.

Property Rights and Efficiency

Although there is no society in the world today in which communal property rights predominate, the concept is central to discussions of economic inefficiency. An economy is efficient when it is maximizing the present value of its current and expected future per capita income and output, with all goods and services priced at their marginal net values to users.[5] With these same prices, efficiency also means maximizing a broad measure of national income or output per capita. In terms of property rights, the three main sources of inefficiency found in the economics literature are described as follows:

1. Some scarce goods, services, or resources do not have complete, well-defined, or well-enforced property rights governing their use or exchange or the distribution of income and other benefits resulting from them. Every economy has examples of ill-defined, incomplete, or badly enforced property rights having effects similar to those of communal rights. Thus, waste or destruction of value results from congestion and overuse, as in the case of pollution and excessive resource depletion, when restrictions on the exploitation of resources are inadequate or not enforced. In other cases, investment is discouraged because no one can claim the income or other benefits resulting from improved use of goods or resources. As noted earlier, communal rights also generate external effects. Some individuals, groups, or firms inflict costs on or fail to provide benefits to others because the absence of well-defined or strictly enforced property rights gives them insufficient incentive to take these costs or benefits into account. A major reason for the failure of past reforms seeking to decentralize economic decision making in socialist countries was the inability of reformers to establish new property rights—and thus a new mechanism for allocating goods and resources—to replace those elements of the old system that were suppressed. This allowed those who benefited from the former centralized control to reestablish it. Such difficulties have persisted in transition economies.

2. There are well-defined and strictly enforced property rights that prevent the movement of goods or resources into their highest-value uses. Such barriers are erected because they allow some people to benefit (potentially at society's expense) from the rights to use inputs in ways that are restricted and/or to buy or sell in protected markets. Monopoly is a standard example. A company with an exclusive right to sell a particular product, use a particular input, or operate in a

particular region has a property right to a market position. More generally, any firm operating in an industry protected by entry barriers—including licenses, franchises, copyrights, tariffs, import quotas, and so forth—has such a right. It is valuable and yields an income, called excess profit, to its owners. In the simplest case, this results from limiting the supply of a good, which drives up its price.

Free access to the market destroys this value, just as free access to a resource destroys its value. But most Western economists would consider the former desirable. Free access to a market—or communal rights to a market position—is a key ingredient of competition, which works when excess profits act like a magnet, luring additional firms into an industry or causing established firms to expand to keep out new competitors. The appearance or threat of new competition helps to keep prices and profits lower, and output and quality higher. Up to a point, it also stimulates innovation. Conversely, losses push firms out of an industry. The forces of competition make it possible for a market economy to be efficient without centralized control or coordination, although the unaided market mechanism never produces efficiency entirely on its own. Efficiency is possible in a decentralized system because decisions have been made to buy and sell and to produce and consume based on prices. When prices reflect marginal values to users and marginal costs to producers, they have the potential to coordinate economic activity in an efficient way, since any decision maker can accurately compute the costs and benefits of one set of decisions versus another. (This is the essence of the "invisible hand.")

Thus, we have a kind of symmetry. Efficiency generally requires well-defined and strictly enforced state or private property rights to scarce goods and resources. Without exclusion, at least part of their value will be lost. But rights to "assets" (such as a monopoly position in the market or favorable tax-subsidy treatment) that have no value in raising production or consumption should not be valuable unto themselves to those who possess them.

Because monopoly power is valuable, moreover, competition to obtain or to establish it (or to gain control over the power to award monopoly positions) will arise. Such competition can take forms ranging from competitive lobbying to bribes to gang warfare for control over the supply of illegal goods and services. Monopoly becomes possible when government does not define or enforce property rights well enough, or when it decides to favor monopoly rather than to enforce competition in the marketplace. In either case, competition to establish or to claim monopoly power uses resources and therefore creates waste analogous to that associated with communal rights, in addition to that associated with the source of inefficiency described under (2) above.

3. Firms, government agencies, or other suppliers of goods and services may be internally inefficient. Economists often refer to this as *X-inefficiency*, which arises when organizations are too large or poorly managed, or when their managements are not motivated to control costs, to innovate, or to tailor their prod-

ucts to users' wants. X-inefficiency is a consequence of the restrictions described under (2), since it results from suppression of competition by smaller production units, better managers, and so on.

A change in property rights will improve efficiency only if it reduces the total losses described under (1), (2), and (3) by more than any additional costs associated with producing and implementing the new rights—including the costs of adjusting to and learning to operate under the new rules. These loss reductions may also be viewed as gains from more closely aligning the rewards of productive inputs in each alternative use with their marginal contributions to national income, broadly defined as above. Differences between rewards and contributions at the margin often relate to separation of use or exchange from corresponding income rights. Separation of ownership (income rights) from control of a large firm is an example, as is a government's right of taxation. The former may lead management to contest owners' income rights, in effect, by taking out the firm's profit in a form (on-the-job consumption, padded salaries and expense accounts, etc.) that only managers can claim. Moreover, to the extent that they are unable to do this, their incentive to manage well may be reduced, because the resulting increase in profit would go mostly to outside owners. Similarly, high marginal taxes on income sometimes cause people to work less, and textbooks contain diagrams to show how taxes or subsidies distort production and consumption decisions by biasing choices toward activities that are more lightly taxed or more heavily subsidized.

Nevertheless, separation of use from income rights is not necessarily inefficient. Governments must raise revenues to pay for public goods and services. Because of scale economies, efficiency often requires firms to expand beyond limits allowed by the personal resources of their managers. This obliges them to raise outside funds, although separation of ownership from control may also be mandated on political or ideological grounds. Any change in property rights will create losers as well as gainers, and there are often trade-offs between efficiency and equity. Therefore, more efficient property rights are not automatically desirable, although economists of diverse backgrounds and viewpoints have assumed that efficiency plays a dominant role in determining the long-run evolution of rights.

A Brief Introduction to Property Rights and Socialism

State Property Rights and Price Controls[6]

When the supply of a good equals the demand for it, access depends on willingness and ability to pay the going price, and available quantities are rationed among users entirely on this basis. If the state wants to directly manage the allocation of the good, therefore, it will keep price below equilibrium, causing demand to exceed supply. Then state priorities—expressed in the form of authorizations or quotas for various users—can determine how demand will be pared down to available supply. In this way, physical rationing of goods via quotas requires price ceilings to overrule market allocation. To a degree, the reverse is also true. Widespread price controls in a market economy require allocation via quotas of some sort to avoid inefficiency, notably that stemming from congestion among prospective users. Thus, they often lead to direct or indirect government involvement in distributing the goods in question. This is because an effective price ceiling must lie below the equilibrium price that equates supply with demand. It causes buyers to want more of the good than is available. (Communal property can be viewed as a special case, with a ceiling price of zero.) The ceiling price prevents the market from allocating the good. Unless there are quotas to complete the task of allocation, price controls will cause waste and will actually harm, rather than help, many potential users.

To understand this, consider the market in Figure 1.2. There the equilibrium price is $\bar{P}$ ($320), but a legal ceiling is set at P_0 ($220). The ceiling reduces quantity supplied, but also seeks to transfer income from sellers to buyers. As a concrete example, let the ceiling be a rent control. At $220 per month, 90,000 apartments are supplied for renting. If this many were put on the market without a ceiling, tenant demand would drive the rent to $370 (the demand price, or P_1, in Figure 1.2). The control therefore attempts to transfer $150 per apartment (a total income equal to $(P_1-P_0) \times 90,000$, or area GAIN) from landlords to tenants. However, this is not likely to happen. Initially, no one will have a firm claim to the income in question (area GAIN). Efforts to establish claims will then cause part of this income to be destroyed—in the sense of being offset by additional costs borne by tenants, landlords, and third parties—while the rest is divided among these groups.

To see why, suppose first that landlords are unable to evade or get around the rent ceiling. With the price held at P_0, a shortage of apartments will develop. There will be *excess demand,* in the sense that quantity demanded (Q_1, or 205,000) exceeds quantity supplied (90,000). Some present or prospective tenants are also willing to pay more than the ceiling rent—indeed, more than the market equilibrium rent ($\bar{P}$)—but have a hard time obtaining or holding onto an apartment. Therefore, they will incur additional costs to this end, including the greater time and expense required to look for, take possession of, and keep an apartment; these are the costs of having to accept an apartment that is less suitable (e.g., of lower quality or farther from work), or simply the costs of doing without one. Let AC be the average monthly cost per apartment borne by those who wish to secure or to preserve use rights to an apartment. AC is an increasing function of the number of people competing for the 90,000 apartments available and of the time, effort, and other resources expended by each. Moreover, by spending more time and effort, one person may improve his chances of occupying an apartment. But since this effort does not increase the supply of apartments, it must also reduce the likelihood that someone else will obtain one.

Figure 1.2 **Price Control and Excess Demand**

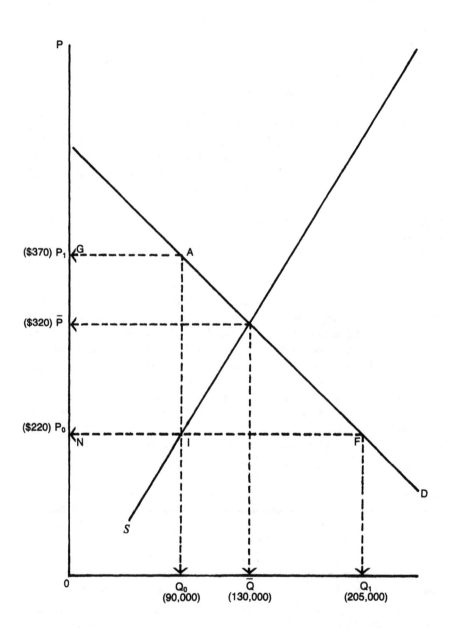

The average gain, or "profit," per apartment to demanders from rent control is roughly the difference between P_1 and $(P_0 + AC)$. Perfect competition on the demand side for apartments (including free entry of prospective tenants into the market) would reduce these profits to zero by driving AC up to $(P_1 - P_0)$. (This is a substitute for increasing the price to $\overline{P}$, but, unlike a price rise, does not encourage expansion of supply.) Total cost to all tenants would be the area GAIN, implying that tenants as a group lose from rent control, since $P_1 = (P_0 + AC)$ exceeds $\overline{P}$, the market equilibrium rent. In practice, however, competition is apt to be less than perfect, if only because there will be some cost to landlords of tenant turnover. Tenants with secure leases when the ceiling is imposed—as well as those with good connections or access to information about vacancies—will have a competitive edge and may therefore gain from rent control, while others are more likely to lose.

Given the shortage, waiting lists will result. Historically, those near the front of such queues have sometimes sold their places to others farther back. If the $150 difference between P_1 and P_0 is expected to continue, a spot near the front of the queue will have a market value of several thousand dollars (or the capitalized value of $150 per month). This is why getting one's name onto such a list has proved to be a good investment, even for people with no desire to rent. If a black market for rental dwellings develops, the average black market rent will probably be closer to P_1 than to P_0, and people may try to acquire apartments at the controlled price simply in order to relet them at P_1. Besides, in countries where goods shortages are widespread, people sometimes make a living by standing in line for others. A serious housing shortage will give rise to intermediaries who specialize, for a fee, in obtaining housing for others.

At some cost, landlords may be able to evade the control. For example, they may convert buildings to uses not covered by rent ceilings. This is wasteful not only because of the resources used up in conversion but also because the most efficient use of these sites is probably for housing. (Otherwise, this use would not have been chosen in absence of rent control.) Alternatively, a landlord may reduce quality and costs by cutting down on maintenance, improvements, or decoration of the building and its grounds. A quality reduction is analogous to a rent increase, and landlords have also been known to demand side payments (such as key money) that effectively raise the rent. At some cost, they can be prevented from doing these things, but such expenses would be unnecessary in absence of rent control. Over time, rent ceilings will discourage construction of new rental housing. Because of the shortage, moreover, builders will be less motivated to take users' preferences into account, and landlords can cut costs through practices such as excessive standardization of apartments. Because many tenants will pay more than the ceiling rent—indeed, more than $\overline{P}$—if we include all their costs of obtaining an apartment and/or of doing without one for a time (or of accepting one of lower quality or in a less desirable location), and because of the waste involved, economists often prefer to avoid price controls. (Instead, it is believed governments should help poor tenants with rent subsidies, for example, and enforce competition among landlords to keep rentals as low as possible.)

Whether price ceilings apply to a few goods or to many, there is a potential for limiting the wasteful behavior associated with them by combining them with the allocation of the affected goods via quotas for buyers.[7] Only authorized buyers of any good would be allowed to pay the low, controlled price, up to the limits of their quota. An effective quota system constrains the distribution of the good and, in the process, supports the controlled price by excluding part of the demand. Suppliers would not be allowed to sell the good above its ceiling price until they have filled the quotas of authorized buyers. One way of doing this is to give targets to producers for minimum deliveries of the good at the ceiling price. The sum of producer targets plus the quantity available to users from previous production should then match the sum of buyer quotas. A system of rewards and penalties will be needed to deter violation of both quotas and targets, and if targets or quotas are too easily influenced by lobbying, efficiency losses will reappear in the form of lobbying costs. Problems will also arise if enforcement costs are too high.

Finally, suppose the above quotas and targets are nontransferable and comprehensive enough to allow the state to use them to control the bulk of exchange among enterprises in a particular economy. This would also be state management of production, since these targets and quotas would play the major role in determining outputs and input usage by each firm. In this way, they would shift production decisions above the level of the enterprise. (State management is the identifying feature of a Soviet-type economy, which also makes widespread use of price controls.) These would then create excess demand that allows targets and quotas to partly overrule the preferences of individual buyers and sellers.[8] Money and prices do not fall out of use, but possession of money alone does not necessarily guarantee access to goods. The targets and quotas received by each enterprise also form a plan to guide production and exchange, and we may therefore think of this as a planned economy.

The Role of the State and the Boundary Between Capitalism and Socialism

Contrasting views of the economic role of the state are related to varying opinions about how well prices and markets work in solving the economic problem. Those who want to put more restrictions on government generally believe that markets, with flexible prices to balance supply and demand, work more efficiently in a wider variety of contexts. Broadly speaking, we can distinguish four versions of the state's economic role. First, the laissez-faire approach would confine government to providing two major public goods—internal order and protection from external threat—plus mediation of disputes as a last resort. In particular, the state would produce and enforce the contract law necessary for efficient market operation. A second version, based on Keynesian economics, stresses the state's responsibility to ensure full employment. Some Keynesian economists also argue for a strong government role in redistributing income and in providing public goods. They believe that reliance on the market alone would lead to an undersupply of these goods.

A still more interventionist view builds on classical reasons for market failure to argue that the state should try to direct economic activity along the lines of national advantage. Such a government may or may not be Keynesian, but it does try to alter the direction of investment and growth within a market economy, often seeking to gain more rapid diffusion of new technology and faster realization of experience or scale economies in the process. Finally, Marxist-Leninists who favor a traditional Soviet-type economy take the most interventionist position of all. They hold that markets work poorly and should be replaced by state management of investment, production, and exchange (at least among enterprises), which is the hallmark of such a system. As such, the state makes major investment decisions, supplies most investment funding to firms, and monitors the use of capital. It also finances most investment from taxes.

In anticipation of later discussion, Table 1.1 summarizes the basic features of a traditional Soviet-type economy, which has been the principal form of socialism in practice. Today this form of economic system is nearly extinct, but as recently as the early 1980s it prevailed in countries accounting for about one-third of the world's population. Since then these countries have adopted *transition* or *transformation economies* that are replacing state planning with free markets. In none of these countries is the transformation complete, and in most the road to a market economy has been long and hard. Our interest in the Soviet-type economy is therefore mainly in the legacy of such a system, which makes transformation to an efficient market system difficult, and in the reasons for its inability to operate efficiently. In addition, we shall see that a capitalist market economy can be viewed as a mirror image of a Soviet-type economy, and therefore our knowledge of such a system helps us to better understand our own.

One major reason for the inefficiency of the Soviet-type economy has already been indicated. In order to prioritize, state officials in control of economic activity kept prices below equilibrium levels and used quotas and targets to govern the production and allocation of goods and resources. This enabled them to replace market choices with their own, but it also created prices that contained almost no useful information about the value of products to users or to state officials or about the true costs of supplying goods and services. Thus the cost of using exclusion based on quotas and price controls turned out to be high. State authorities had no idea how to allocate or use resources in efficient ways. In particular, they did not know the opportunity costs of choosing one use of resources over another. As a result, they often channeled inputs into occupations or uses in which they were relatively unproductive. The Soviet-type economy was

Table 1.1

Basic Features of a Traditional Command or Soviet-type Economy

1. *Public ownership* of most of the material means of production and distribution (capital and natural resources). Except via social insurance, no one was supposed to receive an income from the use or exchange of these means that was uncorrelated with his or her own labor input. Legally, there were two kinds of public ownership: state ownership, or ownership by the "whole people," and collective ownership, or ownership by a specific collectivity, such as the members of a collective farm. In practice, differences between the two declined over time, but collective ownership was supposed to convey greater local freedom to make decisions and greater local responsibility for profits and losses. In addition, members of collective farms and of many state farms were allowed to keep tiny "private" plots (legally, public land) on which they had still greater freedom to grow crops or raise livestock as they wished. Originally, the state used collective ownership to force peasants to market their crops at low prices and, thus, to bear the brunt of harvest shortfalls, although the lot of peasants improved after the 1950s.

2. *State planning and management* of most industry, foreign and domestic trade, and, to a lesser extent, agriculture. The state determined investment and production priorities. Central planners made the most important management decisions, and many others were the responsibility of authorities at the industry and regional levels. At the bottom of the management hierarchy, firms received the results of these decisions in the form of output and delivery targets and input quotas indicating minimum acceptable performance levels. Collectively, these performance indicators constituted the plan for the enterprise, and there were also regional, industrywide, and national plans. Enterprise directors were judged on their ability to meet plan targets, which became their "success indicators," and they generally had decision-making powers somewhere between those of foremen and divisional managers in market economies. Planners used materials balances, which quantified plan sources and uses of each important industrial good, to achieve rough equality between the input quotas and output targets across a nation or region.

3. *No Competition among firms* for market shares. Such competition would have required too much independence from state control. As a rule, each enterprise was assigned a supplier for every material input that it used. Suppliers also had no choice of customers.

4. *Fundamental microeconomic disequilibrium,* in that prices did not balance supply and demand and, on balance, an overall excess demand for goods and services at official prices. The majority of households wanted to consume more goods than were currently available and to hold smaller savings or cash balances. Similarly, firms wanted more productive inputs but were constrained by availability. The access of each industry and region to investment and to other key inputs reflected state priorities regarding the direction of growth. Especially in the case of producer goods, possession of purchasing power alone did not guarantee access to these products, at least through official channels at official prices. Producer goods were formally rationed, as a rule, although consumer goods were often rationed on a first-come, first-served basis and by queuing. The extent of formal consumer goods rationing varied widely across space and time. In some cases, it was widespread; in others, nearly nonexistent. Also, availability of consumer goods depended on a household's location or its political and economic status. If the latter was sufficiently high, it brought access to special stores or

(continued)

Table 1.1 *(continued)*

favors. Typically, inequality was more in the form of differential access to goods and services and less in the form of income differences than in market economies. Since excess demand applied to foreign trade and payments, the domestic currency was overvalued relative to Western currencies.

5. *Official prices were not rational guides to production,* as a rule, and *economic development was not demand oriented.* Excess demand gave the planners some power to overrule the market in allocating resources, so that the state could implement its
industry-by-industry and region-by-region growth priorities. Official prices were not designed to guide production or to allocate goods or resources among users, and relative prices generally reflected neither relative marginal production costs nor relative marginal values of goods to users or to state officials. Nevertheless, major plan targets were aggregates of different goods weighted by physical measures (tons, square meters, etc.) or by prices. Firms emphasized volume, choosing quality and assortment to make plan targets easier to fulfill rather than matching users' preferences or requirements in the best possible way. This reduced the use value of what was produced (and was known as the "problem of success indicators").

6. *Control by the ruble (or yuan, zloty, etc.).* This was use of the state banking system—essentially one large combination central and commercial bank—to enforce performance according to the state plan. Together with efforts to keep down money-supply expansion by controlling budget deficits—and thus to contain inflationary pressures and prevent the erosion of work incentives—control by the ruble was the essence of monetary policy under command planning. There was no fiscal policy as such, although industry-by-industry and region-by-region growth priorities constituted a structural policy. In this context, the state monobank was itself basically a division of the finance ministry. Together the state budget and banking system collected savings, mainly in the form of turnover (sales) and profits taxes, and ensured that they were invested according to state growth priorities. This meant transferring savings generated in sectors whose growth priority was low to high-priority sectors for investment. Broadly speaking, agriculture, light industry, and services had the historical task of subsidizing investment in heavy industry, although agriculture subsequently became a net user of savings.

7. *A large second* or *unofficial economy* of production and trade outside the state planning and management network. Here market exchange, sometimes in the form of barter, predominated; on average, production was relatively small scale and labor intensive. The excess demand for many goods and services at official prices meant that many buyers were willing to pay higher prices to obtain additional supplies over and above what was available through official channels. The second economy arose to satisfy part of this excess demand. It consisted of activities of all shadings of legality. Collective and state farmers grew food on their private plots, for example, and sold it to the public legally. Used car markets, where prices were often higher than for new models (but waiting was avoided), sometimes crossed the border into illegality. Firms often sent out "pushers" (salesmen in reverse) to illegally obtain productive inputs needed to fulfill plan targets or to produce for the second economy.

8. *No electoral competition among political parties.* Elections usually featured just one candidate for each office, with some opportunity for citizens to vote against the Communist Party nominee. In a few cases, two or more candidates ran for government offices or legislative seats, but there was still no competition among political parties.

(continued)

Table 1.1 *(continued)*

Such competition would have caused independent political pressure groups to emerge in order to advance the interests of farmers, wage earners, managers, bankers, etc., by exchanging votes for benefits obtained via the political process. Since excess demand left room for price increases without impairing the ability of suppliers to sell as much as they wanted to, these special interest groups would have generated upward pressure on prices and wages in advancing the material interests of their supporters. Widespread excess demand—and therefore state management of production and distribution itself—would probably have been unable to withstand prolonged political party competition. In addition, periodic elections contested by two or more separate parties with separate platforms would have shortened the decision-making horizons of elected representatives and public officials, especially in periods prior to elections. This is unfavorable to planning because it heightens the tendency to provide short-term benefits— including increases in wages or prices received by strategically-placed voters—at the expense of the long-term.

9. *Planning enterprise output targets from the achieved level.* Next year's target equaled this year's anticipated performance plus a percentage of growth that was a function of current investment in the firm. With irrational prices, planners lacked accurate detailed measures of demand and found no other objective basis on which to set plan indicators. As a rule, enterprises and higher-level planning jurisdictions would incur high costs, if necessary, to reach their output targets. To ensure adequate supplies, they often produced their own inputs on a small scale and maintained large stocks of goods in process. (Relative to value added, inventories in Soviet-type economies tended to be higher than in developed market economies.) But in addition, planning from the achieved level increased their reluctance to exceed output, productivity, profit, and other targets by large margins when they were able, since this made future plans harder to fulfill. Firms would also "storm." That is, their rate of production would rise as the deadline for fulfilling plan targets drew near and would relax just after this deadline—a rhythm that reduced the risk of current targets being raised while fulfillment was in progress.

10. *"Soft" enterprise budget constraint.* High marginal tax on profits and marginal subsidy to compensate losses, that is, the State enterprises were almost never shut down, and enterprise directors were far more likely to be demoted for failing to meet plan targets than for poor financial performance. These economies had no comprehensive unemployment insurance, as a rule, and underemployment within the firm replaced the open unemployment characteristic of most market economies. Moreover, redistribution through the state budget from profitable to unprofitable firms tended to divorce variations in the earnings of managers and workers from variations in enterprise profitability before taxes and subsidies. These profitability variations reflected pricing distortions and management decisions taken above the level of the enterprise, as well as the efforts of managers and workers within the firm. There were also ideological view against tying individual earnings to profits, and the desire to avoid open unemployment limited the emphasis on profitability or cost effectiveness. The soft budget constraint reinforced the effects of planning from the achieved level in making enterprises reluctant to expand output beyond target levels, even when they could profitably do so. But it also increased the willingness of enterprise directors to take on additional workers—especially if they increased a firm's ability to fulfill its plan—and helped to ensure low rates of open unemployment.

(continued)

Table 1.1 *(continued)*

11. *Contrasting sources of economic growth* vis-à-vis Western market economies. In the West, growth of real per capita income and output has been largely *intensive,* in that it results from broadly defined technological progress, which raises the productivity of labor, capital, and land. In Soviet-type economies, growth was mainly *extensive*— resulting from increases in material inputs plus large transfers of labor from agriculture, unemployment, household work, and so on, to industry—or based on imported technology. The level of indigenous innovation was low because firms had captive markets for their products and their success depended, for the most part, on meeting output targets related to past performance. The state brought about higher rates of saving and investment than in most market economies, but at comparable levels of development Soviet-type economies used more capital, energy, and raw material per unit of national income. Growth in the latter went hand in hand with rising ratios of capital and energy to labor, and growth slowed down drastically from initially high levels as a consequence of the law of diminishing returns.

---

inefficient partly because it provided a poor information base for decisions by its state managers. Good measures of value were unavailable, undermining to some degree the ability of state officials to prioritize. As we shall see, the system developed an inertia that made it hard to change priorities or to react in a flexible way to external changes.

If we take a more favorable view of market performance than did traditional Marxist-Leninists, government actions that restrict the autonomy of individual decision makers may still be worthwhile if they prevent some individuals or firms from interfering with production, consumption, or exchange activities of others or if they promote cooperation that increases production or consumption. The main examples of cooperation in production involve specialization and division of labor, which give rise to economies of scale. In consumption, gains from cooperation arise in the financing of *public goods*—internal order, national defense, public parks and roads, television and radio broadcasting, mass transit, environmental improvement, some aspects of education, and many others. These differ from private goods in that public goods are (or can be) jointly consumed, which is the source of scale economies. Many people watch the same television broadcast, use the same highway or park, benefit from the same efforts to provide internal order and protection from external threat, and breathe the same air, polluted or not.

In this context, we have already suggested that a Soviet-type economy is not the only possible form of socialism. In particular, socialist market economies are conceivable in which the government's economic role, including the provision of public goods, would be more familiar to citizens of Western nations. Zhao Ziyang, former leader of the Chinese Communist Party, argued that socialism has just three basic requirements—public ownership of the means of production, payment according to labor contribution, and some form of central planning. This would allow room for more decision-making freedom and responsibility for profits and losses at the enterprise level, as well as a greater linking of rewards to productivity than was usual in Soviet-type economies.

A major theme of reformers in China who want to decentralize control over economic activity has been that state ownership of the means of production need not imply state management. We therefore want to ask what minimum conditions state ownership, in the property rights sense, places on a socialist economy. As noted earlier, the minimum requirement is, in fact, that individual incomes be incomes from productive labor or social insurance payments (and social insurance should be financed mainly by deductions from labor earnings). Other incomes would result from privatization of property rights associated with capital or natural resources, and in this sense would be "unearned." Although small private firms may be allowed, a society that is socialist in the property rights sense would insist that their owners be actively involved in management and that owner incomes be justified as returns to managerial or entrepreneurial labor. In addition, public ownership appears to require at least the following:

1. In a socialist market economy, publicly owned firms may be allowed to "sell" fixed capital or resources in the sense of transferring the use rights over these assets to another firm, or possibly even to private individuals. However, the selling firm cannot then pay out the proceeds as individual incomes. It must either reinvest them or pay them as taxes, in which case the government is obliged to reinvest the tax share of these receipts. Alternatively, no socialist firm may run down the state's stock of capital or natural resources, except possibly via use. Here the intent is to prevent "unearned" incomes, but such a restriction also reduces the incentive to sell assets and may therefore keep them from going to those firms that can make the most productive use of them. In particular, it may hamper small enterprises, which are often buyers of used equipment. If socialist firms are allowed to sell bonds or shares, the proceeds must again be invested. They may not be paid as personal incomes.

2. Individuals would receive labor incomes, as well as social insurance payments related to old age, sickness, disability, and so on, and possibly maintenance of guaranteed living standards for each household. In addition, interest returned on savings that compensates for inflation (or maintains the purchasing power of savings) and allows savers to benefit from economic growth—since the investment financed by their postponement of consumption helps to make growth possible—appears to be consistent with socialism. Similarly, individuals might be allowed to buy bonds and/or shares issued by the government or by socialist firms. However, there would have to be strict limits on capital gains or losses from the sale of such securities or of any publicly owned productive asset. Otherwise, these gains could easily be unrelated to labor contributions to the production of useful goods and services, and therefore "unearned." In practice, socialist governments have usually viewed capital gains as expropriations from the labor of others and required share prices to be fixed in those few cases in

which equity issues were allowed, although the currently operating stock exchanges in China are a clear exception. One consequence is that the market value of socialist firms has generally remained unknown.

The above constraints may make it harder for enterprises, especially in early stages of their organization and growth, to raise money on financial markets. The availability of venture capital in capitalist economies often depends on the promise of capital gains—as no dividends may be paid for some time—in order to allow reinvestment of profits in the enterprise. A shortage of venture capital would deter innovation and the entry of new competitors, except in cases in which the state acted to offset this. Generally, therefore, the state would be more deeply involved in founding firms and in financing their expansion, even under market socialism, than is normal under capitalism. This means that it would more often decide which firms would be founded and allowed to grow.

Therefore, while the state would not manage production and exchange directly under market socialism, it would play a major role as a financial intermediary, as it did in Yugoslavia before 1990. This role results from its control over income rights and the corresponding restrictions on capital markets necessary to preserve socialism in the property rights sense. The absence of secondary securities markets would make it harder for the state to allocate investment funds efficiently, since enterprise value and long-run profitability would be unknown. In principle, nothing prevents a loanable-funds market, with supply and demand governed by interest rates, from being a part of a socialist market economy. However, it is far from clear what would happen if a state-owned firm defaulted on a loan from the state bank; in practice, such markets have been undermined in socialist and transition economies by the soft budget constraint. The state has rescued both borrowers and lenders when loans have gone sour, and political, administrative, and ideological criteria have continued to guide investment allocation.

A major task of any socialist economy, in the eyes of advocates of socialism, is to raise social consciousness to ensure that each individual is less likely to think of his own welfare apart from the well-being of other members of society. If such a transformation were successful, there would be less need to pay managers or workers the values of their marginal products in order to motivate them to maximize their contributions to production. The problem of evaluating these contributions would remain, but individuals would become more willing to work for the collective good and would automatically feel rewarded in doing so, allowing progressive equalization of incomes. (In effect, these would increasingly take the form of social insurance payments.) At last, full communism would be guided by the motto "To each according to his needs." However, this goal did not come close to realization in socialist economies, which over time became more concerned about the problem of motivation. The image of an egalitarian society within which self-seeking has disappeared remains the stuff that dreams are made of.

Historically, the earnings of managers and workers in Soviet-type economies depended on current performance indicators, and notably on the abilities of firms to meet targeted increases in output. If a firm's present management does not expect to remain with the enterprise for a long period, such a reward structure will tend to give it a short decision-making horizon. It will "go after immediate advantage at the expense of the future interests of the enterprise," since it has no claim based on the firm's performance after it leaves.[9] Such behavior is less likely when managers own their companies and can sell their ownership claims at market value, since the value at the time of sale will depend on expected future profitability. In this sense, an owner-manager does have a claim to profits earned after he or she departs from the firm.

The same problem arises in large Western corporations. A Soviet manager's chances of promotion depended on meeting current production targets, while divisional managers in U.S. companies are under pressure to show high rates of short-term profit. Neither has a transferable ownership claim on the unit he or she managed. In theory, active trading of ownership shares at market value will lengthen the time horizons of top managers of Western corporations, but there is also growing suspicion that stock markets sometimes work perversely in this regard. Exchanges are increasingly dominated by institutional investors (mutual funds, pension plans, investment companies) with large portfolios whose managers buy and sell on the basis of formulas that deemphasize long-term performance. This puts pressure on enterprise management to achieve short-term results. In each case, short time horizons are due at least partly to separation of ownership (income rights to property) from management (use rights over property), along with incomplete supervision of managers by owners (since supervision is costly). Large Japanese enterprises make little use of transferable ownership claims as managerial rewards, but they do give most employees, including managers, long-term employment, a close identification with their companies, and the expectation that their own and their families' prospects will depend on present and future evaluation of their current contributions to company success. Potentially, such an approach is available to a socialist market economy as well.

Socialization of Investment Returns

The question of income rights under socialism has always been contentious. By suppressing gains and losses from the use or sale of property, advocates of socialism hoped to reduce or remove a source of inequality under capitalism. However, labor productivity depends on the quantity and quality of capital that each individual has to work with, and if some enterprises have better capital or resource endowments than others, this could be a source of inequality in socialist economies. Historically, however, personal incomes and career prospects were not tied closely to profitability in state-owned firms under socialism, and penal-

ties for poor financial results at the enterprise level were usually low to nonexistent. Most profits were taxed away and losses were subsidized by the government budget, in conformity with the view that returns on investment should be
socialized. This redistribution has been a basic feature of socialism in practice
and has persisted in transition economies.

To put it another way, enterprise budget constraints have been "soft," or
elastic, in that the marginal tax or subsidy on variations in profits and losses has
been close to one. Moreover, since markets and competition were suppressed in
Soviet-type economies, prices were irrational, as noted earlier. It was therefore
nearly impossible to isolate the effect on a firm's profits of the quantity and
quality of its labor input (including management) from other effects on profit,
including those of pricing distortions, different capital endowments, and management decisions taken above the level of the enterprise.

Egalitarian biases toward socializing investment returns also reinforced the
centralization of production and investment decisions. The two went together in
Soviet-type economies because the soft budget constraint reduced the incentive
at the enterprise level to invest rationally or to use capital efficiently without
outside supervision. The right under capitalism to claim the yield on an investment gives an incentive to seek the highest return possible. Although this
scarcely guarantees a socially efficient allocation or use of capital, there is no
obvious replacement incentive as long as people are basically self-interested. If
they can be educated to exchange self-interest for collective or social interest, it
may be possible to break the basic contradiction between egalitarianism and
efficiency. But even then, it would be necessary to estimate yields on alternative
investment opportunities with reasonable accuracy, and this was not generally
possible in socialist economies because of irrational prices. Given this, plus
widespread excess demand, political, administrative, and ideological criteria
crowded out economic considerations in guiding investment choices, as noted
earlier—one reason why capital productivity was low in these economies.

Another example of wasteful use of resources comes from the energy crisis.
In Eastern Europe, the most important output targets were historically related to
the gross value of each firm's output. This value included the cost of inputs used
in production, and therefore rose when the prices of these inputs rose. Thus, it
was often to the advantage of enterprise directors to use more expensive inputs,
and the incentive for firms to conserve scarce resources was weak.[10] East European nations used more energy per capita than Western Europe from 1955
through 1981, and the gap between the two regions widened after the 1973–74
oil price explosion. In 1980, at least 75 percent more primary energy was required to produce a unit of national income in eastern than in Western Europe.

In fact, most East European governments used subsidies to shield domestic
producers for several years from the full effects of energy-price rises. But even
when price increases were passed on, there was little incentive to practice conservation at the enterprise level. Directors could increase their gross output val-

ues, and thus their earnings, by using more energy-intensive production methods, which helped, in particular, to raise the foreign indebtedness of these nations. This generated further pressures for reform during the 1980s in order to increase exports and to make the economy less dependent on imports. Ultimately, wasteful use of scarce resources played a major role in causing the downfall of the Soviet-type economy.

Appendix: Communal Property Rights and Resource Value

In this appendix, I will show that free access or communal property rights to a scarce resource destroy its value.[11] To this end, consider Figure 1.3, which compares the effects of free access with restrictions on the exploitation of a scarce resource. There the horizontal axis measures labor input (L), which we can think of as the number of individuals fishing a stream or other area where the fishing stock is scarce. The vertical axis measures the average or marginal value of fish caught per day. The horizontal line opposite $W = \$200$ gives the opportunity cost (W) to a representative fisherman of fishing this area for a day instead of using his or her time in some other way. It indicates how much the individual's time is worth (here $200). In addition, P is the market price and Q is the total quantity of fish caught. Total output value is therefore PQ.

Of the two solid downward-sloping curves, the upper (ARP_L) measures the average product of labor, or total output value divided by the number of fishermen. As L increases, more and more fishermen are fishing a given area with its scarce fish stock. As a result, the law of diminishing returns comes into play. Each additional fisherman raises the total catch by a smaller amount than the one before, causing the average product of labor to be downward sloping. The law of diminishing returns shows up directly in the value of labor's marginal product (VMP_L), which measures the increase in the value of the total catch that results when the number of fishermen increases by one. VMP_L also slopes downward and lies below ARP_L because of the relation between marginal and average curves.

Suppose that fishermen have free access to the area without being subject to any license or quota or having to pay a fee for the right to fish. Then overfishing will destroy the value of the fish stock and, more generally, overexploitation of communal resources will destroy their value. Under free access, L_C, or 130 fishermen, will fish this area, which is the number that set $ARP_L = W$ or $PQ = WL$. The reason is that a smaller number will leave ARP_L greater than W. A typical fisherman will earn more than his or her opportunity cost, and more fishermen will come to fish here in order to take advantage of this. A number larger than L_C will leave ARP_L less than W, and the number of fishermen will shrink until the average fisherman just recovers his or her opportunity cost.

As indicated, $PQ = WL$ at C, the communal or common property solution.

Figure 1.3 Destruction of Resource Value by Communal Rights

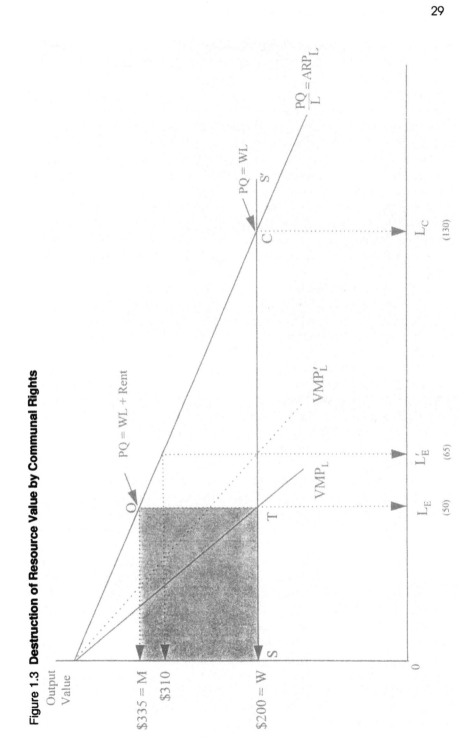

The value of the fish caught equals the value of the labor used in fishing. In general, the value of output (PQ) equals the value of *all* inputs plus profit or loss. Here nothing remains for profit or payment of any other input after paying labor its opportunity cost. In the present context, W includes the opportunity cost of fishing tackle and boats, as well as of direct labor, but nothing is left over from compensation of these inputs to serve as rental on the fish stock. As a scarce input, this stock should earn a return in the form of a rent, and the capitalized value of this rent is then the value of this resource. The communal property solution reduces this rent to zero, and in this way destroys the value of the fish stock through overexploitation.

By contrast, the efficient solution is at $L_E = 50$, where ARP_L exceeds W by $OT = MW = \$135$, and also where the value of labor's marginal product (VMP_L) equals W. The latter pricing rule signals efficient use of any productive input. Less than half as many fishermen are then exploiting this resource as at the common property solution, and the fish stock yields a rent equal to $50 \times \$135$, or $\$6,750$ per day, which is the shaded area, $MOST$. The value of the resource is then positive and equal to $\$6,750$ divided by an appropriate daily interest rate. The latter will be quite small (roughly the annual interest rate divided by 365). If the daily rate is about .0002, the value of the fish stock is around $\$34$ million when only L_E fishermen are allowed to fish. This is the value that communal property rights (or free access) destroy through overfishing. If we set out to maximize the value of the fish stock, and therefore the rental on this resource ($= PQ - WL$), we would also end up at the efficient solution. (When L is less than L_E, an additional fisherman raises $PQ - WL$, since VMP_L is greater than W. When L exceeds L_E, an additional fisherman reduces $PQ - WL$, as VMP_L is less than W.)

The overfishing problem associated with communal property rights can also be viewed as a problem of "externalities." As more and more fishermen exploit a given fish stock, each additional fisherman makes it slightly harder for the others to catch fish. This is analogous to buyers queuing for a good or service. Each additional buyer adds to the congestion and makes it harder for the others to obtain the product. To an average fisherman, it appears as if he or she increases the total value of fish caught by ARP_L, since this curve measures the value of his or her daily catch. However, part of this catch is obtained by reducing the average catch of other fishermen, since ARP_L is falling as the number of fishermen rises. In fact, an additional fisherman raises the total catch by the smaller quantity, VMP_L. Since ARP_L gives the perceived value of marginal product to an average fisherman while VMP_L is the true value of marginal product, the vertical gap between these curves is the value of the negative externality caused when the number of fishermen increases by one.

A second external effect arises because catching too many fish before they are able to breed reduces the future size of the stock. Beyond some point, additional fish caught today will mean smaller future catches, and the true marginal productivity of fishermen should be adjusted downward for this effect. In Figure 1.3, the solid line, VMP_L, is fully adjusted for reductions in future catches, whereas the dashed line, VMP'_L, is not. (Both VMP_L and VMP'_L take the first or congestion externality into account.)

As indicated in the text, we can get the efficient solution in some combination of two basic ways. The market way is to charge each fisherman $OT = MW = \$135$ for the right to fish. Now ARP_L must cover W plus this charge, giving $ARP_L = W + OT$, which occurs where L_E (or 50) fishermen are exploiting this resource. The quota or licensing way is to authorize no more than 50 fishermen on any given day—or to allow more people than this to fish but to limit the catch of each so that the value of the fish caught is no more than $\$335 \times 50 = \$16,750$ per day. To be effective, each type of solution must be enforced, since there will be an incentive to fish without paying a fee or gaining authorization.

Both methods of restricting access in order to preserve the value of the fish stock—and possibly to prevent its extinction as well—have perceived advantages and disadvantages. Suppose that this resource is privately owned. Then the owners of the fish stock have an incentive to maximize the value of their asset. If they are successful, they will end up charging the efficient rent, perhaps after a period of experimentation. The advantage of the market solution is that these owners have a direct incentive to find and to charge the efficient rent, as long as they do not have monopoly power and on the assumption that ownership rights over the fish stock (or the geographical area where it is located) can be bought and sold at a price determined by buyer and seller. In this case, the rental charged to fish the area (OT) indicates both the rental value of the fish stock per fisherman *and* what fishermen are willing to pay for the right to fish. Therefore, it contains useful information.

It is worth emphasizing that the above incentive to maximize the value of the fish stock depends on having two markets. There is a market on which the right to fish is bought and sold, but there is also a potential market on which the fish stock itself can be sold. Without the latter, the incentive to maximize resource value may be diluted. For example, suppose a custodian of the fish stock can gain from exploiting the resource—as when he or she can keep part of the fees charged for fishing rights—but cannot gain from selling it. Then if the custodian expects to remain at this post for a limited period of time, he or she may ignore the second externality above and charge a fee that sets $VMP'_L = W$ or $L = 65$. This fee would be $\$110$, giving a daily rental income of $110 \times \$65 = \$7,150$, greater than the rental of $\$6,750$ when the fee is $\$135$. However, the lower fee yields a greater income only in the short run and does not maximize resource value, because it leads to more rapid depletion of the fish stock.

Despite these potential problems, many will feel that at least some natural resources should belong to society as a whole, in which case they cannot be bought or sold, since the latter implies alienation of ownership. If we apply the same logic, these resources should also be available to all for less than what the market will bear. To preserve the value of such a resource (and possibly the resource itself), we must then restrict access through quotas or authorizations, and we cannot give its public custodians too great an incentive to exploit it. In principle, we can still attain the efficient solution, but in practice this may be difficult or impossible for lack of information. Since we do not seek to charge the maximum rental that fishermen are willing to pay, we are unlikely to be able to determine what this is or to know what value of L maximizes the value of the resource. Since the rental value is not actually paid or received by anyone, it remains invisible.

Nevertheless, even if we do not attain the efficient result, we may still be able to use quotas to restrict fishing enough that the fish stock will sustain itself without "undue" depletion. Although this may not maximize the value of the stock, some would regard the gain in value from moving to private ownership and alienation of the resource to be not worth the cost—always depending on specific circumstances. Even if a resource is not bought or sold, it still has a value to those who benefit from it.

Notes

1. Strictly speaking, these nations were "socialist" rather than "communist." We shall see the difference below.

2. H. Demsetz, "Toward a Theory of Property Rights," *American Economic Review*, May 1967, p. 347. The discussion below elaborates on his classification scheme, esp. pp. 354ff.

3. There is a symmetry here. Below-equilibrium prices produce excess demand and potential congestion among would-be buyers, while above-equilibrium prices produce excess supply and potential congestion among would-be sellers. We shall discuss the latter problem in a labor market context in chapter 4. An analysis of short-run distributional implications of communal property rights may be found in Martin Weitzman, "Free Access versus Private Ownership as Alternative Systems for Managing Common Property," *Journal of Economic Theory*, June 1974. The classic discussion of common property is Scott Gordon's "The Economic Theory of a Common-Property Resource: The Fishery," *Journal of Political Economy*, April 1954.

4. P. J. D. Wiles, "Growth versus Choice," *Economic Journal*, June 1956. We shall explore the Marxian theory of historical evolution of economic systems in chapter 4.

5. This must include nonpecuniary income (e.g., the value of leisure time). By "marginal net value," I mean the marginal value of a good to a user minus any costs other than its price that he or she pays to gain the use of it. (These are called "transactions costs.")

6. The following discussion of price controls borrows from S. N. S. Cheung, "A Theory of Price Control," *Journal of Law and Economics*, April 1974. Concerning experience with rent control, see Sven Rydenfelt, "The Rise and Fall of Swedish Rent Control," in M. A. Walker, ed., *Rent Control: A Popular Paradox* (Vancouver: The Fraser Institute, 1975), and H. W. Morton, "Who Gets What, Where, and How? Housing in the Soviet Union," *Soviet Studies*, April 1982.

7. In the case of rent control, rules making it costlier for landlords to evict or to harass tenants or to convert their dwellings to condominiums have the same effect as a partial quota system, favoring present occupants over those seeking apartments but currently without them.

8. Janos Kornai developed the notion of a state-managed or Soviet-type economy as a "shortage" economy. See his *Anti-Equilibrium* (Amsterdam: North-Holland, 1971) and *Economics of Shortage* (Amsterdam: North-Holland, 1980).

9. Gao Yangliu, "Signs of Capitalism in China? The Shenyang Experiment," *China Reconstructs,* March 1987, p. 41. See as well E. G. Furubotn, S. Pejovich, "Property Rights and the Behavior of a Firm in a Socialist State," *Zeitschrift für Nationalökonomie,* 3–4, 1970, and L. R. Thurow, "Productivity: Japan Has a Better Way," *New York Times,* Feb. 8, 1981, section 3, p. 2.

10. See Istvan Dobozi, "Policy Responses to the Energy Crisis: East and West," *ACES Bulletin,* Spring 1981.

11. This appendix borrows from Scott Gordon, "The Economic Theory of a Common-Property Resource: The Fishery," *Journal of Political Economy,* April 1954.

Questions for Review, Discussion, Examination

1. Compare the notions of private, state, and communal property rights.

    (a) Explain how use, income, and transfer rights would differ under these three different systems. How do we determine "ownership" in the property rights sense?

    (b) What two basic forms of exclusion can we distinguish? Why would we tend to identify one more with state property rights and the other more with private property rights? What is the identifying feature of communal property?

    (c) What is inefficient about communal rights, except in special circumstances? What are these special circumstances? Explain briefly.

2. Why does widespread exercise of state property rights tend to be associated with price ceilings, which create excess demand? (Or why were Soviet-type economies also "shortage" economies?)

3. Why do widespread price controls require allocation via quotas of some sort to avoid inefficiency? Describe the nature of the inefficiency that may result when price ceilings are effective and there are no quota systems of any kind to help allocate goods whose prices are controlled.

4. Suppose that we have an economic system in which there is widespread allocation of goods by means of quotas or rationing. (This was in fact true of the Soviet-type economy.)

    (a) Are prices rational or irrational in such a system? Briefly explain in what ways they are rational or irrational and why.

    (b) Given your answer to (a), what informational problems does quota allocation raise for efforts to allocate goods or to manage the economy efficiently? Briefly explain these problems.

5. What basic condition must an economy meet to be considered "socialist" in the property rights sense? What does this basic condition imply about income rights? What markets would such an economy have to restrict or to suppress? Discuss briefly. What does this imply about the role of the state in a socialist market economy? Would the values of state firms be known in such a system? Why or why not? What further condition does a Soviet-type economy satisfy?

6. Historically, there has been a tendency in Soviet-type economies to di-

vorce reward from performance, as measured by financial indicators, in favor of greater leveling of incomes. One aspect of this has been the "soft" enterprise budget constraint.

(a) What do we mean by the "soft" budget constraint? What are some of its undesirable consequences, and what were some of the reasons for maintaining it in Soviet-type economies despite these? In particular, describe the incentive effects of the soft budget constraint.

(b) Try to imagine the probable effect of introducing a soft budget constraint and associated socialization of investment returns into a market economy. Distinguish a *macroeconomic* effect (or an effect on overall economic performance) from a *microeconomic* effect (or an effect on the efficiency with which resources are allocated and used).

7. Why may *transferable* ownership claims lengthen managerial time horizons? Is this always the case? If not, give an exception. Explain how separation of ownership from management may reduce managerial time horizons. Explain as well how one might try to overcome this problem.

8. Show that communal property rights to a scarce resource have a destructive effect on that resource. Explain exactly what they destroy and how, using a graph if possible.

9. Now assume that the resource in problem 8 is no longer scarce. How will your graph change? Show that the resource is now efficiently exploited under communal property rights. (*Hint:* If the resource is not scarce, there will be more than enough of it to go around among the various fishermen in the common property solution. As a result, the entry of one more fisherman will not reduce the catch of the others, so that diminishing returns will not arise. Now use the law relating the marginal to the average.)

Chapter 2

The Traditional Soviet-type Economy

I once saw in Moscow a sketch in which a well-known Russian comedian went on stage rubbing his hands and saying: "Shortages comrades are what we want. Shortages made me who I am." Of course, he allocates something administratively that is in short supply. "As a result of my position and as a result of shortages, I am a person of influence in society; people bring me cases of cognac, people treat me with respect. What would happen comrades if there were no shortages? I would be as insignificant as any bloody engineer. . . ."

—Alec Nove

The Notion of Planning

In chapter 1, we introduced the idea of a "Soviet-type" economy, so named because it was first installed in the Soviet Union by Stalin in 1928. After World War II, it was extended to Eastern Europe, as well as to China and North Korea, and came to prevail in countries comprising a third of the world's population. This economic system turned out to be inefficient, and today most of these nations have become transition economies in the sense that they are converting to market systems. Even in China and Vietnam, where the Communist Party continues to rule, there appears to be little enthusiasm for turning back the clock. However, all transition economies confront serious challenges that are in large measure the legacy of the Soviet-type economy. In order to understand the problems faced by transition economies, we must first invest some time in understanding the nature of the system that was left behind. As Soviet-type economies were also planned economies, our journey begins with a description of this feature. In what follows, the terms *Soviet-type, command,* and *state-managed* will be used interchangeably. Each refers to the state-managed economy outlined in Table 1.1.

Types of Economic Plans

A national economy is "planned" when its government is able to determine the broad outlines of a strategy of economic development. This means that it formulates and is able to implement a consistent set of priorities over time. Planning thus refers to measures affecting the structure of outputs produced or of inputs used rather than to efforts to raise or lower aggregate demand. However, if we view the setting of priorities as the demand side of planning, there is also a supply side consisting of efforts to improve alternatives available to the economy as a whole and to individual households and firms—for example, through worker training, diffusion of technological information, and investments designed to avoid future supply bottlenecks.

Soviet-type economies were planned, and their central planning staffs drew up three kinds of economywide plans or blueprints to govern future production, investment, allocation of resources, and research and development:

1. *Long-term plans* covered 10 to 15 years and corresponded roughly to the "very long run" in the theory of the firm in a market economy. They tried to predict changes in the main direction of economic development based on expected resource availability and diffusion of new technologies. Thus, "the principles and methods of structural change can best be elaborated in *long-range* plans ... [that provide] guidelines for medium-term planning concerning ... the training and management of the labor force, living conditions, ratios of development in the infrastructure and various fields, main trends in the supply of energy and raw materials, agriculture, and technology, as well as international economic relations."[1] However, long-term plans were the least important of the three categories. They were not greatly detailed or quantified, as a rule, nor were they usually disaggregated to arrive at targets for individual firms.

2. *Medium-term (five-year) plans* were the best known type in the West. They were investment plans corresponding to the "long run" in the theory of the firm in a market economy and were more detailed than long-term plans. The length of the medium-term plan was determined by the ability to see ahead with reasonable certainty and by the gestation periods of capital construction projects. After 1971, the five-year plans of all countries in the Council for Mutual Economic Assistance (COMECON), the economic association that embraced the Soviet Union and her allies, began and ended at the same time. In addition, several joint investment projects involving these countries, most of which were intended to improve the supply of Soviet energy to Eastern Europe, were completed.[2]

3. *Short-term plans* of a year or less were the most important and generally had the force of law. They corresponded to the "short run" in the Western theory of the firm and were by far the most detailed, although they were drawn up in the context of five-year plan targets and prior progress in meeting these. As Tamas Morva states, "The list of investment projects to be started and finished, based on the decisions of the five-year plan and domestic and foreign trade regulations, are generally included in the annual plan, along with [annual credit] policy directives of the National Bank. There is also close coordination between the annual plan and the annual government budget."[3]

Governments can also affect the direction and pace of economic growth without directly managing production and exchange. In fact, there are planned market economies that are quite different from Soviet-type economies, and we shall reserve the term *mixed economy*—that is, a mixture of planning and the market—for this category. Here the role of government is to compensate for perceived market failures—in terms of growth, efficiency, and/or distribution—while leaving most of the market system intact. Such planning has both costs and benefits. Potentially among the latter are the use of a plan as a vehicle for mobilizing efforts and resources to the achievement of national goals. Nations have adopted planning in the past because it gave them at least the illusion of greater control over their destinies. National planning can also help domestic producers get a head start in developing new products and technologies. Here economies of scale or experience are often substantial, and there are frequently technological externalities in the sense that experience gained with one type of production process helps in mastering others based on the same underlying technology. In recent years, the term *industrial policy* has been applied to planning with this kind of objective in a market economy. Planning can also help to avoid environmental problems and to ensure a rational allocation of public goods, as well as to expand political time horizons in a democracy. While planning in a Soviet-type economy tends to replace the market as a coordinator of economic activity, planning in a mixed economy leaves most coordination to the market and therefore presupposes decentralization of most management decisions down to the enterprise.

Planning in a Soviet-type Economy: Targets, Quotas, and Rationing

A Soviet-type economy was built around a hierarchy that extended from the political leadership and central planners at the top to enterprises at the bottom. The political leadership consisted of the top organs of the Communist Party and the state. They notably included the Politburo of the Communist Party, which set basic policy, and the Council of Ministers (or cabinet), in practice the chief government authority. These bodies handed down broad guidelines charting the direction of economic development that were then translated into concrete detail by a state planning agency, formally a staff agency to the Council of Ministers. In practice, the latter had most of the nation's top planning experts and therefore made many major decisions on its own. From the state planning agency, a typical chain of command went to the economic ministries, each in charge of a different sector or group of industries, and from there, via regional and industrial authorities, to the enterprises. Firms of lesser importance were managed largely by provincial or local government bodies.

Figure 2.1 gives a general view of the chain of command in the former Soviet Union, with the arrows indicating the basic directions of orders or commands.

Figure 2.1 **A General View of the Chain of Command in the Former Soviet Union**

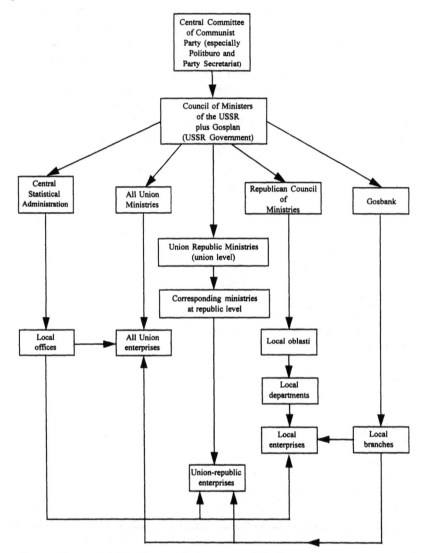

Source: Eugene Zaleski, *Planning Reforms in the Soviet Union, 1962–66* (Chapel Hill: University of North Carolina Press, 1967), chap. 2 (especially chart 2, p. 18).

The entire Soviet Union was divided into union republics (such as Russia, Ukraine, the Baltic states, etc.), which have since become independent countries. These were divided in turn into *oblasti* or provinces. Thus the most important firms were the all-union enterprises, which were controlled by all-union ministries (or ministries whose jurisdiction was the Soviet Union as a whole). Next

came union-republic enterprises controlled by republican ministries, whose jurisdictions were confined to one republic and were themselves coordinated across
different republics by union-republican ministries. Finally, a variety of local
enterprises came under the control of provincial and lower-level authorities.

In this scheme of things, the center made the broadest and most basic
decisions about what and how to produce and, to a lesser extent, for whom.
These were embodied in a set of aggregate production targets specifying a
minimum performance level for the economy that were progressively disaggregated as they filtered down the chain of command. The entire set of
targets was included in a formal document called a plan. There was a plan for
the nation as a whole that was then broken down into plans for each region,
industry, and firm. Enterprise plans included *output targets* giving minimum
expected rates of output, as well as *input quotas* specifying maximum authorized rates of input use, and targets for profitability, cost reduction, innovation, and so on that were usually less important than output targets. In all, a
firm received hundreds or even thousands of targets and generally had to
choose which to meet and which to miss. It also received delivery dates and
destinations for its products. Often the latter were state intermediaries that
supplied ultimate users.

In such a system, producer goods were rationed physically—via input quotas
for each firm—and in some cases by queuing, with precedence in the queue
going to enterprises whose outputs had a high state priority. When done formally, such rationing was called *supply planning by materials balances,* because
the amount of each material available from production, import, and adjustment
of inventory was balanced against the amount used up in further production,
export, and consumption. In this sense, a balance was struck between the input
quotas and the output targets, acting as a substitute for the balancing of supply
and demand via price adjustment in a market economy in which access to goods
depends on willingness and ability to pay going prices. The need for consistency
between input quotas and output targets in the absence of flexible prices—as
well as egalitarian pressures to socialize investment returns—forced some allocation decisions to be centralized to the highest levels of government. Inevitably,
many other decisions remained at lower levels, and there was always some
conflict among the interests of different authorities.

In constructing plans, officials in a command economy often had to add or
subtract quantities of dissimilar goods, and they also used such aggregates to
make the tasks of communicating and enforcing plans manageable. If only for
this reason, all goods had prices, and money remained in use. The most important output targets usually reached firms as aggregates expressed in value terms.
This allowed the enterprise some leeway in deciding how to fulfill its plan. For
example, a rise in the official price of sheet steel, with no change in other prices
or in the plan, would cause steel mills to try to reach the gross or net value of
output targets by producing more sheet steel and less of other kinds of steel.

Quantity supplied, therefore, depended partly on prices, although mainly on production targets.

However, official prices were set by government agencies rather than by sellers or buyers. They remained fixed over fairly long periods—to save the cost of revision and to make the performance of each enterprise more comparable across time and thus easier to evaluate. They were also usually below levels that would just ration available supplies among would-be users. At official prices, there were overall excess demands for both consumer and producer goods, and a typical price was like P_0 in Figure 1.2 rather than $\bar{P}$ or P_1 in the same diagram. In this sense, expansion of production was constrained not by demand but rather by availability of inputs or by organization factors (such as planning from the achieved level, discussed later). The excess demand spilled over into a network of black and gray markets, sometimes called the "second economy." Here prices responded more flexibly to supply and demand and were usually above official levels.[4]

On the "first" or official economy, prices played an accounting-information-supervision role that was designed to simplify the task of state management, and they also had a distribution role. For example, subsidies were used to lower the prices of necessities, while taxes raised the prices of luxuries (which still remained in excess demand). On the "second" or unofficial economy, prices played a role more like that in a market system, and in some cases supplies were available only for Western or other convertible currencies.[5] At the same time, the costs of using the second economy (in terms of effort, time, and risk) were often greater than the costs of similar buying and selling in a market economy. Part of the second economy (including most trade in producer goods) was illegal, and it was restricted in a variety of ways designed to prevent it from dominating the first or official economy.

When desired goods, or those prescribed by the plan, were unavailable, households and firms often had to use substitutes. Such forced substitution created a demand for goods that were of low quality or otherwise ill-adapted to user requirements but that were relatively easy to produce and make available. Shortages of goods and of consumer credit also gave rise to an excess supply of savings. People saved more than they wanted to at going prices and interest rates because consumer goods were not readily available and/or because the low availability of credit to households forced them to build up their savings in advance of large purchases. In most Soviet-type economies, there was less formal rationing of consumer goods than of producer goods. That is why we speak of official markets for the former but not the latter. Yet the reduced role of prices in rationing consumer products led households to spend a lot of time searching, standing in line, and otherwise trying to obtain goods. The opportunity cost of this time was probably lower for relatively low-income households.

However, key officials, directors of major enterprises, and others with high status also enjoyed a wider access to goods, including the right to shop in special stores, and they sometimes received part of their paychecks in Western currencies. Because of shortages, the state was able to control the rewards given to these people by granting them favorable access to luxuries as long as their performance was judged acceptable. Differential access raised effective inequality in such a society, although this was not reflected in statistics on income distribution.

Because shortages reduced the value of money and increased the time devoted to obtaining goods in a Soviet-type economy, they also reduced the willingness to work. To offset this, the state often required satisfactory job performance as a prerequisite to access to housing and other consumer durables, which were sometimes distributed through the workplace. Each worker had to carry a labor book or similar document that contained a variety of personal information, including information on formal and on-the-job training. This allowed the government to keep track of workers. The regime also tried to make it hard for employees to get medical excuses for absence from work, and there was some pressure to work during vacation periods. "Parasitism," or living off the labor of others, was a crime for any able-bodied male of working age, and in some cases for able-bodied females. As a result, most command economies had higher labor force participation rates than did most Western market economies.

The Financial Plan

Because each flow of goods from one enterprise to another (or to a household or for export) was compensated by a flow of money in the opposite direction, a network of financial flows lay behind the physical flows associated with any plan. Thus, there was a financial as well as a physical plan. A disruption of physical flows (e.g., failure to receive planned deliveries on time) potentially gave firms an incentive to ask for departures from the financial plan (specifically, that they not be charged for such deliveries) or else disrupted financial flows. Consequently, the financial plan was used to monitor compliance with the physical plan; this was called "control by the ruble" (or yuan, zloty, crown, forint, etc.). Such control was the essence of monetary policy under command planning.

The government had no independent control over the supplies of money and credit, which were dictated by the requirements of the physical plan and by "extraordinary" or above-plan needs of state firms. In the years leading up to the downfall of command planning, the latter became larger and larger and helped to generate inflationary pressures that contributed to making the system dysfunctional. There were few banks in a Soviet-type economy—mainly the National Bank and specific banks for investment, agriculture, and foreign trade. The first of these was a combined central bank and commercial banking system. State enterprises kept their accounts with the National Bank, which monitored flows of funds and enforced control by the ruble. There were two types of money, each of which was segregated from the other. Within the state sector, all payments took the form of bookkeeping entries that transferred credit from one state firm or agency to another. Between households, units of collective agriculture, and other nonstate entities, as well as between the state and nonstate sectors, payments were made in cash. Households could hold cash and savings deposits only. As a rule, they could not have checking accounts and had little access to credit, if any, through official channels.

The priorities of a Soviet-type economy were etched in its financial flows. Let us say that heavy industries are those producing basic inputs, such as iron, steel, coal, chemicals, cement, fuel, electric power, and machine tools, while light industries are those producing consumer goods or inputs into the production of consumer goods. Traditionally, heavy industrial output had the highest priority, followed by light industry, with agriculture and services last. The prices of many heavy industrial outputs and inputs were set well below production costs, and firms producing them received large subsidies. By contrast, most light industrial goods were priced to yield profits, which were mainly taxed away, and large sales or turnover taxes were levied on them as well. The budget also absorbed the difference between low prices paid to farmers for produce raised on collective farms and higher prices charged to households. In addition, obligatory delivery targets were required to ensure a supply of agricultural produce at the low procurement prices.

Such priorities meant that the basic task assigned to heavy industry was to expand flat out—to an extent heedless of cost considerations. The task of light industry and agriculture was to generate savings—in the form of profits and turnover taxes—to finance the growth of heavy industry. The state budget and banking systems had the job of siphoning funds from low-priority sectors and funneling them mainly into basic heavy industries.[6] This funnel replaced financial markets, which were virtually nonexistent in Soviet-type systems. Priorities did change to some degree over long periods of time. For example, after being starved of funds for many years, farming subsequently received a higher priority, because the supplies of food, raw materials for industry, and (in some cases) farm exports could not otherwise have been maintained. Agriculture became a net user rather than a net supplier of savings. In addition, modern, high-technology sectors came to have a high priority, especially when these were useful to defense-related production.

Finally, besides monitoring financial flows, the state supervised production in other ways. There were agencies charged with enforcing plan compliance through direct inspection, for example, and local Communist Party members were charged with enforcing the spirit of the plan. Each workplace had a party secretary in charge of a committee of employees who were party members. Their task was to enforce quality and cost control, labor discipline, and a correct political line, as well as to promote innovation and a longer managerial time horizon. The party committee was therefore a kind of board of directors to which the enterprise manager had a general responsibility, on top of his specific responsibilities to his planning superiors. However, in some of these countries, including the Soviet Union itself, the party secretary was judged by the same production indices as the director, which tended to undermine the former's supervisory role.

In addition, Communist Party youth groups visited factories, farms, and construction sites, noting poor performance and exhorting managers, engineers, and workers to build socialism by improving performance. Newspaper and magazine articles often complained about poor performance and could sometimes put pressure on those responsible, as long as their complaints did not touch on the basic nature of the system or reach too high in the planning hierarchy. Labor unions had no independent bargaining power over wages, although they could often protect workers from dismissal or job transfer, and they controlled the allocation of enterprise housing and social benefits. They also helped to monitor managerial performance.

Pressure from planners, Communist Party officials, and others was designed to motivate firms to make good use of the resources at their disposal. It replaced the competitive pressures of a market economy. Yet the successful enterprise director in a Soviet-type economy was able to build reserves of labor, materials, and production capacity in order to be able to meet output targets with room to spare. Consequently, he often produced inside his production-possibilities frontier. Let us look at this phenomenon more closely.

Planning from the Achieved Level

State management of production and distribution placed a heavy decision-making load on the planning hierarchy. Ministries or subordinate agencies required some detailed knowledge of the production capabilities of every enterprise of consequence under their supervision. While knowledge of individual firms could be scattered among lower-level planning authorities, this had to be brought together at the top in order for state management to be effective. Each year, the planners coordinated millions of flows of goods among firms, the household sector, and the foreign sector, and the optimal value of each flow depended in a complex way on all the others. Even in the short run, they had to choose from an almost unlimited number of possible plans—each with a somewhat different array of output targets and input quotas, and thus a different matrix of flows linking the former to the latter.[7]

Consequently, the amount of information needed to calculate an optimal plan was too great; optimizing was largely confined to Western textbooks on planning. Yet plan targets had to be set on a simple and objective basis in order to keep down the volume of resources devoted to calculating them and to lobbying or bargaining over them. Therefore, in practice next year's targets were usually based on this year's performance, with markups for expected increases in capacity or other inputs, as well as for expected productivity gains. There were also adjustments for changes in central priorities, for new information, or as a result of enterprise requests. Nevertheless, as Igor Birman has written, "The well-known words, 'from the achieved level,' denote that plan indicators are derived by adding to the relevant figures [of expected current performance] a certain percentage of growth. That is the foundation of all the technique, all the methodology of Soviet planning. The rest is secondary."[8]

The tendency to base next year's plan on this year's achievement profoundly influenced the way a command economy operated. Since plan targets gave minimum acceptable performance levels, a manager whose enterprise consistently fell short of these risked losing income and chances for promotion. Therefore, it was crucial to reach the most important output targets, even at a high cost. But the tendency to proceed from the achieved level also made an enterprise director reluctant to overfulfill his output targets by large margins. Suppose he were to exceed his major output target by 25 percent. As future targets depended on present performance, they would be set higher than if he had overfulfilled by only 5 percent—a phenomenon known as the "ratchet effect." Similarly, he would be reluctant to overfulfill profitability, productivity, or cost control norms. Since prices were irrational and planners did not know what values of profit or cost corresponded to efficient performance, they had to assess each firm in relation to its own past record rather than against an external standard.

The ratchet effect put a discount on the value to managers of production beyond target levels. Surviving directors would produce inside their production-possibility frontiers and be reluctant to deviate too much above or below their target levels. As a result, supply curves were quite inelastic for those products and aggregates of products whose output targets were important. They could even be backward bending, since an increase in the price of a good made it possible to reach value targets with a smaller output. Directors also tried to hoard inputs in order to ensure target fulfillment. The soft budget constraint reinforced these tendencies by divorcing the earnings and career prospects of a firm's management and workforce from its financial success.

The ratchet effect also increased the importance of the plan as a guide to performance, thereby strengthening the bond between past, present, and future output assortments and production methods. Command economies tended to lock themselves into a particular strategy of development—such as priority expansion of traditional heavy industries—from which changes in direction were difficult. This reduced their ability to adapt to changing supply and demand patterns or to change priorities, thereby offsetting a potential advantage of planning. New products with no history of production and use tended to be frozen out of plan formation. These economies had low rates of innovation. The ratchet effect also forced the central planners to guard against tendencies to "lead a quiet life." This referred to a manager who succeeded in getting easy plan targets year after year, thereby wasting resources. To countervail such behavior, planners tried to challenge firms with targets that were hard to reach. However, such taut planning also increased the incentive to hoard inputs. Thus, it worsened shortages of key inputs and led to two additional phenomena—ministerial self-sufficiency and "storming."

Under taut planning, ministries had to worry about meeting their own targets, defined in terms of the aggregated outputs of firms under their jurisdictions. This gave each ministry an incentive to make its own firms supply other firms under its jurisdiction before allowing similar inputs to go to firms under other ministries. Ministries also tended to integrate backward—or to produce their own supplies—which led to duplication of production among them. Moreover, enterprises producing at a rate faster than necessary to fulfill their annual or quarterly output targets risked having these raised while fulfillment was in progress. This encouraged them to "storm"—that is, to maintain a relatively slow production pace until near the end of the planning period and then go flat out to meet their targets. When the new period started, they again took things easy. (To some extent, this is human nature in the face of a deadline; university students have been observed in a similar pattern with respect to their course work.)

Plan construction was even more complex when it came to choosing among alternative capital spending programs over a horizon of five years or more. We recall that relative prices of different goods were irrational in that they reflected neither relative costs of production nor relative marginal values to planners or to users. Any ranking of alternative investment projects on the basis of their expected yields or rates of return could therefore be far from accurate, since the computation of such yields invariably depended on prices. However, investment yields were still calculated and used to a limited extent under command planning because they were a common denominator, allowing comparison of proposed capital spending projects even across diverse sectors of the economy. Without them, such comparisons would have been staggering beyond imagination. Billions of uncertain, dissimilar, and multidimensional physical flows—the outputs in physical terms of proposed investment projects—would have had to be evaluated and compared. It would have been necessary for the planners to envisage several alternative complete industrial sectors, each in highly complex physical detail, evolving several years into the future. From there, they would have had to choose a preferred alternative with its associated investment programs, but such a procedure was far too complex to be practical. In addition, because of the decision-making overload at the center—which increased rapidly as an economy expanded—Soviet-type economies often tried to "reform" or to decentralize, although usually with quite limited success.

Planning in Market Economies: The Common Denominator

By letting each firm be an independent decision maker, a market system breaks up the economic problem facing society into a multitude of subproblems, each of which is comparatively tiny in terms of the scope and number of variables involved.

This is an advantage, and it brings us to the mixed economy, which leaves most coordination of economic activity to the market and thereby tries to capture potential benefits of both plan and market.

Within an economy that is "mixed" in the sense of combining planning and the market, enterprises have greater freedom to decide how much of each good to produce and what production methods to use. In most cases, competition is the main force relied on to ensure that firms make intensive use of the resources available to them. The state nationalizes fewer property rights, and when it does formulate production targets, these usually remain aggregated at the level of the industry or region. They are not broken down by firm, since the lack of control over individual enterprises renders their behavior too unpredictable. Such targets are mainly forecasts or indicators rather than commands. Quantitatively, they may turn out to be wide of the mark. In a market economy, however, it is not as important for government to have an accurate, detailed breakdown of future production by industry and region as it is to perceive basic directions of change and to know which sectors to promote in order to achieve state goals.

Planning in a market economy usually costs less than command planning. The government tries to influence the direction of growth by relying on its control over expenditures, taxes, and insurance; its regulatory authority; its ability to raise or lower barriers to entry; its ability to influence the allocation of investment; and its facilities to promote the exchange and spread of information. These can alter the behavior of firms and households by changing their property rights environments. Command planning potentially gives the state more direct control over the assortment of goods produced. Nevertheless, when successful, the two approaches have as their common denominator government's ability to exercise leverage over the availability and allocation of key productive inputs. Even in mixed economies, these have often been in excess demand.

Under command planning, the state gains some control over the direction of economic growth through its ability to set output targets, but it must also control the allocation of essential inputs. Soviet-type economies hardly ever fulfilled all of their main output targets in a given year. In the Soviet Union, farm production goals were usually not met, and light industry had a worse record than heavy industry. By and large, it was low-priority sectors that most often failed to meet their targets. In this context, we recall that enterprise managers were reluctant to overfulfill output targets by large margins because of planning from the achieved level. At the start of any year (or quarter, month, etc.), production possibilities for that year were partly unknown. As a result, the planners tried to challenge firms with difficult targets in order to keep their managements from leading quiet lives (or from producing too far inside their production-possibility frontiers). This helped to ensure that not all targets could be reached, and managers sometimes underfulfilled their plans deliberately in order to conceal input reserves.

Consequently, in allocating inputs planners often had to decide which targets would be made easiest to fulfill. By controlling input supplies, they tried to confine most shortages, forced substitution, and bottlenecks or other disruptions to low-priority sectors. These industries and their customers (historically, mainly households) bore most of the risk of failure to fulfill the plan by acting as residual claimants to goods and resources. By controlling the allocation of key productive inputs, the state was able to control which targets were met and which were missed. The more profitable, low-priority industries were well placed to bid for scarce inputs in a market setting and were usually the main buyers on black and gray markets for producer goods. Insofar as this trading simply reduced inventories of productive inputs (which were usually too high), it was desirable. But when it reduced high-priority outputs below target levels in order to allow low-priority sectors to increase production, it thwarted the central planners' intentions. Restrictions on the second economy served to reduce its scope—in part, to protect state priorities.

Control over supplies of key inputs under conditions of excess demand thus helped to keep the planners in command. However, shortages also caused goods to be more readily acceptable, even with defects in quality or design. Thus, excess demand covered up mistakes of planners or enterprise managers and helped the planning network to isolate producers from users by reducing the latter's bargaining power. Firms produced to meet plan targets rather than to satisfy user preferences, causing quality problems and supply-demand mismatches that increased prevailing shortages. Input inventories were high, and firms that fulfilled their main targets year after year usually succeeded in building reserves of labor and capacity. Because it was costly to use the second economy, firms sometimes failed to meet output targets for want of essential inputs, even though other enterprises were holding reserves of the same or of substitute goods. Moreover, firms came to depend on their planning superiors for delivery of supplies. Efforts to decentralize the economic systems of Eastern Europe, the Soviet Union, and China—and, in particular, to raise enterprise autonomy—foundered on this dependence.

Under market planning, excess demand is confined to a narrower class of goods, such as investment finance, but government again relies on its ability to influence access. Once a Japanese steel producer who was complaining about state interference in his expansion plans was asked why he did not ignore the government and go his own way. His answer, "Because in that case I wouldn't get the money I want to finance the development," shows how the state can utilize excess demand plus leverage over the allocation of investment loans to overrule the individual preferences of households and firms in charting a course of economic development.[9] In some countries (including Japan), foreign currencies have been rationed among prospective importers in a similar fashion, or the same effect has been achieved through informal barriers to imports. Those firms with best access to investment funds or imports receive an effective subsidy, while others are penalized.

We can also view information as a productive input whose availability potentially affects costs and product quality. Government activities to improve the flow of information about products and production methods, as well as public authorities' leverage over the availability of investment credits or of imported goods, represent efforts to influence the direction and pace of economic growth without resorting to direct control over the allocation of thousands of different kinds of producer goods.

Centralization versus Decentralization

Some Gains from Centralizing Control Over Production

Because the excess demand for goods and services—together with effective wage ceilings—tends to produce an excess demand for labor, Soviet-type economies usually had low rates of open unemployment, although with some notable exceptions. In addition, they paid wages whose purchasing power was low. In place of unemployment, these countries had relatively high rates of underemployment, or surplus labor employed in factories, offices, and farms, as a result of the emphasis on reaching output targets and the deemphasis of cost control. Workers were not fully occupied, but they usually had jobs, which removed the psychological costs of unemployment. Moreover, the strong job protection extended to most workers—which was buttressed by insulating the domestic economy from world markets—removed most of the need for unemployment-related social welfare. In a sense, this part of the welfare system was shifted inside the enterprise. When high rates of open unemployment were observed in Soviet-type economies—as in Chinese cities during the late 1950s and late 1970s or in Soviet Central Asia during the 1980s—the unemployment in question was mainly structural. It resulted from high population density or growth in combination with investment concentration on heavy industry. Here, labor absorption (number of jobs created) for a given capital outlay is lower than in light industry or services, even with an allowance for overstaffing.

When the Communist Party came to power in countries that developed Soviet-type economies, party leaders believed they had a historic mission to generate rapid growth, which they did for a time mainly by accumulating capital at a breakneck pace. The command planning mechanism was suitable for this in that it provided readily accessible vertical channels downward to every important firm. This gave the state control over the supply of savings—generated mainly in the form of taxes on enterprise profits and on wholesale trade—together with leverage over the industry-by-industry and region-by-region assortments of investments and outputs. These translated into leverage over the direction and pace of economic growth. In most instances, Soviet-type economies also began with a pool of surplus labor that they could combine with capital, and they used a variety of means to increase labor force participation rates. For a number of years, they achieved rapid economic growth and even considered themselves to be in a growth race with capitalist nations. However, the improvement of living standards always lagged behind the expansion of output, and the difficulty in obtaining growth via traditional command economy methods eventually began to increase. This highlighted the inefficiencies of Soviet-type systems.

Marx, Engels, Lenin, and other founding fathers of socialism were greatly impressed by the gains from large-scale factory production that were first realized during the industrial revolution of the nineteenth and early twentieth centuries. These played a decisive role in shaping their visions of socialism. Thus, economies of mass production, marketing, product development, and so on are in the first instance gains from specialization and cooperation, known as the division of labor. To realize them, the entire task of producing a good or service must be divided into simpler subtasks that are carried out by cooperating individuals and/or by cooperating divisions of a larger organization. In effect, many units specializing and cooperating can often produce far more output than they could if each unit were to make the entire product. Up to a point, opportunities for further specialization and cooperation will arise as output expands. This will mean producing more of given goods, as well as (in some cases) diversifying into technologically related products. The benefits from a highly specialized division of labor are great only when production exceeds some minimum scale.

Picture 1,000 workers along an auto assembly line where the job of making a car is divided into thousands of subtasks as minute as repeatedly turning a screw. Each worker becomes a specialist in one or more subtasks. Now imagine the same 1,000 workers, each operating a small shop within which he or she builds entire motor vehicles. While the second experience may be more enjoyable, the division of labor will make the level of output many times higher in the first case. A similar advantage often arises when an enterprise subdivides its activities into research, design, production, accounting, and marketing and assigns each to a specialized department. To realize gains from specialization and cooperation, a central coordinator and supervisor must restrict the autonomy of members of the organization as individual decision makers to ensure that they cooperate. This requires management to determine and to implement through administrative means an allocation of resources within the organization. As long as gains from further specialization and cooperation in production exceed additional costs of extending management's control over a larger organization, there will be cost savings from expanding this centralized organization.

Conceivably, a division of labor within a factory could be arranged through many voluntary contracts between the cooperating individuals. That is, it could possibly be transacted through the market, but the cost would usually be prohibitive. Suppose that such a market solution is tried. For example, suppose a group of workers collectively agrees to rent or buy an auto assembly plant together with its machinery. Worker A then buys a partially completed vehicle from worker B, alongside him on the assembly line, and proceeds to tighten his screw, weld his joint, fasten his bumper, or whatever, after which he sells the vehicle to worker C, also alongside him, at a higher price. Worker C then adds his value and sells at a still higher price to worker D. Each sale transfers ownership of the vehicle from one individual to another. Thus, every price must be periodically renegotiated, and all prices are interdependent. Each price depends on the contribution of every worker to the final product, which is difficult to measure in at least some cases. Moreover, whenever two workers disagree over price, quality of workmanship, or whatever, they can disrupt an entire assembly line. This possibility increases the required number of contracts between workers and forces each to hold larger inventories.

Therefore, it is less costly to organize an elaborate division of labor under central coordination and supervision—that is, within a firm whose owners also own the intermediate goods passing through its production process. The problem with a division of labor organized through market contracts is that ownership of intermediate goods changes as they pass from worker to worker, in the sense that income rights to the product are transferred. Yet each worker's output is partly specialized to the entire production process. Each therefore has some monopoly power vis-à-vis the others, and the factory becomes a chain or web of bilateral monopolies. The result is a high cost of negotiating and enforcing contracts plus interdependency between contracting parties in the sense that contractual problems between any two workers will cause financial injury to third parties. This is compounded by difficulties in measuring worker productivity, which is a job for specialists (i.e., management).

From another viewpoint, the value of a car rolling off the assembly line can no more be uniquely divided into a sum of values created by each worker than a baby can be divided into parts created by father and mother. Part of the value creation stems from cooperation among workers. There is no unique way of dividing this "cooperation surplus" among them, and with the prevailing bilateral monopoly, supply and demand forces do not determine a division. Consequently, rights to the cooperation surplus are communal within the group, and the surplus is dissipated by wasteful competition among workers to claim it.

We can imagine other situations of this nature that often lead to vertical integration. Suppose that an oil field, a pipeline, an oil refinery, a wholesale gasoline distributor, and a network of service stations are all owned by different companies, each of which enjoys some market power vis-à-vis the others. The retail value of the gasoline is partly created by cooperation among these companies, and this value cannot be uniquely divided among them. In competing for the cooperation surplus, the companies involved will wipe at least part of it out, not only in bargaining over prices but also in reinterpreting contracts or even in violating them outright. This is why we often find companies that are vertically integrated from raw materials to final consumers, thus reducing or eliminating such wasteful competition by reducing or eliminating the transfer of income rights (changes in ownership of an intermediate good as it proceeds toward the final user). As a result, parties to transactions in which there is a potential for bilateral monopoly lose their financial interest in the terms on which exchange occurs.[10] The management of the vertically integrated firm must then ensure that supplier divisions respect the requirements of user divisions; as long as the enterprise does not grow too large or complex, the costs of this will be less than the gains from eliminating wasteful competition to claim the benefits of cooperation.

More generally, centralized organizations arise and grow in any type of economy to realize the benefits of cooperation among different productive inputs—cooperation that cannot be efficiently transacted through the market. Often such cooperation results in "physical" scale economies, which involve indivisible capital inputs—factories, assembly lines, complex machinery, and so forth—that cannot be divided up or miniaturized without some loss of efficiency. Economies may also arise from diversification into technologically related products and may be based in part on human capital or on knowledge of and experience with basic technologies that are shared by several different products. In addition, there are "informational" scale economies, which arise mainly from increasing returns on the uses of information.[11] To understand the basic idea, suppose that for a given cost a firm obtains estimates of the optimal ways to combine labor, capital, and other inputs in a certain production activity, such as an assembly line. Each time the enterprise expands horizontally by adding another activity like the first, the value of these estimates to its management will grow (or the average cost, per unit of output, of obtaining the estimates will fall). Informational scale economies are especially likely when expansion involves no new products or production methods and when each production process can be standardized, concentrated in space and time, and subdivided into routine tasks. When production is of this nature, for example, such devices as time and motion studies can be used to set precise productivity norms, and the cost of setting these norms is about the same regardless of the scale of output.

Many production activities display both informational and physical scale economies. Frequently the development of a complex division of labor depends on the ability to subdivide an activity into routine tasks. Work that is repetitive and requires little exercise of independent judgment—especially if it results in a continuous flow of a standardized product—can be monitored by observing samples either of the product at various stages of completion (as in a quality control examination) or of the finished work itself. This type of monitoring is a major source of informational economies. As output increases, the cost of sampling to determine, within a given margin of error, exactly how to produce a product and whether production meets quality standards or productivity norms will often rise much less rapidly than the value of this information to the firm—again a consequence of increasing returns to the use of information and also of the Law of Large Numbers. The more monotonous and repetitive work is, the less independent judgment it calls for, and the more standardized the resulting product is, the greater are the scale economies in supervising and coordinating production.

By contrast, when work requires independent judgment, supervisory scale economies tend to disappear. An inability to remove the need for discretion implies that work effort cannot be efficiently reduced to a routine that is standardized across workers. This obliges a supervisor to become familiar with the conditions faced by each worker and to separately monitor the efforts of each to cope with his or her particular circumstances. When work constantly requires independent judgment, supervising just a few workers may be a full-time job. More generally, the less standardized production activities are, the less valuable are inferences about one activity from observations or measurements of others and the smaller are the associated informational scale economies. This helps to explain why firm size in a market economy is usually smaller in sectors in which job performance depends on successful exercise of independent judgment. It also helps to explain why industry was more tightly controlled from above in Soviet-type economies than was agriculture or services.

In this context, the structure of incentives or rewards facing an employee of a centralized organization usually differs qualitatively from the rewards associated with self-employment. A factory employee receives a wage that is at least partly divorced from the profitability of the specific operation that he performs. His pay may depend on the rate at which he processes material, but he has no direct financial interest in the difference between the value of goods in process when they arrive at his station and their value when they leave. That is why his work is supervised within the firm. The common denominator of all employment contracts is acceptance, within limits, by the employee of such restrictions on his or her autonomy as management may prescribe. This is what allows management to organize and to supervise the cooperation of many individuals.

However, it is also true that an employee has a smaller incentive to hold up or disrupt production than he would have if his wage depended on the profitability of his specific operation. A self-employed worker needs no supervision to make him work hard—since he automatically bears the cost of his own laziness—but he will have some incentive to mislead product users; therefore, within a factory, self-employment of each worker is apt to lead to high negotiation costs. Enterprise directors in a Soviet-type economy were employees of a centralized organization. Accordingly, their incomes and promotion prospects did not depend on profitability for the most part, which reinforced their orientation toward fulfilling plans that were handed down to them. Target fulfillment plus subjective assessment by superiors determined their rewards, and the targets in question became managerial piece rates or "success indicators." Command economy managers were therefore evaluated more like foremen or divisional managers in Western companies, but in keeping with the scope of their decision-making roles. Because they were less profit oriented, they had a smaller incentive than managers in a market economy to try to manipulate the preferences of users or to create wants, although the state of excess demand plus the primary need to satisfy hierarchical superiors often led them to disregard these preferences.

Problems of Supervision and Coordination:
Some Disadvantages of Centralizing Control over Production

Control Loss

Conditions are favorable for combining production activities into a larger centralized organization when these activities can be reduced to standardized routines that are concentrated in space and time and/or when they are partly specialized to one another and share indivisible plant space and equipment or use similar basic technologies. As this organization grows, however, economies of scale eventually start to weaken, and gains from further expansion become smaller and smaller. The major advantages from a division of labor are realized, and indivisible capital inputs are utilized close to their optimal capacities. Gains from further product diversification will also decline or disappear when new products are based on quite different underlying technologies than those on which the old products were based.

Sooner or later, expansion also brings offsetting diseconomies of large size, which arise in part from increases in the number of individuals (including managers) within the organization who must exercise independent judgment to perform their jobs well. The reduced number and complexity of voluntary contracts associated with centralization go hand in hand with rising informational and decision-making burdens on management. In response, management itself is likely to expand. However, this causes more and more managers to be supervised and coordinated by other managers. Because the most important management decisions require independent judgment, initiative, subjective use and interpretation of data, and so on, efficient management cannot be fully standardized, nor can it always be concentrated in space and time. This raises the cost of vertical supervision of managers or planners by other managers and planners within a Soviet-type economy and helps to limit efficient firm size within a market economy.

As a firm expands, the increasing size or declining efficiency of management will give rise to diseconomies that eventually dominate any unrealized economies of scale or product diversification. If market size is large enough, the only efficient way to expand production further is to add a second firm that is independent of and competes against the first. Markets allow the management problem to be broken up into smaller, more tractable components. Although centralizing management often facilitates the division of labor, markets facilitate the division of management and make it possible to limit the pyramiding of authority. Loosely speaking, the greater the need for independent judgment, the greater is the advantage of supervision by the market (or by customer purchase decisions) over supervision of the same individuals by superiors within a chain of command. If there is vertical supervision, nonetheless, we get a combination of over-routinized subordinate behavior and over-reliance on assessing subordinates

Figure 2.2 **A Three-Level Chain of Command**

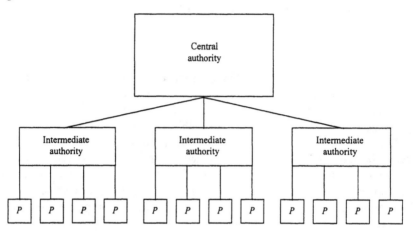

according to their performance in meeting a few quantitative targets. Either approach simplifies the task of monitoring, but both leave supervision incomplete and encourage counterproductive behavior.

The declining efficiency of management as a centralized organization expands is a consequence of the "control loss" phenomenon.[12] Within a Soviet-type economy, the bulk of industry, together with part of agriculture and services, was in some ways like a giant firm managed by its planners and enterprise managers, with central planners in the role of top management. Using this as our example, suppose we have a chain of command with central planners at the top and workers who carry out production at the bottom. Figure 2.2 shows a chain with two levels below the central authority. In its simplest form, control-loss says that the larger the hierarchy and the greater the variety of tasks it must perform, the smaller the percentage of central planners' intentions that will be realized in production. As orders filter down from the top, there will be a loss of understanding at each level, and intermediate planners, as well as enterprise directors, will tend to insert their own preferences.

These losses will be greater, the greater the number of subordinates supervised by each superior and the greater the variety of subordinate tasks—for example, the greater the product variety within a Soviet-type economy and the greater the duplication of products from one ministerial or regional jurisdiction to another. (Moreover, the latter will increase over time due to efforts by intermediate-level authorities to enlarge their jurisdictions and to achieve self-sufficiency.)

In part, our knowledge of control loss is based on a famous series of psychological experiments by F. C. Bartlett in which subjects were asked to reproduce line drawings from memory. In one instance, eighteen individuals successively redrew what was originally an Egyptian version of an owl facing the viewer, with each drawing based on the one before. By the ninth drawing, the owl had become a cat with a ribbon and tail, its back to the viewer. The intentions of the original artist (analogous to the central planner) were successively altered at each stage until they were no longer recognizable.

Suppose there are six levels in a chain of command below the central planner, including firms. By and large, this was true of much of the Soviet economy. Suppose further that at each level 5 percent of the original intentions of the central planners is lost in the process of receiving instructions from above and translating these into new directions for the next level. Since control loss cumulates across levels, only 77 percent of the central planners' original intentions will be transmitted to the workplace, 23 percent having been lost in filtering through the chain of command. If 10 percent of the original intentions is lost at each hierarchical level, the cumulative control loss will come to over 40 percent. Generally, this will mean some loss of efficiency, as well as a partial thwarting of planners' goals. Because the extent of loss increases with the length of the chain of command, the length of the chain down to any given workplace in the Soviet economy tended to be shorter the higher the central planners' priority for the goods being produced.

The above example assumes a rigidly vertical organization and ignores enforcement measures available to the central planners to reduce control loss.[13] It also ignores the use of devices such as feedback to clarify commands. Therefore, let us try for a more general view of control loss. As market signals do not coordinate the activities of enterprises and lower-level planning jurisdictions within a Soviet-type economy, these must ultimately be coordinated by instructions from superior authorities. (Moreover, loss of control will result in such problems as excessive duplication of effort and too little specialization and exchange among subordinate units, as well as poor work discipline, production of goods not in demand, low quality, and others.) With this in mind, we divide the total management input supplied by all planners and enterprise managers into two parts. One part will consist of the flow of orders, suggestions, monitoring, and so forth used to organize, coordinate, and supervise labor and other non-management inputs. (In the rigidly hierarchical model, this would come entirely from management at the workplace.) The other part will consist of managerial input used to organize, coordinate, and supervise other managers and planners. This part is entirely consumed within management.

As production and exchange expand or grow more diversified and complex, a command economy (or any centralized organization) will increase its management input, along with its inputs of capital, raw materials, and labor. Then some combination of two basic tendencies will eventually set in. The efficiency of management as a supervisor and coordinator of production will fall, and/or the percentage of total input of all managers and planners used to organize, coordinate, and supervise other planners and managers will rise. In fact, the latter must grow with the number of planners and managers if the former is to remain constant. Greater numbers make the management function harder to organize efficiently, requiring more channels of communication, more messages, more complicated decisions, and more costly supervision. The need for planners and managers to exercise independent judgment in order to perform their jobs well limits the possibilities for offsetting scale economies in organizing the management function. Instead, this function grows more complex and cumbersome, which is the essence of overcentralization. Thus rising costs of management eventually dominate any further gains from scale economies.[14]

The Problem of "Success Indicators"

Control loss implies incomplete supervision, which allows subordinates a significant freedom of choice. Under command planning, we have seen that enterprise directors could often choose, within limits, their assortments of outputs and inputs. The incompleteness of supervision has some benefits. Managers usually know the production capabilities of their firms better than anyone else, are first on the scene when production problems arise, and are often first to spot opportunities to improve performance. Therefore, they need some room in which to exercise initiative.

But managerial discretion also imposes costs under command planning. Earlier, for example, we noted the tendency to hoard scarce inputs as insurance against the risk of not being able to reach output targets. In addition, since managers have restricted transfer rights, but more extensive use rights over the assets of their firms, incomplete supervision often leads them to overexploit or misuse these assets in order to capture the income from them. For example, to reach their output targets, Soviet oil producers started too many wells and left too much oil behind in wells already drilled because further recovery eventually became more difficult and time consuming than drilling new wells. Similarly, managers have tended to overexploit capital and natural resources in order to meet output targets.

In order to reduce their supervisory costs, planners cut down the number of targets sent to firms by aggregating and omitting some detail, and they enforced some targets more closely than others. The resulting managerial leeway led to the famous problem of success indicators, also a problem of adverse selection.[15] This was the problem of furniture that was made too heavy to get up the stairs (plan targets expressed in tons), of cloth in strips that were too long and narrow (targets expressed in meters), of tractors that were ill-adapted to the soil and crops of the regions to which they were sent (targets insufficiently detailed), and of unending spare parts shortages. (As a rule, spare parts targets were not closely enforced, and spare parts were underpriced. Therefore, producing them was a relatively hard way to meet gross or net value of output targets.) Often specific difficulties were solved by changing the success indicators. But in the absence of rational prices, there was no ideal way of aggregating targets. As a result, the basic problem continued and grew worse as the economy became more centralized or complex.

Historically, central planners also sought to reduce their supervisory costs by building large production facilities (*gigantomania*) and by consolidating firms into larger units (called combines or industrial associations), each subject to one-man management and responsibility. Vertical integration was also viewed, both at the enterprise and at the ministerial level, as a way of dealing with the tight supply situation, which was made more unreliable by the success indicator problem. To protect themselves from output losses when inputs arrived late, in the wrong assortment, or with any of a variety of unsuitable characteristics, many firms diversified into production of their own inputs, often on an inefficiently small scale. For example, as Alice Gorlin wrote, in the Soviet Union "Lifting-transport equipment [was] produced by 320 enterprises subordinate to 35 ministries and departments; about 250 of these factories produce[d] it for their own use. . . . [Moreover,] the ministry in charge of lifting-transport equipment produce[d] only 14 percent of it."[16]

The Problem of Innovation

If a Soviet-type economy were to use similar production and distribution methods year after year and produce similar assortments of goods and services from similar input combinations—and if this caused no serious disruptions—the above problems of command planning would probably become minor. In time, the planners would adjust to the human and technological constraints facing them, and the loss of central planners' intentions at each hierarchical level would become minimal. In Bartlett's psychological experiments, a major cause of distortion was a tendency to reinterpret the unfamiliar so as to make it progressively more familiar. Once the Egyptian owl had become a cat, it remained a cat through the next nine drawings, although it lost its whiskers and ribbon, and its tail moved from one side to the other.

Indeed, if a command economy could expand or contract along unchanging lines, it would become possible, in time, to routinize the operation of at least the industrial sector, including the functions of most planners and managers. The need for these people to exercise independent judgment would decline as formulas were devised for them to follow that would maximize the productivity of the system. The number of planners and managers would also fall, and the average span of control would rise. Fewer resources would be needed to organize the management function efficiently for any given size and complexity of the economy. Moreover, as the size of industry grew—which in the present example would mean more production, with the assortments of inputs and outputs remaining nearly the same—management input could grow at a slower percentage rate than output without reducing efficiency. Aside from dealing with the problems created by greater geographical dispersion, it is nearly as easy to supervise and coordinate a large economy as it is a small one when the large economy is an upscale version of the small. This is because of informational scale economies.

However, an economy cannot remain efficient in modern times and expand along unchanging lines. Instead, its range of products must increase, and the matrix of flows of goods among firms, their customers, and their suppliers must grow more complex. Over time, new resources will be discovered, and supplies of old ones will run out. An efficient modern economy will also introduce better products and production methods on a continuing basis, so that production and distribution will improve qualitatively as well as quantitatively over time.

In this context, medium-sized and even small firms whose internal procedures are informal and subjective—and whose research workers enjoy open, direct lines of communication with top management—do most of the basic innovating in market economies. Also important is a willingness by management to have faith in an unstructured and often disruptive process (innovation) whose payoff is highly uncertain. By contrast, the Soviet-type economy relies on routinization, excess demand, price and structural rigidity, planning from the achieved level, and quantitative evaluation of subordinates on the basis of current output. These factors simplify the task of centralized management, but they also suppress innovation. An individual obliged to follow a routine is greatly limited in exercising independent judgment; this is the reason for routinizing his or her work in the first place. The stress on quantitative evaluation tends to cause potential benefits from a prospective investment to be ignored unless they can be readily quantified. This introduces a bias against investing in new products and production methods. Instead, managers and intermediate-level planners, knowing how they will be judged, tend to play it safe by maintaining behavior patterns that have led to successful evaluation in the past.

The incentive to introduce new products is further diluted by the existence of captive markets guaranteed by excess demand and lack of competition among suppliers. Producers have no need to innovate to keep their customers, but they do need to worry about evaluation by superiors. The latter will not spot most failures to innovate, but they will notice when plan targets are missed, and the introduction of new products or production methods is bound to slow production until sufficient experience is gained with the new technology.

If an enterprise director in a Soviet-type economy were to install a new type of machine, try out a new product design, or reorganize his firm, he could easily miss his output targets and lose his bonus or chance for promotion. His workers would lose their bonuses as well. Therefore, he usually preferred to go on meeting targets with the old technology—even if users were unhappy with his products—as long as he could satisfy his superiors. His direct links were mainly to them. In order to bring about changes, users had to go through the chain of command and persuade the producer's planning superior to order and enforce these changes. At best, this took time because of the roundabout nature of the required information flows. But the state bureaucracy was often less than enthusiastic about promoting new products or technology as well, since this usually required new links among the enterprises involved and their suppliers (who might be foreign), as well as some reorganization of domestic firms. The jobs of planners and managers were easier when interenterprise relations and enterprise organization remained static over time.

Planning from the achieved level also tended to freeze out new products with no past history of manufacture or use. If innovation led to higher output, the firm's targets would likely be boosted in consequence. Together with the soft budget constraint (whereby the greater part of any increase in profits was usually taxed away), this deprived managers and workers of most of the financial benefits of innovation. Irrational prices, in combination with excess demand, also made innovations hard to evaluate.

Of course, the number of new products or inventions could be made an explicit success indicator. We would then expect more "inventions," although with usefulness a secondary consideration—an expectation apparently borne out by Soviet experience.[17] Authorities cannot simply order innovation to occur; this activity, more than any other, needs a favorable environment in which to flourish. A market economy dominated by monopolies is also unlikely to have a high rate of innovation. A monopolist would probably not suppress innovation altogether. But with its captive market, it would be reluctant to take risks and might try to slow down and smooth out the flow of new products and technologies in order to protect the profits still being earned on past investments.[18] Nor would the perfectly competitive economy of the textbooks be innovative, since managerial decision-making horizons of firms would be too short, owing to the high risk of failure.

If innovation is to flourish, four basic criteria must be present, all of which are missing in Soviet-type economies. First, firms must be free to take initiatives. Investment decisions must be depoliticized and decentralized to the enterprises. Second, managers of firms must be motivated to put up with the necessary risks and frustrations. This will require their rewards to be linked to long-run profitability. Third, the success of new products should depend on their acceptance by users. This will require horizontal ties between producers and users to be stronger than vertical bonds between producers and controlling government agencies. Finally, the "Red Queen" effect should prevail. That is, competition among firms for market share should force them to keep improving their products and lowering their costs as a way of holding on to their customers. An oligopolistic market structure with low barriers to entry and active competition, but within which firms have enough financial strength to survive some failures, is probably the one most favorable to innovation.[19] In the economics literature, this is sometimes called "workable competition." Unfortunately, if one were to design a system intended to suppress innovation, one might well come up with a Soviet-type economy.

Extensive versus Intensive Growth

The basic problem of the Soviet-type economy was its overcentralization. This type of system extended administrative control far beyond the point at which rising costs of management exceeded further gains realized from increasing the size of the unit under state control. Most efficiency-oriented complaints against it can be traced to this problem. As noted above, low-cost supervision of production within a chain of command usually requires routinization and spatial concentration of the activities being supervised, as well as standardization of products. When supervisees must exercise independent judgment to perform their jobs well, vertical supervision becomes costly, and the alternative of supervision through the market (based on purchase decisions of product users in a context in which sellers compete for market shares and prices balance supply and demand) becomes more attractive.

This insight helps us to understand why Soviet-type economies were poorly managed, as well as why the advent of computer-assisted production and design and more flexible manufacturing processes actually reduced their comparative efficiency vis-à-vis market economies and made their rigidities more apparent and costly. These changes reduced routinization, scale economies, and product standardization and increased the importance of independent judgment in the workplace. Many manufacturing processes are still highly routinized, but as we move up the chain of command from the production floor, the importance of independent judgment by managers increases. Yet these individuals are subject to vertical supervision within a Soviet-type economy, with its substantial pyramiding of authority. The "excess demand" umbrella in such a system tended to shield all decision makers from supervision via the purchase decisions of product users. In effect, sellers had captive markets. Moreover, the process of innovation cannot be routinized, and successful innovation requires sensitivity to demand pressures. The Soviet-type economy's low rate of innovation ensured its eventual stagnation and technological backwardness.

From what has been said, we can conclude that Soviet-type economies have their greatest efficiency potential when the economic environment and the government's preferences are relatively simple—in the sense that a few key goals stand out above all others—or when the direction and pattern of economic growth can efficiently remain static over time. Centralized management is also a way to spread the best managerial talent over many firms, and it therefore represents a short-term answer to shortages of competent managers. However, opportunities for on-the-job training in situations in which the full range of management skills can be tested without serious consequences when mistakes are made are also relatively few in a centralized economy. This factor impedes reform and helps to perpetuate the bureaucratic structure of such a system after decentralization has become advisable on efficiency grounds.

More generally, Soviet-type economies have a comparative advantage in generating extensive growth rather than intensive growth. They work best under three conditions: the initial level of development is low and government goals stress the growth of basic heavy industries; there is a shortage of industrial capital plus an underutilized labor force; improved technologies that embody substantial scale economies are available from abroad and can be adopted and duplicated rapidly without much need to adapt to local conditions. Under these conditions, centrally planned economies have been able to generate large forced savings and to lavish them on industries with low capital-to-output ratios, which for a time produced dramatic increases in output. In the process, they transferred unemployed workers or underemployed farm labor into the factories being created and successfully exploited natural resources for raw materials and energy. As a rule, these things were done rapidly, but also wastefully.

The combination of high rates of investment, duplication of existing technology, exploitation of natural resources, and transfer of labor to relatively high-productivity sectors constitutes extensive growth—basically, output expansion due to expansion of productive inputs. By contrast, intensive growth results from the introduction of new technologies and better ways of organizing production or motivating people. Growth is usually partly extensive and partly intensive, but extensive growth will eventually die out, on a per capita basis, without a transfusion of new technology. Sooner or later, it becomes harder and harder to expand some inputs, such as labor or energy, relative to the total population. Expansion of other inputs, such as capital, is then subject to the law of diminishing returns.[20]

In Figure 2.3, suppose a Soviet-type economy is moving upward along path T_1 as economic growth occurs because it is able to expand its stock of industrial capital more rapidly than its industrial labor force. In this graph, we have plotted capital per worker in industry along the horizontal axis and output per worker in industry along the vertical axis. These types of economies increased their stocks of industrial capital per worker dramatically between the early 1950s and the early 1980s. The slope of path T_1 is a measure of the yield on investment—specifically, the average increase in output resulting from a given net investment or increase in the capital stock. As the economy moves up T_1, the yield on investment, so defined, eventually begins to fall (in the vicinity of A) owing to the law of diminishing returns. Since Soviet-type economies have followed energy- and resource-intensive strategies of growth, rising costs of fuel or of basic raw materials may reinforce this decline. In the vicinity of B, the curve becomes nearly flat, signifying that the yield is close to zero.

At B, further increases in capital per worker will not by themselves generate additional economic growth in the form of increases in output per worker. The possibilities for extensive growth, measured along path T_1, are now exhausted. Thus intensive growth, resulting from broadly defined technological progress, becomes the only alternative to stagnation. Intensive growth would move the economy upward from path T_1 to path T_2 by increasing the productivity of labor,

62

Figure 2.3 **Extensive versus Intensive Growth**

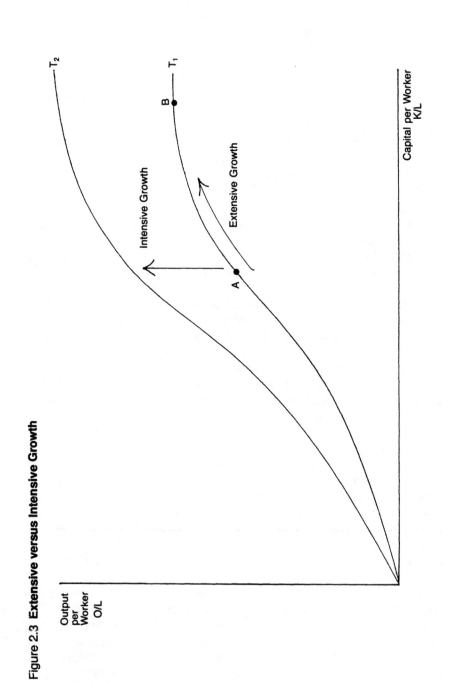

with no increase in capital. However, we have seen that a Soviet-type economy provides a relatively poor environment for innovation and technical progress. The usefulness of this type of system in generating growth has come to an end.

We should not overlook the ability of centralized planning to generate rapid growth for a time, but its days are numbered by the law of diminishing returns. Additional drawbacks of command planning have been summarized by Chinese economists from their experience.[21] "Under such a system," writes one, all activities of an enterprise are subject to norms, quotas, and directives passed down from higher administrative organs. In actual fact, no higher authority, even with the most sophisticated computers, can calculate accurately the production needs of hundreds of thousands of enterprises and the everyday needs of hundreds of millions of consumers (needs which are not only highly diverse, but are also constantly changing). Even less can it issue in good time production and distribution plans which conform to these needs. Enterprises have no right to revise plans or to improve their management in line with the needs of the market. Thus, a centralized, directive type planning system is inevitably accompanied by dislocations between supply and demand, lack of variety of products, technical stagnation, and a low level of efficiency.

"Products needed by society are often in short supply," writes another Chinese economist, "while those unwanted by society are plentiful." Moreover, enterprises are divided up by economic departments (or ministries) and regions, and economic activities have to proceed according to the divisions and levels of this administrative framework. Direct economic relationships among enterprises belonging to different departments or regions are lacking. Each department and region seeks to create its own self-contained system, which seriously hampers the division of labor and cooperation. This causes a great deal of duplication in production and construction.

"In recent years," relates a third Chinese economist, "the unwieldy, over-centralized system of goods allocation allowed little flexibility, provided little stimulus for improvement, and in fact afforded a soft berth for producers who simply wanted to 'get by.' Goods were allocated and sales outlets had to take things, whether they were popular or even saleable; with little direct sales connection, producers paid insufficient attention to market research and often went on producing unsaleable goods; a lot of goods piled up in warehouses, either because of the unwieldy distribution system or because they were unwanted. . . ." In one of his last speeches, Yuri Andropov, the Soviet Party leader for 1982–83, complained that an enterprise director who takes a risk and introduces new technology "frequently comes out the loser, while the manager who shuns innovation loses nothing."

Organization and Motivation

Incentives are extrinsic to the extent that an individual is motivated by linking income in money or in kind to job performance. Incentives are intrinsic to the extent that a worker is motivated to do a job well, independently of present or prospective income. Motivation may come from the job itself, the job environment (including a desire for acceptance or approval by fellow workers), a desire to be creative or of service to the community, or any combination of these. One way of describing Marx's full communism is to say that scarcity is overcome with intrinsic incentives alone. In a world characterized by scarcity and specialization, however, extrinsic incentives have always proved necessary, although intrinsic motivation may play an important role. Conventional economics distinguishes two ways of tying extrinsic rewards to performance depending on whether an individual is directly supervised by superiors within a chain of command.

First, employees of an enterprise receive wages or salaries geared to their work effort, as evaluated by foremen or managers. Doing a job "well" in this context means following a superior's directions with accuracy and speed, and we have seen that such supervision is more efficient when work can be routinized. One of nature's ironies is that mass production economies usually depend on standardizing production and subdividing it into simple tasks that are repeated over and over. The production of great wealth thus implies the impoverishment of much of the work effort that goes into production. This is the source of alienation, of "blue-collar blues," and of efforts to humanize the workplace, which usually entail less direct supervision of labor.

Second, the owners and top managers of a firm in a market economy are supervised indirectly by product users when the latter decide whether and how much to buy. Purchase decisions have a decisive effect on enterprise profit, which is why markets work best when buyers can choose among suppliers and vice versa. As a rule, the rewards of top managers depend more closely on profitability than do the earnings of other employees. The textbook version of such a firm carries this distinction to its limit by assuming that a company's top managers are also its owners. They hold all use and income rights in the form of residual claims to enterprise profit, whose size depends on how well they manage. This is what motivates them.

In the textbook version, moreover, claims to a firm's profit residual should not be spread over too many owner-managers. Spreading dilutes the incentive based on residual claimancy, since part of any increase in profit due to one manager's increased effort goes to others. If a manager is lazy, part of the resulting loss of profit is borne by others. Suppose the top management of a corporation owns just 10 percent of its shares, while 90 percent belongs to nonmanaging owners. Each time management is able to raise after-tax profit by $1, it is able to keep only 10¢. The incentive effect is the same as that of a high marginal tax on incomes. In addition, managers may try to claim company profits in a form shareholders cannot "tax"—for example, by padding their salaries or expense accounts or by consuming on-the-job benefits in kind, such as free company-paid transportation or pleasant work surroundings.

Competitive pressures on profit can limit the extent of this problem but will usually not eliminate it.

Any collectivization of material rewards based on the sharing of income residuals will contain the same built-in dilution of incentives.[22] An efficient incentive structure therefore suggests small firms, in terms of staff size, when products cannot be standardized or when jobs require the exercise of independent judgment in order to be performed well. This is the only way to hold down both the number of individuals who are directly supervised and the number sharing a given profit residual. In practice, however, there is a wider sharing of income residuals than the above considerations would imply—not only within, but across firms (even across industries and regions)—and we can identify three basic reasons for this:

1. Many enterprises would be unable to expand far enough to realize economies of scale (more generally, to realize economies of large size) without acquiring investment funds beyond the personal resources of their managers. This is especially true since efficiency also requires management to be specialized in the hands of individuals with a comparative advantage in managing. This leads to separation of ownership from management in the sense that all or part of a firm's profit residual is shared by nonmanaging owners, which reduces the part available to be shared among managers. A firm also acquires more managers as it expands.

2. Intrinsic motivation linked to a workplace, enterprise, or even a larger entity can widen the sphere of efficient sharing of income residuals. This is more likely if intrinsic motivation increases with the right to exercise independent judgment on the job.

3. All governments use taxes and subsidies to redistribute income between households and firms. Such redistribution is motivated by some combination of political, ideological, and moral considerations.

Because of (1), separation of ownership from management is a fact of economic life under both socialism and capitalism despite its perverse incentive effects. This is also why modern industrial societies feature the separation of decisions to save from decisions to invest as well as a range of financial intermediaries (notably banks) that can transfer funds from savers to investors. The nature of these institutions—in particular, the state's involvement in the transfer—plays a major role in determining the kind of economic system. There is no way to make the transfer without cost, since the interests of managers and of suppliers of finance are bound to diverge to some degree.[23] The board of directors of a modern corporation protects its owners—who are really suppliers of finance for the most part—via limited supervision of management. For example, a board will probably try to close off the easiest ways of diverting profit from the owners. This implies limits on expense accounts, job perquisites, and managerial salaries, as well as some control over major investments. An independent audit can provide assurance to the owners that management is following legitimate business practices and incurring no unreasonable expenses. The board is also likely to have power to hire and fire top managers.

Therefore, no one working for a large enterprise, whether publicly or privately owned, will be motivated solely by a residual claim to its profits and losses. Everyone will face some form of direct supervision, although the cost of this is still greater when the supervisee must exercise independent judgment. As a result, it is potentially valuable to be able to find good managers who are intrinsically motivated and able to instill a team spirit in other employees. The stronger the intrinsic rewards for managing well, the lower the efficiency cost of weakening the link between a manager's performance and his or her financial reward. The greater the employee team spirit, moreover, the greater the prospective benefits from employee profit sharing. To better understand this combination, let us delve briefly into the psychological theory of motivation.

According to Maslow, individuals try to satisfy a fivefold hierarchy of wants.[24] The lowest order consists of purely physiological impulses—food, water, sex, and so forth—followed by the drive for safety or security and freedom from anxiety. Belongingness and love constitute third-order drives or sources of motivation, while the desire for achievement and mastery—in the sense of attaining self-esteem and the esteem of others—is the second-highest source of motivation. Highest of all is the drive for "self-actualization" or full realization of a person's capabilities, meaning that the individual is performing to potential and doing what he or she is best suited for. The lower-level wants must be satisfied, in Maslow's theory, before the higher-level wants can be attended to. If we lack love and a place in a social group, for example, we will ignore our self-actualization wants. (Moreover, Maslow felt that only a small percentage of individuals would completely fulfill this drive within their lifetimes.) Conversely, as their lower-level wants are satisfied, people become harder to motivate simply with higher incomes. Instead, they require intrinsic incentives, which often rest directly or indirectly on social ties.

By contrast, Western economists stress the motivation inherent in a person's claim to individualized material rewards. They tend to ignore identification with a group, product, ideology, industrial empire, etc., as a motivating force. Thus, they treat a high correlation between an individual's income and the quantity and quality of his or her work as a prerequisite to efficiency. An entrepreneur is assumed to build an industrial empire for profit, not for the inherent prestige, self-fulfillment, or social satisfaction. And yet, most creative work is probably motivated intrinsically, at least in part, and it is a strength of any society to be able to rely on individuals who are mission oriented and so ignore risks that customarily deter innovative effort. Increases in the division of labor that further impoverish the level of work may also reduce intrinsic motivation and thus be inefficient, even if we ignore the costs to the workers involved. This is more likely to be true when individuals can afford to satisfy their first- and second-order wants.

Then there are potential gains from allowing employees to share in profits. When combined with job security, profit sharing raises employee enthusiasm for adopting new technology. Moreover, it establishes an interdependence among a firm's workers in the sense that the income of each depends on the combined efforts of all the others—provided that enterprise profitability depends on these efforts. If team spirit at the workplace is high, employees will be willing to monitor one another. Horizontal supervision by coworkers will partly substitute for vertical supervision by management, resulting not only in peer group pressure on shirkers but also in feedback that management can use in assigning jobs, determining promotions, and deciding which employees to keep on. The number of foremen and managers can be reduced as well. The effectiveness of peer group pressure is greater when efficient production depends on close cooperation and on learning as a team and/or when each employee values social acceptance by his or her coworkers. It is reinforced by any inherent motivation on the part of each to try to raise the incomes of fellow workers. Given bonds of loyalty, trust, and respect among workers, these factors can more than offset the dilution of managerial incentives caused by wider income sharing and turn the stereotyped peer group pressure to slack off on its head.

To develop team spirit and intrinsic motivation, a firm's products should be a source of prestige within the community, and more efficient production should result in higher after-tax profits for employees to share. The soft enterprise budget constraint may be unfavorable to team spirit because it dilutes the link between team effort and team reward. Ideally, the enterprise will be a social as well as a production center, and its employees will identify closely with it and its products. For example, a Japanese firm considers itself a family, with its top management as a father figure. Large companies occupy their employees in social and cultural activities from which outsiders are barred. Under these conditions, an employee's profit share is both a sign of and a reward for being a group member in good standing. If cooperation within the group is to be high and discord low, employees should generally view the reward structure as fair.

The standard theory of the firm ignores the roles played by intrinsic motivation and by bonds among employees based on loyalty, trust, and respect. When horizontal ties among coworkers are strong, there is a potential for team spirit, cooperation, and greater productivity on that account that may require profit sharing. Table 2.1 summarizes the linkage between nature of work, rewards, and supervision.

Table 2.1

The Relation Between Nature of Work, Method of Reward, and Method of Supervision

Nature of work and work milieu	Suggested method of reward	Suggested method of supervision
(1) Independent judgment and/or spatial dispersion of workers crucial to efficient performance.	Residual claimancy based on customer (user) acceptance.	Market supervision by customers (user acceptance), ideally with competition on the supply side plus regulation to prevent negative externalities, dangerous products, etc. Vertical supervision should be cut down, as when a firm is divisionalized into profit centers on the basis of product line and/or territory.
(2) Work can be routinized and spatially concentrated. This does not seriously interfere with—or even increases—worker productivity.	Wage or salary geared to efficiency with which the routine is repeated.	Vertical supervision based on observation of the work itself and/or of the product (as in quality control).
(3) It is possible to develop substantial team spirit at the workplace among workers from management on down, based on identification with the company and its products.	To some extent, conformity with (1) and (2). Those doing work requiring more independent judgment will have incomes more closely tied to residual claimancy. But the development of team spirit makes possible a greater sharing of profit residuals.	Again, conformity with (1) and (2) to some degree. However, intrinsic motivation to do each job well should be relatively strong. Moreover, with good team spirit, workers will monitor one another. This horizontal supervision will at least partly determine each worker's acceptance by his or her colleagues as a team member and potentially serves as a partial substitute for vertical supervision.

Notes

1. Lajos Faluvegi, "Economic Development, Economic Structure, New Phenomena in the World Economy," *Acta Oeconomica*, vol. 14, 2–3, 1975, p. 146.

2. Over ten joint investment projects were launched, of which the most important was the $10 billion, 1,700-mile-long Soyuz natural gas pipeline, which supplied Eastern Europe with natural gas from the Orenburg gas fields in the Soviet Union (now Russia). Hungary, East Germany, Bulgaria, Czechoslovakia, and Poland each built one of the pipeline's five sections. Much of the equipment came from the West, and its purchase was mainly financed by the International Investment Bank of COMECON. The Soviet Union provided technical data, construction supervision, and half the capital—although the East European countries, which badly needed the natural gas, paid most of the cost.

3. Tamas Morva, "Planning in Hungary," chap. 8 of Morris Bornstein, ed., *Economic Planning: East and West* (Cambridge, Mass.: Ballinger, 1975), p. 293.

4. Some exchange on the second economy took the form of barter. These unofficial economies resembled "underground" economies in Western countries, that have arisen to escape taxes. For more on the notion of a "shortage" economy, see the references to Kornai in note 8 of chapter 1.

5. The governments of Soviet-type economies claimed to be presiding over "classless" societies. However, anecdotes that circulated in several of these countries claimed that there really were two classes. The "upper" class had access to Western currency, and therefore to an increasingly superior range of goods and services of higher quality than the "lower" class, which had to make do with the local currency.

6. It used to be said that agriculture was at once the least and most important sector of a Soviet-type economy—least important because farm output had the lowest priority, and most important because farming was the chief source of investment funds for heavy industry.

7. The sum of output targets over all firms producing a good, plus imports, should equal exports plus the sum of input targets over all firms using the good plus the amount of the good earmarked for final domestic use. A plan would also include projections of labor and natural resource inputs, along with the balance of payments, the budget balance, the balance of income and expenditure of the population, and other items.

8. Igor Birman, "From the Achieved Level, " *Soviet Studies*, April 1978, p. 161.

9. The anecdote about the Japanese manager is told by G. C. Allen in the Toronto *Globe and Mail*, Aug. 26, 1971, p. B6.

10. See A. A. Alchian, R. G. Crawford, and B. Klein, "Vertical Integration, Appropriable Rents, and the Competitive Contracting Process," *Journal of Law and Economics*, October 1978.

11. R. Wilson, "Informational Economies of Scale," *Bell Journal of Economics*, Spring 1975. See as well J. C. Panzar and R. D. Willig, "Economies of Scope," *American Economic Review*, May 1981.

12. See Gordon Tullock, *The Politics of Bureaucracy* (Washington, D.C.: Public Affairs Press, 1965); O. E. Williamson, "Hierarchical Control and Optimum Firm Size," *Journal of Political Economy*, April 1967; and E. Ames, *Soviet Economic Processes* (Homewood, Ill.: Irwin, 1965), chap. 14. The example that follows relating to the Soviet economy comes from Ames. The psychological experiments were conducted by F. C. Bartlett. See his *Remembering* (Cambridge: Cambridge University Press, 1932), especially chap. 8.

13. These enforcement measures combine two principles known as "redundancy" and "bypassing." Overlapping jurisdictions are the main example of redundancy: the subordinates whose jurisdictions overlap tend to check on one another's activities—as in the case, for example, of an enterprise director and a party secretary whose job it is to enforce the "spirit" of the plan. One cost of this may be wasteful competition between these officials

to expand their control. On-site inspections by the Soviet Ministry of Supervision, as well as "control by the ruble" and use of the press in a watchdog role, are examples of bypassing one or more levels in the chain of command. See Anthony Downs, *Inside Bureaucracy* (Boston: Little, Brown, 1967).

14. For further discussion of this problem, see Karl Wittfogel, "Communist and Non-Communist Agrarian Systems," in W. A. D. Jackson, ed., *Agrarian Policies and Problems in Communist and Non-Communist Countries* (Seattle: University of Washington Press, 1971), pp. 3–60, and R. Carson, "The Optimal Size of the Competitive Firm," *Journal of Economics and Business,* February 1984.

15. See Alec Nove, "The Problem of 'Success Indicators' in Soviet Industry," *Economica,* February 1958. See as well Nove's book, *The Soviet Economic System,* 3rd ed. (London: Allen and Unwin, 1986), pp. 87–94.

16. Alice Gorlin, "Industrial Re-organization: The Associations," in U.S. Congress, Joint Economic Committee, *Soviet Economy in a New Perspective* (Washington, D.C.: U.S. Government Printing Office, 1976), p. 8.

17. See Joseph Berliner, *The Innovation Decision in Soviet Industry* (Cambridge, Mass.: MIT Press, 1976), and James Dearden, Barry W. Ickes, and Larry Samuelson, "To Innovate or Not to Innovate: Incentives and Innovation in Hierarchies," *American Economic Review* 80, no. 5, December 1990, pp. 1105–24. See as well the other references cited in Dearden et al.

18. For example, the silicon chip revolutionized the construction of electronic cash registers and calculators. It cut the cost of making them to a fraction of that of the old electromechanical models, in addition to which the newer silicon chip models were smaller, lighter, faster, and less complicated. One result was the National Cash Register Company's 1972 decision to write off more than $130 million in shareholders' net equity. Without competitive pressure, it is doubtful that National Cash Register would have ended production of electromechanical equipment so soon.

19. The "Red Queen" effect is named after the character in *Through the Looking Glass,* chap. 2, by Lewis Carroll. She had to keep running just to keep from going backward.

20. See Martin Weitzman, "Soviet Postwar Economic Growth and Capital-Labor Substitution," *American Economic Review,* September 1970, for an early analysis of growth slowdown in the Soviet Union owing to diminishing returns. Weitzman writes (p. 685), "Accounting for somewhere around 15 to 25 percent of average output increases, technical change [in the Soviet Union] is not nearly so significant a determinant of economic growth as in some other economies."

21. The references are (in order): He Jianzhang, "Basic Forms in the Socialist Economy," *China Reconstructs,* January 1982; Dong Fureng, "Some Problems Concerning the Chinese Economy," *China Quarterly,* December 1980; Cai Wuyan and Liu Hongfa, "Marketing Changes in Beijing," *China Reconstructs,* January 1981. The reference for Andropov's quote below is to *The Current Digest of the Soviet Press,* July 20, 1983, p. 4. (The speech originally appeared in *Pravda* and *Izvestia,* June 16, 1983.)

22. By way of analogy, compare the incentive effects of the following approaches to penalizing air travelers for carrying too much baggage: (a) China's national airline once followed the practice of weighing all luggage together and dividing any penalty equally among passengers; (b) Western airlines assign a penalty to any traveler whose baggage exceeds an individual weight ceiling.

23. For an extended discussion of this point, see M. C. Jensen and W. H. Meckling, "Theory of the Firm: Managerial Behavior, Agency Costs, and Ownership Structure," *Journal of Financial Economics,* October 1976.

24. Abraham Maslow, *Motivation and Personality* (New York: Harper and Row, 1954).

Questions for Review, Discussion, Examination

1. What two broad categories of planning can we distinguish? Briefly describe the two, explaining their differences and common denominators. Which type of planning is compatible with a market economy, and, roughly speaking, when is a market economy planned?

2. Why do all goods have prices in a Soviet-type economy? Why have these prices tended to be fixed over long periods and below levels that would balance supply and demand? What is the cost of maintaining prices that are "irrational" in this way?

3. How are the priorities of a Soviet-type economy indicated by its financial flows? What is "control by the ruble"? How (briefly) does the banking system of a Soviet-type economy differ from that of a market economy? Can we speak of legitimate capital or financial markets in Soviet-type economies? Why or why not?

4.   (a) What problems arise from the tendency to plan "from the achieved level"? Explain what is meant by this and how it tended to increase shortages in a Soviet-type economy as well as vertical integration at all levels of the planning hierarchy and the tendency for firms to invest in producing their own inputs.

    (b) Given these problems, why were plan targets set from the achieved level? How did the soft budget constraint reinforce planning from the achieved level in terms of its effects on supply? In terms of its effects on efficiency?

5. What do we mean by the "second economy" of a Soviet-type economy? Why did the second economy arise, and what role did it play? Did it make the economy as a whole function more or less efficiently? Why did state authorities often seek to limit its scope?

6. Although Soviet-type economies did not systematically gather unemployment statistics (claiming to have eliminated the "capitalist evil" of unemployment), rates of open unemployment were generally lower there than in Western market economies.

    (a) What was the basic reason for this? Does it automatically mean that workers were "better off" in the Soviet Union and Eastern Europe than in capitalist economies with relatively high unemployment? Explain briefly.

    (b) In what major way did the role of labor unions in a Soviet-type economy differ from their role in a Western market economy?

    (c) In what sense did Soviet-type economies shift part of their social welfare system inside the doors of producing enterprises?

    (d) In a few cases, high rates of open unemployment were observed in the Soviet Union (notably in Central Asia) and in China. What aspect of the economic development strategy followed by these countries *could* produce open unemployment? Under what conditions would this be most likely?

7. What are some of the gains from combining production activities into a larger centralized organization? How does the structure of incentives or rewards facing a factory employee differ from that of a self-employed individual? What is the reason for this difference?

8. What limits efficient firm size in a market economy? If efficiency is the determining factor, what conditions are most favorable to large firms (with extensive pyramiding of management authority), and what conditions are most favorable to small firms (in the sense of units that operate independently)? What implications does this have for management efficiency in a Soviet-type economy? Finally, the text states that "while centralizing management facilitates the division of labor, markets facilitate the division of management and limit the pyramiding of authority." Why is the latter important?

9. What is the problem of "success indicators," and how does it relate to the pyramiding of authority in a Soviet-type economy?

10. Why were Soviet-type economies large net importers of technology?

11. What basic property rights features of an economic system are most favorable to innovation? What features are unfavorable to innovation? Explain why the features you have selected are favorable or unfavorable. What does this imply about innovation in a Soviet-type economy?

12.   (a) From the standpoint of generating economic growth, what are the basic advantages and disadvantages of centralizing control over the industrial sector of an economy? When are the net advantages of centralized control likely to be greatest? Discuss briefly. Explain how these advantages and disadvantages are related to the distinction between *extensive* and *intensive* growth.

    (b) Why did growth slowdowns in socialist countries generate pressures to decentralize? Over time, did inflationary pressures tend to rise or decline in Soviet-type economies? Briefly explain why.

13. What is the difference between *extrinsic* and *intrinsic* motivation? Which of the two does conventional economics emphasize, and how does this help to account for the "ideal" textbook organization of the firm? How can intrinsic motivation overcome some of the potential disincentive effects of separating performance from extrinsic reward?

14. Under what conditions would profit sharing by a firm's employees be part of an efficient way of rewarding them for their work? Explain why this is the case.

15. Explain why we find widespread separation of ownership from management under both capitalism and socialism. In answering, be sure to explain what this "separation" means in terms of property rights.

Chapter 3

Political Rights and the Role of Government in a Market Economy

Democracy is the worst of all possible forms of government—except of course for those others that have been tried from time to time.

—Winston Churchill

The Political Dimension of an Economic System

Economic and Political Decisions Contrasted

From the standpoint of economic phenomena, a society's political decisions are those that formulate its socioeconomic goals, both directly and indirectly, as well as those that determine the nature of the economic system. All decisions, including the making and interpreting of laws that help to shape the distribution of property rights, are political decisions. By contrast, a society's economic decisions determine specific quantities of inputs and outputs or specific prices within the organizational and goal framework created by its political decisions. For example, decisions by the manager of an enterprise or an industrial ministry that set specific output targets or determine specific production methods are economic decisions. However, a law defining a policy on taxes and subsidies is the result of a political decision, as is a law granting monopoly power to firms or labor unions. The same would be true of the five-year plans (whose targets were expressions of intent rather than orders to produce) in Soviet-type economies. When a firm takes advantage of its monopoly position to raise prices and restrict output, it is making an economic decision. Economic and political decisions are interdependent, and the boundary between them is not always precise.

Earlier discussions of property rights, markets, and chains of command relate to economic rather than to political (de)centralization. Political decision making is more decentralized, or democratic, the more diverse elements in society are able to have a voice in social goal formation. Alternatively, it is more centralized, or dictatorial, the more a small group (ultimately, an individual) is able to impose its will on the rest of society. As with economic decisions, political decentralization implies competition—here between political parties or coali-

Table 3.1

Basic Political Rights

I.   Right to vote
II. Right to participate in electoral competition
     A. Right to run for office
     B. Right to organize a political party, faction, or coalition
     C. Right to organize an election campaign
III. Basic freedoms (bill of rights)
     A. Freedom of thought, belief, and expression
     B. Freedom of peaceful association and assembly
     C. Freedom of the press
     D. Basic human rights
     E. Basic legal rights, including the right of contract

tions for votes in periodic elections—while political centralization implies monopoly control over government, and thus an absence of electoral competition among political parties.

We can also talk about "political rights," which are the political counterparts of property rights. Table 3.1 indicates three kinds of basic political rights—the right to vote, the right to participate in electoral competition, and the right to basic freedoms (which are sometimes embodied in a constitutional bill of rights). The most fundamental political right, which gives voting a social value, is the right to participate in electoral competition. This forces parties to compete for votes by fielding candidates and designing policies, programs, and laws that will be attractive to voters. It also tends to be a necessary, but not a sufficient, condition for insuring basic freedoms, because support of such liberties will often gain votes for parties or candidates. Rights-related grievances have a way of becoming campaign issues.

The right to participate in electoral competition embraces a range of more narrowly defined rights, including the right to run for office, the right to organize a political party or coalition able to field election candidates, and the right to organize particular election campaigns. Without the right to compete in elections, the right to vote has no value, and basic freedoms are apt to be precarious. Nonelected rulers are sometimes benevolent, but they do not rule forever, nor do they always remain benevolent as long as they rule.

Command Planning and Political Democracy

Most Soviet-type economies held periodic elections, but all serious candidates for office had to support the platform of the Communist Party and be approved by the party. In most cases, a single candidate stood for office. Although it was possible to vote against the party's nominee, the outcome was not in doubt. There have never been political democracies—in the sense of universal suffrage and competing political parties—that were also Soviet-type economies, and two basic problems would arise in trying to combine the two.

The first results from the natural monopoly of government. Usually, it would be grossly inefficient for two governments to compete in administering a given nation or region or in providing it with other public goods. This is why political democracy implies electoral competition for temporary control over the reins of government. However, avoidance of monopoly, in the form of dictatorship, is then possible only at the cost of shorter time horizons for elected government decision makers, who must face reelection every few years. This tends to discourage long-range planning and initiative.

Instead, the political party currently in power wants to provide benefits that will appear in time to help its chances in the next election. It is less willing to invest in projects that will bear fruit afterward—a strategy that it is apt to view as a formula for losing that election. Moreover, if Party A invests in long-term benefits, they may arrive when Party B is in power, allowing the latter to claim part of the credit for them. Since no individual voter can affect election outcomes, the right to vote, by itself, does not give enough incentive for most people to become sufficiently informed about issues or candidates for political office. Nor is it easy to identify the long-term economic consequences of different policy mixes. Economists disagree about these as much as the general public. Therefore, people tend to associate the government in power with current economic successes or failures, which are the decisive economic influence on election outcomes.

By contrast, if political party competition becomes institutionalized, it will prevent the systems of law enforcement and interpretation from coming under the control of any single party. The police and judiciary become independent, allowing the rule of law to take precedence over rule by individuals. Political party competition thus makes it harder for government officials to act arbitrarily and, in particular, to change property rights or to interfere in the formation and implementation of contracts in an arbitrary way. As a general rule, but with exceptions, due process protection for property and lives is greater and basic freedoms are more secure when there is political party democracy than when there is dictatorship. The time horizons of private individuals and organizations are therefore likely to be longer in mature democracies. For governments, however, the need to face periodic elections shortens time horizons, and this influences the property rights environment (laws, regulations, etc.) within which other decision makers operate.

A partial solution to the time horizon problem is to shift decisions into the hands of a civil service bureaucracy with lifetime employment guarantees. However, if carried too far, this is no longer compatible with a basic prerequisite for democracy—namely, that major policies and programs must at least be approved by elected public officials. To lengthen the decision-making horizons of the latter, one proposal would have members of the legislature elected for longer terms—say, twelve to fifteen years—and no legislator would be allowed to serve two terms in a row. At some cost in terms of the increase in decision-making horizons thereby achieved, the terms of legislators could be staggered to make it possible to change political parties or coalitions more frequently. To date, however, successful long-term planning by democratically elected governments has usually required one political party to remain (and to expect to remain) in power for a long period.

The political requirements of excess demand are also the source of a fundamental contradiction between Soviet-type planning and political democracy. We recall that excess demand is a common denominator of all planning, because it allows the state to play a decisive role in determining the direction of economic growth. The relatively widespread excess demand of a Soviet-type economy has political implications, especially in light of the short time horizons of elected officials under political party competition. Suppose that a Soviet-type economy were to be democratic in the sense of allowing universal suffrage and competing political parties, more than one of which has a realistic chance of gaining control over the central government at election time. Such a society will contain a number of lobbies or political pressure groups representing business, labor, farmers, consumers, and other special interests. In single-party states, such organizations are part of or are controlled by the dominant political party. But when two or more parties compete, special interest groups are able to maintain some independence. They can vary the intensity of their support for or opposition to parties and candidates as they see fit. As a result, they play a major role in social goal formation because they are able to influence—or to give candidates for office the means of influencing—the voting habits of the public. Some of the most powerful pressure groups (business, labor, farmers) are based on means of earning a living.

As noted earlier, special interest or political pressure groups arise because the right to vote does not give most people enough incentive to become informed about issues or candidates. In addition, politicians will often be unable to identify consensuses emerging within the population or to rationally weigh one consensus against another. Special interest groups thus serve as intermediaries—with their own values, norms, ideologies, and goals—between the public and the politicians. Like successful advertisers, they help to shape and to crystallize preferences at both ends. They both reflect and create public opinion, and they play a role in the implementation of government policy. While they are imperfect, it is not clear that democracy could be effective at all without some way of rallying voters into groups large enough to have an impact on election outcomes.[1]

In this context, let us focus on the political role of labor unions and large firms or groups of firms. In a Soviet-type economy, the state of excess demand could not be preserved if these entities exercised independent bargaining power over wages and prices. They would take advantage of the excess demand for many goods and for labor to bid up prices and wages, thereby undermining part of the basis of command planning. If a democratic society is to retain its command economy, pressure groups will have to agree not to exercise the full thrust of their bargaining strength, making a kind of social contract to this effect. They will also have to keep their memberships in line. Their reward for restraint will be a higher growth rate—when state management can generate this—and/or a redistribution from that part of society with the least effective political representation. But each interest group must feel better off staying in the social contract than bargaining for higher prices, wages, or interest rates on its own. Thus the lower an economy's growth rate relative to its perceived potential, and the less widely shared its benefits among the strongest political pressure groups, the less enduring the social contract is likely to be.

An economy is also more vulnerable, the greater is the number and variety of independent political pressure groups in society and the more pervasive is the state of excess demand. If political parties must regularly compete for votes, they have every temptation to do so by offering to raise incomes. Given widespread excess demand, this can always be done for some voters by raising prices or wages. Special interest groups representing different segments of society or different sectors of the economy will have an incentive to make parties compete for the votes they control in this way. As a result, the excess demand for most goods and services will be eroded and will eventually disappear.

Historically, centralized economies have been created to address the goals of a single dominant political party or group. The dominant party does not end lobbying. However, short of war, revolution, a serious split in the leadership or the emergence of a political force outside the party, no rival organization can hope to gain control of government. The dominant party can use its monopoly over the organs of the state to keep political pressure groups under its control and to confine competition among special interests within bounds that do not threaten the system. For example, labor unions in Soviet-type economies were subordinate to the Communist Party and had no independent bargaining power over wages, although they did have some power to protect workers' interests. (They were also supposed to promote productivity.) To give them independent bargaining power would risk inviting them to take advantage of the excess demand for labor, thereby weakening planners' control over the distribution of wages, as well as their ability to control the allocation of labor. Moreover, social priorities would have to be negotiated with the unions, which would come, in effect, to constitute a political party rival to the Communists. Priorities would therefore change. The share of national income devoted to consumption would have to rise in order to translate wage increases into greater purchasing power. Many Marxians view a "plural" society, with its independent special interest groups, as the political counterpart of the anarchy of the market, and the appearance of pluralism under socialism was treated as a threat (as in Hungary in 1956, Czechoslovakia in 1968, and Poland in 1981).

During the period of rapid extensive growth, the containment of special interest group pressures within a single political party plus the longer political time horizon also helped Soviet-type economies to control inflationary pressures—including hidden inflation in the form of a growing excess demand for goods and services.[2] Inflation is mainly caused by increases in the money supply, and images are sometimes evoked of too much money chasing too few goods. But governments create money in response to political pressures. In the short run, this is the least-cost way of financing government spending and tax forgiveness and the benefits that flow from these for specific groups. The tendency for the money supply to expand more rapidly in periods leading up to elections and less rapidly afterward produces what is known as the "political business cycle."

Thus inflation and business cycles in Western democracies result partly from special interest group political pressures and partly from the short political time horizon created by periodic elections. Once inflation is under way, firms, labor unions, and individuals—expecting it to continue—begin to bid up future wages and prices in contract negotiations. These expectations require the money value of the aggregate demand for goods and services to keep on growing just to maintain the current level of employment and to accelerate if unemployment is to decrease further. Since the growth of aggregate demand is linked to the growth of the money supply, this increases the political cost of reducing the latter. At the least a short-term rise in unemployment would result, until people revised their inflationary expectations downward. Once started, therefore, inflation has a tendency to persist, and even to increase, until its political cost exceeds that of accepting higher unemployment.

A Soviet-type economy requires a political monopoly by a single party with a pervasive grassroots organization. By contrast, political party monopoly (or dictatorship) can coexist with either a Soviet-type or a market economy, although command planning potentially provides the economic base for more enduring control of government by a single party. Within a Soviet-type economy, it is harder to develop alternative networks of power that can become strong enough to challenge the principal network based on loyalty to the party elite. Career advancement requires party approval, and alternative career paths are circumscribed. Many people will make money on the second economy, but their wealth is precarious and always in danger of expropriation—unless, perhaps, they gain influential positions within the party. Factions develop inside the party, but they are not officially tolerated, and periodic purges are used to suppress them, just as periodic campaigns against fraud, theft, corruption, bribery, and so on, are used to suppress potential power networks based on the second economy.

In a market economy, firms and other economic organizations must be free to compete if the system is to be efficient and, in particular, if it is to generate technological progress. This means they are free to grow and to prosper, thereby providing alternative career advancement paths. Loyalty to a political elite is less important to economic success or accumulation of wealth (and, therefore, power). This makes political monopoly harder to sustain over the long haul, and raises the likelihood that it will depend on having a charismatic leader at the helm.

Social Insurance

If we take a general look at the economic role of government in a market economy, we find that it always includes enforcement of internal order and protection of citizens from external threat. As well, most modern governments provide an array of additional goods with public qualities—parks, roads, schools, mass transit, health and medical care, and so forth—in the sense of paying for them from tax revenues and supplying them to ultimate users free of charge or on a subsidized basis. Finally, they try with varying degrees of success to regulate markets, to promote full employment, to control inflation, to promote and direct economic growth, and to redistribute income and other benefits in specific ways. Inevitably, these goals turn out to be partly contradictory—for instance, because growth-promotion incentives become tax loopholes or because redistribution divorces rewards from productive contributions, which may reduce the incentive to increase production. Nevertheless, there has been a dramatic expansion of government's role in redistribution and in the provision of public goods and other social benefits since World War II. This has occurred in both capitalist and socialist economies, but especially in modern welfare states such as the Scandinavian and Benelux nations, Austria, Germany, France, and Italy. These are "social market" economies with so-called womb-to-tomb social insurance protection of individual citizens from financial distress.

By *social insurance* we mean compulsory, state-run insurance against poverty resulting from old age, poor health, unemployment, and other calamities, that is usually financed by obligatory contributions tied to an individual's income from work. Because of its importance, we shall briefly examine its effects on distribution, public finance, and the provision of benefits paid for by the insurance. The ground rules of social insurance programs usually work to redistribute income from the rich to middle-income groups, and to a lesser extent the poor, although such categories as foreign "guest" workers are much less likely to come out ahead. Among those covered by social insurance, redistribution is also directed toward individuals whose consumption of benefits relative to their contributions (and, hence, their incomes from work) is greatest. Since the ratio of contributors to beneficiaries tends to decline over time, there has also been a historical tendency for redistribution toward early participants in these programs.

An efficiency argument can be made for social insurance based on *adverse selection*. This argument is not decisive, however, because there may be other ways of dealing with adverse selection and because social insurance, which is more widespread and comprehensive than voluntary private insurance, also aggravates the problem of *moral hazard*. To explain these phenomena, consider first a program of voluntary health insurance. The amount of the premium that each insured person must pay will depend on his or her age, state of health as determined by a medical doctor, family status, and other measurable characteristics. On the basis of these measures, each insured person is put into a risk category, and everyone in the same category pays the same premium, even though some will, in fact, make greater use of insurance benefits than others. Consequently, within any given category, those who will buy the most insurance are those who value it most highly—in effect, because they are relatively high-risk cases and know it, or because they overestimate the value of the protection to themselves. Those who will buy the least or opt out altogether are those who value the insurance least, either because they are low-risk cases or because they underestimate the value of the protection.

This is adverse selection. Within any given category, the relatively high-risk users are the ones most likely to opt into a voluntary insurance program, a factor that increases the cost per subscriber of providing the insurance. The relatively low-risk users—who expect the lowest pay-out to pay-in ratios—are the ones most likely to opt out. It is often possible to reduce adverse selection by refining insurance categories so that each person's premium depends more closely on his or her expected benefits. However, refinement is costly and also tends to increase insurance rates. The upshot is that in order to cover costs rates will have to be set high enough to exclude some potential customers, who will tend to be the relatively low-risk users within each insurance category. As insurance rates (or prices) increase, moreover, it is always the lowest-risk users who opt out of the market, with the consequence that the average risk associated with insurance applicants keeps increasing, which in turn keeps raising the cost of coverage. Thus it is possible that no voluntary insurance will be provided at any price.

One solution to this problem is to tie insurance coverage to employment, or alternatively to membership in a club or other organization. Companies often advertise medical and/or dental plans as employee benefits. One can opt out of such a plan only by leaving the firm in question. Since employees rarely quit their jobs in order to end their insurance coverage, the basic problem is resolved, although many people may still find that insurance is unavailable. Thus a more comprehensive solution is to "socialize" the insurance—that is, to make participation in the program compulsory and to administer it through the state. Social insurance is a public good in the sense that its consumption by any one low-risk user lowers the cost of providing it to other people.[3]

However, widespread social insurance also leads to overuse of insurance benefits, which results in soaring costs, and frequently in shortages or reduction on quality. A German anecdote—that, in time, the average worker will be so healthy that he will starve to death trying to keep up his health insurance premiums—illustrates, in part, the effect of moral hazard. That is, the greater and more widespread the insurance against some event's occurring (such as a visit to the hospital), the more often will this event, in fact, occur. The reason is that insurance largely severs the link between consumption of a good or service and its cost to the user.

To illustrate, consider the demand for and supply of hospital care in Figure 3.1. Without insurance, these are D_1 and S, giving an equilibrium price of P_1. Now let the government introduce compulsory medical insurance, financed by a payroll tax that covers most of the cost of such care. As a result, P_2, the new price, is far below P_1. At each price, quantity demanded will depend on the disposable incomes of prospective patients. The payroll tax tends to reduce incomes and so causes a small downward shift in the demand curve in Figure 3.1, from D_1 to D_2. Nevertheless, with P_2 well below P_1, the quantity of hospital care demanded rises from Q_1 to Q_2, illustrating the moral hazard phenomenon—which has less to do with morals than with the fact that most demand curves slope downward. Hospital care is frequently a necessity, but when it is available at lower prices, people will tend to go more often, to stay longer, to have more tests, and so forth.

With supply curve S, Q_2 units of hospital care will be forthcoming only at a supply price, including the subsidy, of P_3. Following the introduction of the program, therefore, the total cost of care jumps from P_1Q_1 to P_3Q_2, requiring a subsidy of $(P_3 - P_2)Q_2$ (or area ABCD), which is financed by the payroll tax and other public revenues. The government is then likely to look for ways of holding down this subsidy. At some cost, for example, it may try to screen out and exclude those who don't really "need" the care. It may also raise the average price, say to P_4, as further insurance against "unjustified" use of the care. Ideally, the most elastic segment of the demand curve will lie below P_4. The quantity demanded then falls to Q_3. Finally, governments often try to put a ceiling on P_3, which has the effect of moving the supply price down the supply curve. This causes a shortage to develop (the quantity supplied becomes less than the quantity demanded), and individuals pay in part via longer queues and waiting times.

When all is said and done, the state will be subsidizing an expanded supply of the good. Yet because of the greatly reduced price, it will still be in excess demand, which requires rationing by nonprice methods such as queuing. Patients will have to go on a waiting list for nonemergency care and may face quality deterioration or other inconveniences, such as not being able to see the doctor of their choice. In practice, the definition of emergency treatment is also likely to become broader. The cost of waiting is less for the poor than for the rich—whose time is worth more in purely monetary terms—so that rationing in this manner is potentially more egalitarian than rationing by price and ability to pay. At the same time, by paying a higher price (which may take the form of a bribe), it may be possible to obtain better or faster treatment.

Potentially, social insurance also helps to stabilize (or to reduce variations in) individual incomes by raising the covariations (or correlations) between the incomes of different individuals. At any point in time, someone who is becoming better off in terms of earning potential or health is likely to be increasing his net payments into the system or reducing his net benefits from it, while someone becoming worse off is likely to be doing the reverse. Macroeconomic policy

82

Figure 3.1 **Social Insurance and Moral Hazard**

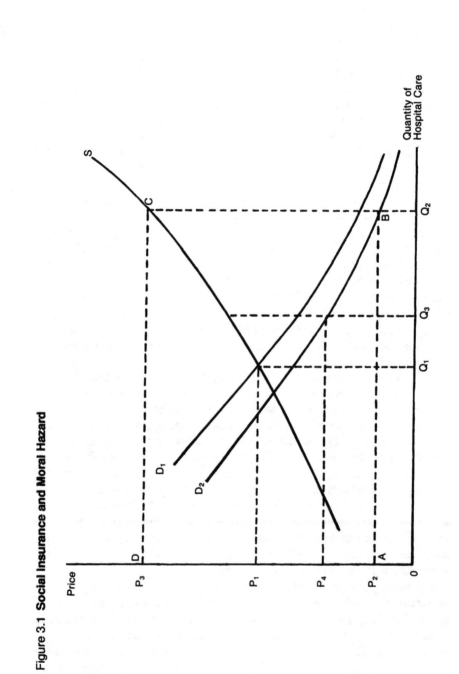

seeks to reduce variations in individual incomes by decreasing the variation of national income over the business cycle—that is, to stabilize the parts by stabilizing the whole. Statistically speaking, there may be a greater potential for reducing the variations of the parts (individual incomes and other benefits) by increasing the correlations between them, although this may also weaken the link between individual reward and productive contribution, as noted above. Together with other progressive taxes and subsidies, social insurance is in this way part of contracyclical policy. Finally, compulsory pension plans and health insurance have also lowered population growth rates in several countries by reducing average family size. In the absence of such insurance, parents have traditionally relied on their offspring for security.

Expansion of the Public Sector in Market Economies

All modern economies depart from classical laissez-faire, in which government does little beyond ensuring internal order, protection from external threat, and a smoothly functioning market system. In developed nations, there have been few more striking phenomena than the growth of the public sector relative to the total size of the economy since World War II. This expansion is now largely over, although in some countries, the aging of the population will cause further growth. The ratio of government spending on goods and services to GNP in the United States was 7 percent in 1909 and 11 percent in 1925. By 1954, it had risen to 20 percent, since which it has shown little net tendency to rise or fall. In West Germany, the same ratio rose from 17 percent to about 25 percent between 1955 and 1990, while in Sweden, it more than doubled, from 17 percent to about 35 percent, between 1950 and 1990.

However, the greatest public sector growth has come in the provision of social insurance—covering mainly pensions, health care, employment creation, unemployment benefits, and vocational training and rehabilitation. Since World War II, Western market economies have become "social market economies," many of which spend two-thirds or more of their total public outlays on social welfare, mostly in the form of transfer payments rather than direct purchases of goods and services. In 1994, the ratio of total public outlays to GNP came to 33 percent in the United States and to 36 percent in Japan, where social insurance expenditures were still relatively low, but where the population was also aging rapidly. This ratio was 43 percent in the United Kingdom and over 47 percent in Canada. It came to between 49 and 54 percent in Italy, France, Germany, and the Netherlands, and to 56 percent in Norway. It was over 64 percent in Denmark and in Sweden. By the 1990s, all these countries had large budget deficits, which in 1994 came to 9 percent of GDP in the case of Italy and to over 10 percent for Sweden.

We can identify five basic causes of public sector expansion.[4] (1) An explosive growth in technology and cost has affected a number of products that are publicly financed, notably defense and health care. In the former case, the cost of protection from external threat has soared far above pre–World War II levels. For example, the Spitfire (the plane that saved England from the Luftwaffe in World War II) cost around $16,000 per copy. In the Gulf War, Stealth bombers went for over $1 billion each. Nevertheless, the greater cost of defense is a relatively minor source of public sector expansion relative to the rest of the economy, and worldwide defense expenditures have fallen since the end of the cold war in 1989. Health care technology has also undergone explosive growth. Unlike the growth in defense technology, the growth in this area has benefited the human race by providing treatments and cures far beyond what was possible before World War II. Like the growth in defense technology, however, this has meant soaring costs.

(2) Economists make two arguments related to the elasticity of demand for publicly financed goods and services:[5]

(a) Over some ranges of income, education and social insurance protection are plausibly luxury goods in the sense that the demand for them rises at a faster percentage rate than income. Because economic growth from 1950 to 1994 was greater than ever before in world history, the "luxury goods" effect increased the share of income spent on these products. (In effect, the income elasticity of demand for them was greater than one.) The basic rationale is that, when incomes are low, peoples' time horizons are short. They are mainly concerned with surviving and getting along from day to day. When their incomes rise, their time horizons expand. They can now afford to ensure their future and that of their children. As a result, the willingness to spend on and/or to be taxed for education and social insurance benefits increases rapidly as incomes rise from low levels.

(b) However, the foregoing applies only to some publicly financed services and may apply to these only over (relatively) low to moderate income levels. Recent studies suggest that the income elasticity of demand for all government-supplied goods and services is around one or even lower in developed market economies. While it may have exceeded one earlier in the postwar era, some economists advance a different elasticity argument to explain the relative growth of public spending. They argue that the effective *price* elasticity of demand for publicly financed services has been low.

This view holds that it has been mainly the relative price of publicly financed services that has gone up, instead of the relative quantity. Citizens do not pay these higher prices directly. Instead they take the form of higher taxes and payroll fees, which governments have been able to raise without reducing the quantity demanded very much, if at all, because of the low price elasticity of demand. This argument also holds that the real costs of tax collection have fallen since World War II, and that the resulting cost savings have been used to increase the size and power of government (and thus to pad public sector costs and payrolls) rather than to cut taxes. Where there has been expansion in the volume of publicly financed services relative to output that is privately bought and paid for, this has resulted largely from transferring the financing of such services from the private to the public sector (as in the case of health care, where most Western nations are concerned).

A more benign version of the foregoing view holds that production of these services is labor intensive. Thus they have benefited less from productivity growth than has privately financed output. As a result, the relative cost of publicly financed services has risen, and the low effective price elasticity of demand for the latter has allowed these cost increases to be passed on more easily in the form of higher taxes and payroll fees.

(3) A third cause of public sector expansion has been the greater political power of labor movements, which first increased their strength in Western countries over the late nineteenth and early twentieth centuries. The Great Depression speeded this evolution. By causing record levels of unemployment and bankruptcy, it also raised the perceived riskiness of economic life in a modern industrial society dominated by private property rights and market relations. People not only became more receptive to and even more insistent on social insurance protection, they became more receptive to a larger economic role for government. Since World War II, labor-oriented political parties have enjoyed more power in the West than ever before, and the fifteen to twenty years following the war can be viewed as the heyday of Keynesian economics, which became the intellectual justification for giving government a larger economic role.

Based on J. M. Keynes's *General Theory of Employment, Interest, and Money,* Keynesian economics argued in particular that government could use its leverage over the economy to reduce (or possibly even eliminate) business cycle fluctuations in output, employment, and inflation. The basic idea was to run a budget deficit during recessions by raising government spending relative to tax revenue, and to run a surplus during boom times (or periods of relatively rapid growth). The deficits would increase aggregate demand, thereby combating recessions by stimulating higher levels of output and employment, while the surpluses would restrain aggregate demand in booms, thereby combating inflation. In the process of "fine-tuning" the economy, the public sector might not balance its budget in any given year but could still do so over the course of the business cycle. While the economy would not necessarily live happily ever after, in time it might become possible to realize maximum sustainable growth with low inflation and unemployment.

Today economists are more skeptical about the power of government to achieve such a goal via discretionary fiscal or monetary policies. The major barrier is the role played by expectations. If suppliers of goods and services believe that the government will try to raise aggregate demand, they will respond by raising prices and wages. Part or all of expansionary policy, therefore, goes to produce inflation—rather than output and employment expansion—when this policy is foreseen by rational decision makers. Such policy is therefore most effective when it surprises (or fools) suppliers of goods and services, but this may be a difficult feat to bring off. Thus expansionary policy may be frustrated, leaving both inflation and unemployment above desired levels, a matter to which we shall return in chapter 5.

In fact, the combination of left-of-center political action and Keynesian economics has caused governments to grow during recessions, often creating public sector employment in the process, but not to contract—or to contract by smaller amounts—during relative prosperity. The net result has been public sector expansion over the business cycle. Labor-oriented political parties have also been more willing than rival parties to their right on the political spectrum to use government as an instrument for redistributing income, including the provision of social insurance. Their constituents have been major beneficiaries of this insurance (and are likely to bear the burden of future cutbacks), although they have also paid for most of it via payroll taxes or fees.

The shift from voluntary to compulsory social insurance has dramatically increased the demand for insurance-financed benefits, independent of the above elasticity arguments, because these benefits are provided at subsidized prices or free of charge to many more people than ever before. As a result, the demand boost from moral hazard ($(P_3Q_2 - P_1Q_1)$ in Figure 3.1) has become greater than ever. In addition, social insurance has lowered birthrates and increased longevity. This has raised the ratio of people receiving benefits from social insurance to those paying into the system. If these systems do not undergo basic changes, the viability of many of them will be threatened within the first third of the twenty-first century.

(4) The post–World War II era has witnessed an explosive growth in world trade, as well as in international technology transfer. World trade growth has been greater, for most countries, than the growth of national income and output.[6] This serves as a climax to several centuries of increasing specialization, division of labor, and exchange in the Western world, without which the growth of output would have been far slower. However, it has also intensified the demand for social insurance and related public benefits. By producing for the world market, many small Western nations (such as Belgium, the Netherlands, Sweden, Norway, Finland, and Denmark) have realized industrial scale economies and gains from specializing according to comparative advantage that would otherwise be out of reach.

But there is also a price to be paid in the form of increased exposure to shifts in demand and supply on world markets. These shifts are hard to foresee and impossible for national governments to control. The latter have therefore tried to cushion the resulting blows—through unemployment benefits, subsidized retraining and relocation of displaced workers, subsidies to tide over firms in temporary financial distress or to help them alter their product mixes or production technologies, and programs to help domestic producers become less dependent on export markets or imported inputs. Rapid technology transfer and other factors that contribute to technological change have reinforced the need for such programs by increasing the rate of job obsolescence as well as the investment required to achieve a competitive edge in many occupations. The same is true of the long-term trend toward freer trade and larger free-trade areas. These trends have increased specialization and trade and caused many jobs to be moved from one nation to another. A given nation loses some kinds of jobs and gains others, with the result that many of its citizens have to change careers and go through spells of unemployment while they try to acquire new skills and find new work. Jobs have also become more sensitive than ever before to movements in exchange rates, which further increases the need for occupational mobility.[7]

(5) Finally, two factors that derive from the nature of representative government and public expenditure have magnified the foregoing causes. Earlier in this chapter, we saw that political time horizons tend to be short in Western democracies. This increases the likelihood that governments will create programs (including social insurance) whose costs are relatively modest at first but then tend to escalate over time. In addition, the output of a public agency is nearly impossible to value from the demand side, since user access does not depend on a willingness to pay prices that reflect marginal costs of supply. The agency is apt to have a monopoly, and its product will usually be a service that is difficult to quantify. An objective basis for setting its budget will therefore be hard to find unless budgeting is from the achieved level. Because future budgets depend on current expenditure, a public agency will rarely underspend its budget, even when there are better uses for these funds. It knows that underspending will cause next year's budget to be cut. But it will overspend and press for more funds if it believes it can make a case for this spending. Toward the end of a fiscal year, agencies with unspent funds rush to "use it or lose it," which recalls the phenomenon of storming in Soviet-type economies. Similarly, a contractor to the government will rarely supply goods or services for less than his cost allowance, but he will often run over this amount in hopes of getting it raised.

As the reader will have guessed, economists and political scientists disagree over the nature and main causes of the relative expansion of the public sector. Disagreement is possible in part because separate measures of prices and quantities of publicly financed services are often unavailable. Neither do we know the opportunity costs of these products or their marginal values to users in many cases. All we know are the outlays made by government to pay for them. Thus we can identify two underlying views of public sector expansion. To some, government has become leviathan, exercising a growing monopoly power over its citizens. For these observers, the growth of government is mainly a price effect in which citizens pay higher and higher tax prices for publicly financed products, plus a nationalization effect in which services such as health care come to be paid for, and in some cases to be supplied by, government agencies or enterprises. Nationalization also leads to higher effective prices. To others, relative prices of publicly financed products may have risen, but quantity and quality increases have also occurred, well beyond what can be accounted for by the nationalization effect. To these observers, democratically elected governments have reflected voter preferences and carried out the wishes of their citizens.

When buyers face higher prices in the marketplace, they cut back on products whose prices have gone up the most and switch to lower-priced substitutes. In this way, they economize. If customers are sufficiently successful at economizing, product demand curves will be elastic. A given percentage increase in price will be offset by a larger percentage decrease in quantity demanded, resulting in a lower total expenditure (price times quantity) on the good in question. A typical customer, then, is spending a smaller percentage of his or her income on the product whose price has risen.

To the extent that the expanding share of national income accounted for by the public sector is a price effect, government must therefore be able to act like a supplier facing an inelastic demand curve—and in some cases, even an upward-sloping demand curve—for its services. Inelastic demand would result from government's role as a monopoly supplier and from the fact that higher prices are not always perceived as such by voters when they take the form of higher taxes (or simply of a failure to lower taxes when costs of tax collection fall), as is nearly always the case for publicly financed products. Other issues may also influence voting patterns, with the result that politicians in power when such price increases occur may not feel pressured to roll them back as a condition of survival at election time.

In addition, expansion of social insurance substitutes tax and payroll fee financing for direct financing in the form of prices charged to users, as noted earlier. The drop in the latter reduces the incentive to economize on insurance-financed services, as was explained in connection with Figure 3.1. The result may be an expansion of the quantity demanded, even though the price received by suppliers rises as well (e.g., from P_1 to P_3 in Figure 3.1). This produces the effect of upward-sloping demand. If the state exercises monopoly power over price, the latter will in fact rise above P_3 for a quantity supplied of Q_2. Suppliers of publicly financed products will then receive supernormal returns on their labor and/or capital or returns above their opportunity costs. (In this sense their costs are "padded.")

Regardless of how we view the expansion of government, it is clear that the public sectors of nearly all developed market economies are now in fundamental disequilibrium. Expenditures exceed revenues even during relatively prosperous times, and tax avoidance is widespread and well organized. Governments regularly borrow large sums, mainly in the form of interest-bearing debt (bonds) rather than money creation, resulting in cumulative net debts that ranged in 1994 from 9 percent of GDP in the case of Japan to 23 percent for Sweden; 32 percent for France; 35 to 40 percent for Denmark, Germany, and the United States; 45 percent for the United Kingdom; 64 percent for Canada; and 121 percent for

Italy. Of the nations in the Organization for Economic Cooperation and Development (OECD), only Norway and Finland had cumulative net surpluses. Since 1980, interest payments on these debts have grown faster than any other category of public expenditure.

As these fundamental disequilibria have emerged, voters have become more critical of government spending and less willing to pay higher taxes to close deficits. Higher tax rates do not necessarily generate more revenues, because they increase the incentive to avoid them and reduce the incentive to use resources in a productive way. Modern welfare states have created "soft budget constraints" at the household level, since the combination of high taxes and social insurance or welfare payments weakens the link between productive effort and reward, part of the price that must be paid to reduce the likelihood of extreme financial distress for individual households.

Since budgets are in deficit and tax revenues have hit a ceiling as a share of gross domestic product in most Western countries, the expansion of the public sector relative to the rest of the economy is also over or nearly over in most nations, as noted at the outset of this section. Indeed, the first hints of downsizing have appeared. Privatization of public enterprises and of the supply of services once reserved to public agencies has gained in popularity, allowing competition to be reintroduced in supplying these products. Although they may still be publicly financed, at least in part, user fees have become more widespread as well. Social insurance benefits and the welfare state are being trimmed, although there is no sign that they will be abandoned as major governmental responsibilities. Moreover, cutbacks in some areas of government expenditure are partly offset by increases elsewhere. The aging of populations in most developed market economies implies greater outlays on pensions and health care, and increases in vocational training are now popular among some politicians—in part because of the dislocations caused by freer trade. In this context, economic theory does not tell us exactly where the private sector should end and the public sector begin, and we are likely to continue to see variation in the size and role of the public sector from one country to another.

In the years following World War II, many people had faith in government's ability to do far more for its citizens than formerly, especially in the areas of education, health care, pensions, and insurance against income and job loss. Keynesian economics, then in its heyday, provided the intellectual underpinning for the public sector expansion that was under way or about to occur. Arguably, governments over-reached themselves, and people are now more aware of the limits as to what politicians and public institutions can do. In such a climate, we must be careful not to go overboard in the opposite direction, as an example may show. Today the United States is nearly the only developed Western nation in which most citizens must rely on private health insurance or else have no insurance. Yet this country spends a greater share of its GDP on health care (in 1993) than any other OECD nation, in return for which it has one of the highest infant mortality rates in this group of nations and one of the lowest life expectancies at birth. Socialized health insurance is fraught with problems, but it may still be preferable to the patchwork of systems currently in place in the United States.

Industrial Policy in a Mixed Economy

> Your free capital market is mythological. Capital markets are perverted by investors' expectations of what governments will do. In America, investors know that the government will protect industries that grow beyond a certain size. Government aid to large, dying enterprises is politically inevitable unless advanced economic planning renders such rescues unnecessary. . . .
>
> —An official of the Japanese Ministry of
> International Trade and Industry (MITI)

The Nature of Industrial Policy

Historically, the discipline of comparative economics was defined to no small degree by the contrast between Soviet-type and market economies. This was a sharp contrast, with many clear-cut as well as subtle differences. As long as these two archetypal systems appeared competitive, moreover, the contrast fascinated many observers. However, as the deficiencies of Soviet-type economies became more and more apparent, interest in this type of system waned and transferred to the problems of transition from a Soviet-type economy to a market economy. We shall take up this issue in chapter 7.

At the same time, to say that an economic system is a market economy leaves much room for variation, notably in the role of government. Two ways in which this role can vary are in the provision of social insurance and welfare benefits, which we have just discussed, and in formulating and implementing an industrial policy. This section considers the latter. If such a policy is successful, measures to develop and exploit key technologies and sectors based on them (which could include agriculture or services, as well as industry narrowly defined), are apt to constitute its driving force, although it may also include measures to promote the orderly decline of some industries whose demand is waning. If industrial policy is unsuccessful, it will subsidize the growth of sectors that never achieve a competitive edge, as was the case in Soviet-type economies and, unfortunately, in many market economies as well.

Because it requires competition among political parties, democracy puts constraints on the extent of economic planning and is, in particular, incompatible with state management of the economy over the long run. The short political time horizon created by periodic elections tends to militate against long-term planning of any kind. Yet the existence of competent long-range plans can also have the effect of lengthening political time horizons by expanding the range of alternatives open to political decision makers. Jobs can more easily be created by speeding the growth of promising new industries rather than by propping up industries that are over the hill. Competent advance planning can also lead to more fruitful worker retraining and to better regional specialization according to comparative advantage. Such programs would be provided in the context of industrial policy, the best known example of which is that of Japan, where it is widely credited with playing a major role in the post–World War II economic miracle. More recently, several Asian "tigers," including South Korea, Singapore, and Taiwan, have evolved their own industrial policies based partly on the Japanese model. After World War II, some West European countries used such policies to launch their own periods of rapid economic growth.

We recall that a mixed or market-planned economy combines government influence over the direction of economic growth with independence on the part of individual firms, whether publicly or privately owned. While government can change incentives and alternatives facing individual producers, it must realize its priorities in an environment in which enterprise management is largely independent of direct state control. By allowing markets to solve most of the details of the economic problem, it hopes to escape the high information costs of command planning. It may have to accept less leverage over the direction and pace of economic growth in return, although the less bureaucratic nature of planning should make it easier to change priorities.

However, a mixed economy also requires cooperation and trust between government officials and groups that participate in policy formation, as well as a substantial pooling of information. Ideally, plan participants will develop dedication and team spirit at all levels, but such cooperation will be harder to come by the more aggressively the state seeks to redistribute benefits away from some of these groups. As well, planning should increase supply elasticities in both product and factor markets by raising the mobility of resources between industries and regions and enable domestic firms to compete more effectively, although planning will often promote cooperation in research or diffusion of technical information as well.

One reason for unemployment in "free-market" economies is that such systems are vulnerable to shocks that disrupt existing production and employment patterns. The freedom to compete, and in particular to innovate, is capable of generating such shocks. When trade barriers are low, shocks will often originate in a country's trading partners. We have seen that it is possible to reduce the cost of dislocations caused by shifts in demand and supply via social insurance. However, this cannot be the entire solution. It is equally important to keep a nation's industries on the cutting edge of efficiency and to take advantage of potential shifts in comparative advantage that can enable it to exploit new opportunities for growth of output, employment, and earnings.

This is how industrial policy would make the alternative of protecting declining sectors less attractive and reduce lobbying pressures to this end. In Figure 3.2, suppose that the demand for a particular type of labor, which has been *DD*,

Figure 3.2 **Relationship Between the Elasticity of Supply and the Cost Imposed by a Fall in Demand**

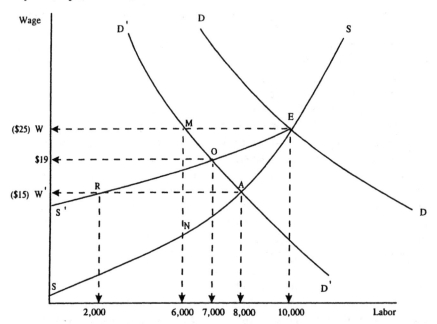

threatens to fall to $D'D'$ because of a downward shift in the demand for the goods or services that this labor helps to produce. With supply curve SS, hourly earnings threaten to fall from $25 to $15 and employment from 10,000 to 8,000 if wages are flexible downward. When a union or other bargaining agent keeps wages from falling but takes no other action, job loss is twice as great (to 6,000 remaining places), again with supply curve SS.

This fall in demand imposes a penalty on affected workers whose magnitude depends on the shape of their supply curve, which indicates the alternatives available to them if they do not supply this particular type of labor. When supply is relatively inelastic (SS as opposed to $S'S$), the penalty is relatively large. The fall in demand causes a 40 percent cut in wages. Just 20 percent of workers would then withdraw their labor and seek alternatives. With supply curve $S'S$, a 40 percent wage reduction would cause 80 percent of workers to go elsewhere. The fall in demand from DD to $D'D'$ would cause 30 percent of workers to leave this employment and would reduce wages by only $6, or 24 percent. Thus the more inelastic the supply of labor, the harder a union or other bargaining agent would lobby for measures to prevent the fall in demand.[8] This might be done via subsidies to this industry, an increase in government orders, or restrictions on foreign competition via tariffs or import quotas.

Measures such as these may reduce efficiency and technological progress, especially if done on a regular basis. A better option will often be to increase elasticity of supply by improving the alternatives available to workers. This will reduce lobbying pressures to keep demand from falling but may still result in measures that reduce competition and efficiency. Unemployment compensation based on the $25 wage will cushion the cost of a fall in labor demand but will hardly resolve the problem by itself unless the fall is expected to be temporary. (Even then, suppliers of labor may bargain for higher wages than they would if unemployment benefits were less generous and deliberately accept longer spells of joblessness in industries with seasonal or cyclical fluctuations in demand.)

A permanent solution to unemployment caused by structural shifts in demand should therefore include measures to increase occupational and geographical mobility of displaced workers. Subsidized retraining is now politically popular, but today's unemployed may be more educated than ever before, even though the rate of return to education also appears to be higher than in the past.[9] Vocational or professional training is successful only when the skills being acquired are also in demand. This requires information about trends in product demand that it is, in part, the task of industrial policy to provide. Lacking this information, governments may use retraining programs to warehouse people who would otherwise be unemployed, especially in periods before elections, even if the courses in question do little to improve long-term career prospects. By contrast, since products go through life cycles of growth, maturity, and decline, efficient policy would speed the transfer of resources from declining to advancing sectors.

Potentially, industrial policy requires the equivalent of four basic institutions in order to set and implement priorities and to improve supply alternatives for households and firms: (1) An economic planning council or similar body to organize and lead the goal-forming process, which in particular involves the generation and dissemination of information about alternatives; (2) an agency (such as a department or ministry of industry or of technology) to help implement priorities and to promote technological progress and/or diffusion of technical information; (3) an agency to promote labor mobility (including retraining) and to ease adjustment costs for workers; and (4) an investment bank to help give the government some leverage over the allocation of investment resources. Today most governments have at least some of the elements of these institutions.

As indicated, a major role of government in industrial policy is to increase the flow of information about costs, product standards, production methods, and the like, as well as about future shifts in demand and supply. Since this information has public-good properties, cases will arise in which its diffusion is in society's interest, but not in the individual interests of firms that would prefer to keep such data confidential. The state may also try to increase access to technology from abroad. To implement its priorities, the government could use incentives and controls that affect the magnitude and direction of investment, including investment in human capital and in research and development. These incentives may take many forms, including a variety of direct taxes and subsidies. To illustrate them, we shall show how some governments have influenced the allocation of loanable funds as well as access to imported goods and technology. In the process, banks or other lenders have often served as agents of the government, in effect, by helping to diffuse technical information, as well as to finance investments that exploit the technologies in question.

A major function of financial markets is to attract savings and channel them into investment. In Figure 3.3(a), I_p and S_p refer, respectively, to intended gross investment and saving by firms, households, and government bodies, while Y indexes gross national product. I_p/Y and S_p/Y are therefore the shares of GNP that decision makers collectively intend to invest and to save. These will depend on the interest rate, r, in a fashion shown by the solid curves, because r indexes both the reward paid for savings and the cost of loan financing for purchases of capital goods and consumer durables. In this section, r will measure the *real* interest rate—that is, the difference between the nominal rate (or the rate actually paid) and the expected rate of inflation.

As a rule, S_p/Y slopes upward but is believed to be inelastic. The net effect of changes in r on savings is positive but small. (A household saving toward a fixed goal, such as buying a car, may even save less when the interest rate rises, since higher interest earnings will offset some amount in decline in savings.)[10] Moreover, governments have been known to offset any negative effect of low interest rates on saving through policies that tax consumption and subsidize saving and/or by restrictions on borrowing that force households or business firms to save more than they would like to at existing interest rates in advance of purchases of durables or other large outlays.[11] These policies would shift S_p/Y outward to S'_p/Y. By contrast, I_p/Y slopes downward because, as r falls, more investment projects become cost effective. To a borrowing firm, the expected profit on an investment is (roughly) the amount invested times the difference between the project's expected yield and the cost of borrowing. Firms are more willing to invest when the state bears part of the risk, a practice followed to some extent in most market economies, and many governments effectively subsidize investment. These policies would shift I_p/Y outward to I'_p/Y.

With savings and investment schedules at S'_p/Y and I'_p/Y, the equilibrium interest rate is 4 percent, and the equilibrium share of GNP saved or invested is 16 percent. With r at 4 percent, access to credit depends entirely on a willingness and ability to pay this rate. However, the government may assert its priorities in part by keeping the interest rate below equilibrium—for instance, at 3 percent in Figure 3.3(a)—creating an excess demand for loanable funds. This allows government influence over lenders to help determine how loans will be allocated among prospective borrowers. (Moreover, as we saw earlier, a quota system of some sort is necessary to keep down the efficiency losses associated with an interest rate ceiling.) That part of demand with lowest priority ranking will have the lowest access to credit on official markets.

Rationing of foreign exchange (or of foreign currencies) works similarly.

Figure 3.3 **Rationing of (a) Investment Funds and (b) Foreign Exchange**

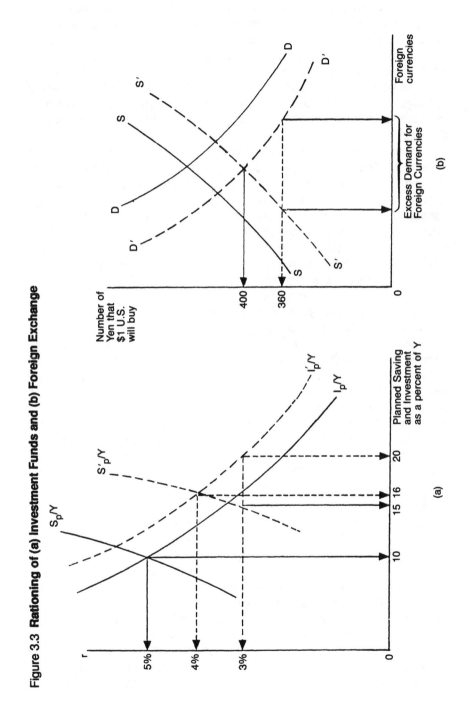

Once again access depends on the use to which the funds are to be put. In Japan during the 1950s and 1960s, for example, foreign exchange rationing was thorough and systematic. A holder of yen could not exchange them for dollars or deutsche marks if his or her intended use of the funds had a low state priority. In addition, many imports were restricted by licensing procedures. While the Japanese government removed most exchange controls during the 1970s, a similar (although weaker) effect continued to be achieved through a variety of informal trade barriers that suppressed the demand for some kinds of imports more than the demand for others.

Consider Figure 3.3(b). There DD gives the demand for foreign currencies by Japanese holders of yen who want to import goods or to invest or travel abroad. The supply of foreign currencies (SS) comes from foreigners who want to buy Japanese goods or to travel or invest in Japan. The more expensive foreign currencies are in terms of the yen—measured along the vertical axis as the number of yen needed to buy $1 U.S.—the more expensive foreign goods are and the smaller is the volume that Japanese will wish to buy. Thus DD slopes downward. By contrast, the greater the number of yen exchanged for $1 U.S., the cheaper Japanese goods are priced in yen to foreigners. Thus SS slopes upward. The Japanese government undertakes a number of policies that cause DD or SS to shift—notably, the range of subsidies for exporters, including low-cost loans, risk absorption, and public assistance in promoting exports. Export subsidies make Japanese goods cheaper to foreigners at any exchange rate, causing SS to shift out to $S'S'$. Tariffs, plus red tape in handling imports (e.g., in the form of drawn-out inspection and registration procedures), and other discriminatory costs make foreign goods more expensive to Japanese at any exchange rate and thereby shift DD down to $D'D'$. Given $D'D'$ and $S'S'$, equilibrium occurs where 400 yen equals $1 U.S.

In order to ration foreign currencies among would-be buyers, however, it is necessary to keep the yen prices of foreign currencies below equilibrium, as shown in Figure 3.3(b).[12] This makes imports cheaper for those firms and individuals able to obtain them, while others are not allowed to import goods or foreign capital even though they are willing and able to do so at official exchange rates. Thus high-priority industries have enjoyed good access to imports and to low-cost loans, as well as protection from foreign competition, accelerated depreciation, and other subsidies. The easiest goods to import have been key raw materials and equipment embodying advanced technology. Imports of manufactured consumer goods and of food have been strictly limited—the latter through formal barriers designed to protect domestic agriculture. Both credit and foreign-exchange rationing subsidize expansion in industries or regions with a high government priority and penalize it in low-priority sectors, where access is comparatively low. When monetary policy becomes tighter, the excess demand for loans is apt to increase as a partial substitute for increases in interest rates. Priority becomes more important in determining access to funds.

During the 1970s, and to a greater extent during the 1980s and 1990s, governments in Japan and Western Europe have relaxed controls on financial markets and international trade. This has been part of a general trend toward reduced government regulation of economic activity, which serves as a Western counterpart to the reform of former Soviet-type economies. However, governments continue to promote investment in priority sectors via concessional credit terms, tax forgiveness, loan guarantees, improved access to information, and other forms of subsidy. In Japan, consumer credit restrictions have fallen slowly, and households continue to maintain high rates of saving, which has financed much of Japan's overseas investment. Economists, the general public, and even government officials now take less favorable views of the kinds of intervention shown in Figure 3.3. Increasingly, economists tend to favor policy options that limit these interventions and restrict government's role to that of producing and spreading information. Japanese industrial policy has also become less interventionist and more information-intensive as Japan has shifted toward more knowledge-intensive production.

By reallocating investment finance or access to imports, a government may reduce economic efficiency. For example, suppose an interest ceiling of 3 percent in Figure 3.3(a) is combined with credit rationing. Then investments with a high government priority may be undertaken when they have expected yields of just over 3 percent, while projects yielding 6 percent or more but with a low state priority are starved for funds. If these are true rates of return to society, the result will be a loss of future income and output. Part of the 6 percent profitability may result from the exercise of monopoly power. However, the existence of excess profits is a sign that users want more of the products in question, and that their supply should expand. Credit rationing will sometimes prevent this, reinforcing the effect of other barriers to entry. When interest ceilings and other restrictions are severe, moreover, banks will try to confine themselves to relatively safe loans, which are attractive even with constrained interest earnings. Thus, without government support, loans to finance entry into new markets or innovative products and production methods may be harder to come by under credit rationing.

A similar cost may arise from the rationing of foreign exchange or imports, and officials have made some famous gaffes in allocating import quotas and investment funds. For instance, from 1952 to 1954 Japan's Ministry of International Trade and Industry blocked the application of a small Japanese radio manufacturer to import transistor technology on grounds that the company, the Sony Radio Corporation, lacked the know-how to develop cost-effective uses for it. (It should be pointed out, however, that the system was not so inflexible as to hold up Sony for long.) More generally, an industrial policy is usually a policy of import substitution—or of restricting imports and replacing them with domestic production—since otherwise government assistance to promote their growth would be unnecessary. Such measures are risky, as they could leave a nation with problem industries that never become competitive. When industrial policy has been successful, it has usually included or coincided with measures that alter a country's resource endowments by increasing the quantity and quality of physical and human capital. This has helped to reduce costs and increase quality in industries that make intensive use of these inputs, thereby creating a new comparative advantage. Successful industrial policies have also been able to correct rather than reinforce market failure. We shall now look at how this might be done.

Industrial Policy and Market Failure

Standard economic analysis reveals two potential sources of market failure in the sense that investment yields to society may diverge from the private yields foreseen by an investing firm or supplier of investment finance in the absence of corrective measures. We shall identify shortly a third potential source. A task of industrial policy is then to compensate for market failure by channeling resources into areas in which social investment yields exceed private yields. Traditional sources of market failure are in the provision of public goods (or goods that are jointly consumed), as well as in the realization of scale and experience economies in production.

For example, a chemical plant may find it profitable to pollute the environment, thereby shifting part of its costs onto firms or individuals who want to use the air or water it is befouling. This is the classic case of social cost, and governments sometimes use subsidies, together with penalties, to get firms to alter their production technologies and to steer resources into research and development of pollution-preventing devices (which are public goods). A more frequent use of credit rationing is to channel funds into housing and public works. Up to a point, social investment yields here will exceed rates of return to private investors. A plentiful supply of good housing will help to lower social tensions, the incidence of disease, and the crime rate—and is thus, in part, a public good.

In addition, the profile of industries in which one nation has a comparative (or cost) advantage over others will shift over time—often from labor-intensive to physical capital–intensive and then to knowledge- or human capital–intensive production. Thus there is an advantage in being able to foresee specific directions of change and in speeding up this evolution, especially for resource-poor countries, since the result potentially may be to raise value added per worker more rapidly. The ability to spot potential comparative advantage early and to speed the movement of resources into sectors with future growth prospects is more valuable the greater is the influence of experience or scale economies on production costs. Scale economies cause the average cost (AC) of a particular product to fall as its rate of output rises (or, perhaps, as the output of related products rises) within a given factory or firm. Up to a point, increases in output require smaller percentage increases in total cost, and we have given reasons for this in chapter 2. Experience economies result from learning about production processes and usually depend on cumulative output from the time an enterprise begins to use a new technology. A firm's AC curve for a given product will be lower, the greater its past experience with the basic technologies it is now using and the greater its access to experience gained by other enterprises using these technologies. The same is true of product quality. For example, over a fifteen-year span Japanese companies reduced the cost of making a videotape recorder to about 1 percent of its original level and greatly improved quality at the same time.

While some benefits of experience with a given technology are hard to communicate, the cumulation of experience by one firm does generate knowledge that can be passed on to others. Thereby, each enterprise using a given technology can help others to bring down their costs or to improve their quality more quickly. Without such information exchange, there will be more duplication of learning, and firms will have higher unit costs than they would if the results of each company's experience were made available to others. Enterprises will be reluctant to pass on technical information that could benefit competitors. However, if firms can be induced to exchange such knowledge, the cumulative output of each will be a good with public properties. The greater this output, then, the more valuable will be the experience-related information passed on to others using the same basic technology and jointly consuming this information.

Potentially, therefore, efficiency requires subsidies to promote the achievement of experience economies on two grounds: (1) the cumulative output of one firm can provide jointly consumed (public) benefits for others, and (2) over any given time period, experience economies are also scale economies, and acquisition of experience via current production lowers the cost of future production. For either reason, production may be socially worthwhile, even if it is not currently profitable.

To realize the public benefits, subsidies must be tied both to output expansion and to good-faith provision of technical information, which also gives a firm access to the information collected from all participating enterprises. The government can promote such an information exchange most freely when the nation in question obtains most of its basic technological advances from abroad. Communal property rights (in the form of free access to technical information for domestic producers) will maximize the spread of technology at the cost of lowering the private return on (and thereby discouraging) domestic research and development aimed at achieving basic breakthroughs. Gains from free access may still be high, not the least because new technologies often have unforeseen applications beyond initial uses. The discoveries that originally made high fidelity possible, for example, turned out to have applications for the whole range of consumer as well as producer electronics and to other industries. This amplified the need to begin accumulating experience with such a technology as soon as and as rapidly as possible. If a nation relies on its own development of basic new technologies, it can still promote the exchange of experience-related technical information among enterprises that already have access to the underlying technology, but it will have more critical choices to make about when to penalize and when to subsidize the spread of such information.

Scale economies are a classic reason for market failure when the smallest output that will minimize average cost is more than a small percentage of total market size. If a good is produced, efficiency requires its output to expand to the point at which its price (P) equals the marginal cost (MC) of supplying it—for example, to Q_0 in Figure 3.4—if the firm's demand curve crosses LMC at M. But as long as scale economies persist, MC must be less than AC.[13] Such expansion therefore requires the firm to take a loss—equal to area P_1AMP_0 in Figure 3.4—in the absence of a subsidy (or, possibly, of some form of price discrimination). If government assistance tied to expanded production is not forthcoming, the scale of output will be too low, and the good may not even be produced when it should be on efficiency grounds.[14] As a rule, scale economies are greatest in heavy industry, transportation, and other capital-intensive sectors. Experience economies (basically the same as the Japanese term *Kaizen*, or continuing improvement) are important in a variety of industries, and notably in knowledge-intensive sectors. Over time, they would cause the average cost curve in Figure 3.4 to shift downward. Both types of economies have played a key role in the strategy of economic development followed by Japan since World War II and in the development experience of many other nations.

The Problem of Collateral and the Role of the State

Scale and experience economies, including technological spillover benefits from one product to another, are reasons why market failure may occur in the sense that the social rate of return on investment in new products or methods may exceed the private yield foreseen by an individual investor. Another potential problem arises when firms must finance their investments from outside funds— that is, when they must borrow or sell shares. Suppliers of outside funds may foresee a lower return on their outlays than the best yield available to the investing enterprise. That is, they may further discount the returns on risky investments, curtailing the flow of venture capital to prospective growth industries. As noted earlier, large institutional investors increasingly dominate the equity markets of North America and Western Europe. Their money managers thrive or fall on their ability to earn large, fast returns, which puts pressure on corporate managements to achieve short-term results. This militates against the provision of equity financing for development or introduction of basic new technologies and products, which usually require long decision-making horizons, especially when experience economies are large.

Under laissez-faire, firms that have been profitable in the past may have the best access to investment financing in the form of loans because they possess valuable assets and established reputations that constitute collateral or security for lenders. On this basis, lenders will ration credit on their own, even in the absence of government intervention. To see why, consider a firm that values its credit rating at $20,000 and has used a machine worth another $20,000 as security for a loan. A banker would be irrational, in an economic sense, to lend $40,000 or more on this collateral, since repayment of principal and interest would come to over

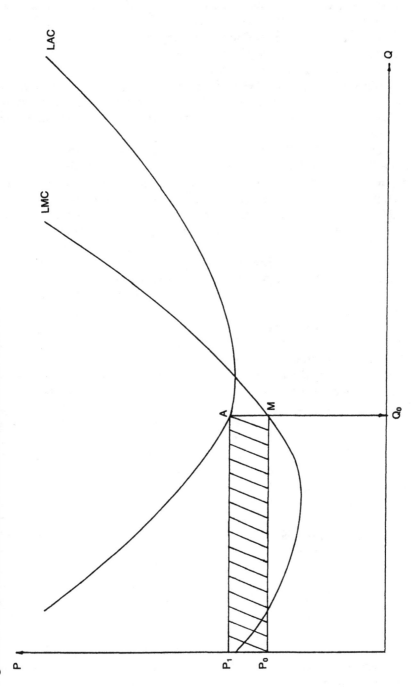

Figure 3.4 Scale Economies as a Classic Reason for Market Failure

$40,000, and the machine may depreciate further. If a bank did make such a loan, the borrower would be rational, economically speaking, to default, even if he had to sacrifice all his collateral. This implies credit rationing. Firms with expected yields of 15 percent, but that lack sufficient collateral, will on that account fail to obtain financing. Others with expected yields of 10 percent, but also with better security to offer, will get the credit they are seeking because they pose a lower default risk for lenders. In the absence of collateral, the returns foreseen by lenders on their loans are reduced by any positive probability that borrowers will default (or fail to repay on time).

According to D. K. Benjamin, "Collateral . . . helps make the debt self-enforcing: since the debtor forfeits the collateral in the event of default, his wealth is less dependent on his repayment decision."[15] From another viewpoint, collateral affords protection to suppliers of savings in the form of debt, much as a board of directors and independent auditing provide protection to suppliers of savings in the form of equity. Collateral can also be intangible, consisting largely of borrowers' expectations of a continuing relationship with lenders. Kinship, ethnic, religious, ideological, geographic, and long-term business ties have acted as collateral. For example, business-government-bank relationships in the former Yugoslavia had an ethnic and regional basis, and banks there were reluctant to lend across ethnic frontiers. A lender's participation in the management of a borrowing firm is a form of collateral, which helps to explain the close ties between banks and firms that sprang up in the late nineteenth century in Japan, Germany, and other European countries—creating the economic system known as "finance capitalism."

Explicit or implicit government guarantees to lenders that their loans will be repaid constitute a form of collateral and could serve to reallocate credit according to state priorities that are partially substituted for the guidelines of bankers and other lenders. If left to their own devices, banks would make loans only for which borrowers could offer good collateral as security. Normally, physical assets must serve as collateral, since the lender must be able to acquire income or use rights over them. Human capital cannot play such a role in societies in which human bondage is outlawed. On these grounds alone, a case can be made for subsidized loans to help finance education, vocational training, and occupational mobility.

Moreover, because they are well endowed with collateral, established enterprises usually have the best access to outside funds, while younger, smaller firms generally have relatively low access, especially for risky investments or investments with delayed payoffs—for example, because of experience economies. The result could be a shortage of financing for new products, entry into new markets, or new production technologies. This shortage would be greatest during periods of relatively rapid structural change—in the sense that some industries are declining, while others have growth potential—when capital is tied up in declining industries. If collateral destroyed by permanent shifts in demand or supply is not replaced—probably through some form of government intervention—the transition will be slowed, the economy will go into recession, and the country in question may be unable to establish itself in growing industries or to gain sufficient experience with basic new technologies that will serve as the foundation of future product development and economic growth. Recessions often begin in times of rapid structural change, when destruction of collateral owing to the concentration of wealth in declining industries is apt to be relatively high.[16]

The less mobile resources are shifting out of declining and into advancing sectors, the greater will be the cost of structural shifts in demand in terms of unemployment and reduced growth. As a result, there are potential gains from subsidizing resource mobility (and penalizing immobility) that are greater, the sooner and more accurately sectors of future growth and decline are identified. In this context, it should be noted that credit rationing can be used to break down barriers to entry, as well as to reinforce them. Once public officials are convinced that an effort to break into a market is worthwhile, the firms in question—taking advantage of government guarantees as collateral—can frequently raise far more capital than they would be able to mobilize on their own.[17]

The central role of government in industrial policy arises from its position as the largest and financially strongest actor in any modern economy as well as its position as the only decision maker to share ownership rights with and represent all others and with a comparative advantage in producing and enforcing property rights. It also has the best-developed facilities for promoting compromise. Therefore, it is in the best position to develop an economywide perspective, to organize the goal-forming process, and to bring other decision makers into social goal formation.

In an age when people demand insurance against income and job loss, the question is not whether, but how best to provide this. A successful industrial policy will compensate for market failure, but because of the influence of special interest lobbies plus the short political time horizons of elected representatives, the alternative is apt to be a poor industrial policy instead of none at all. Governments are bound to influence the direction of production and investment, but governments frequently fail to get value for their assistance in terms of output expansion, cost reduction, new product development, or public benefits. There is always a risk that they will react too late to crises and prop up declining or inefficient industries with political clout, thereby delaying necessary adjustment and even increasing long-term unemployment. Advance planning can make it possible to transfer resources and provide retraining for displaced workers sooner while still promoting the development of promising new industries. Here the ability of government to exercise leadership will be crucial in determining how much benefit a nation derives from its evolving comparative advantage and in giving different groups in society a stake in economic growth.

Per Capita GNP in Developed, Transition, and Rapidly Growing Asian Economies

To close this chapter, Table 3.2 gives 1994 data on gross national products for several developed market economies, along with five transition economies and

Table 3.2

Per Capita GNP, Growth, Inflation, and Unemployment

	GNP per capita (1994) (U.S. dollars) (purchasing power parities)	Growth* (1985–94) (in percent)	Inflation** (1985–94) (in percent)	Unemployment (1994) (in percent)
Developed economies				
United States	25,860	1.3	3.3	6.1
Switzerland	24,390	0.5	3.7	4.7
Japan	21,350	3.2	1.3	2.9
Canada	21,320	0.4	3.1	10.4
	E 9,340			E 13.5
Germany	19,890	1.9	2.9	9.6
	W 22,360			W 8.2
France	19,820	1.7	2.9	12.4
Australia	19,000	1.2	4.1	9.7
Italy	18,610	1.8	6.2	11.3
United Kingdom	18,170	1.4	5.4	9.2
Sweden	17,850	0.0	5.8	8.0
Transition economies				
Czech Republic	7,910	−2.1	11.8	3.2
Hungary	6,310	0.9	19.5	10.4
Russia	5,260	−4.4	124.0	7.1
Poland	5,380	0.9	101.7	16.2
China	2,510	6.9	9.6	2.7†
Asian "tigers"				
Hong Kong++	23,080	5.3	9.0	1.9
Singapore	21,430	6.9	3.9	2.6
Taiwan	12,220	6.9	2.8	1.6
South Korea	10,540	7.8	6.8	2.0

Sources:

For all economies except Taiwan: World Bank, *World Bank Atlas, 1996* (Washington, D. C.: U.S. Government Printing Office, 1996), pp. 18–19.

For Taiwan: Council for Economic Planning and Development, *Taiwan Statistical Data Book, 1995* (Taipei: June 1995), pp. 1, 27; and Robert Summers and Alan Heston, "The Penn World Table (Mark 5): An Expanded Set of International Comparisons, 1950–1988," *Quarterly Journal of Economics*, May 1991, table II, p. 353.

Unemployment data come from *OECD Economic Outlook*, June 1995 (Paris: OECD), pp. 111–A24; and statistical yearbooks of Asian "tigers."

*Per capita GNP growth, 1985–94, as annual average.

**Annual average growth of GNP deflator, 1985–94.

+Data refer to united Germany except where indicated by E (former East Germany), W (former West Germany).

++Per capita gross domestic product. Growth and inflation refer to GNP per capita and to GNP deflator, as with other economies.

†Urban areas only.

four Asian "tigers" (or rapidly growing nonsocialist Asian economies). Except for China and Vietnam, transition economies generally had the slowest growth rates from 1985 through 1994 and the highest rates of inflation, first, because their Soviet-type economies had exhausted possibilities for extensive growth by 1985 and, second, because transition has been a painful and disruptive experience. By contrast, China's growth rate has been one of the highest in the world, and the same is true of the Asian tigers. Growth in developed market economies was slow to moderate. In order to make per capita GNP as comparable across nations as possible, purchasing-power-parity comparisons have been used. These take into account differences in price levels, as well as differences in per capita income, from one country to another.

Notes

1. We may be tempted to conclude that if special interest groups are inevitable the legislature itself should be made up of their representatives. Generally, however, this is wrong. For one thing, the need to face periodic elections would shorten the time horizons of these representatives. Beyond this, most governments face a need to separate interest articulation from interest aggregation. Pressure groups articulate interests and try to rally their supporters behind various positions and points of view linked together by group ideology, values, and norms. The government then takes responsibility for synthesizing interest group preferences into policies and laws. This relieves group leaders of part of the onus, in the eyes of their supporters, of retreating too far from group values or goals when compromise requires this.

Moreover, in any society the struggle over distribution always threatens, at best, to occupy too many resources and, at worst, to create chaos or to paralyze the economy. Pressure groups will generally form around those special interests that are most active in this struggle—business, labor, farmers, professionals, and so forth. Compromise between them becomes easier to achieve if the legislature is chosen on a different basis—normally by geographical district—so that each member's jurisdiction cuts across these interests to some degree. This makes the prosperity of each jurisdiction more dependent on efficient compromise, although inevitably—since each district contains a different mix of farmers, blue-collar workers, businessmen, and so on—the struggle over distributive shares will spill over into the legislature.

2. In the long run, however, this potential advantage may be more than offset by two other factors. First is the soft budget constraint, or practice of shielding enterprises from the profit-and-loss consequences of their actions. This reduces the incentive to earn profits, which are a major source of budget revenue, and thus increases the pressure on money supply expansion to help finance state expenditure. Over time, falling profit returns on investment resulting from diminishing returns or declining opportunities for extensive growth will intensify this pressure. For a discussion of the political business cycle (defined below), see E. R. Tufte, *Political Control of the Economy* (Princeton: Princeton University Press, 1978).

3. The basic theory of adverse selection is from George Akerlof. See "The Market for 'Lemons'," *Quarterly Journal of Economics,* August 1970. Regarding the discussion of moral hazard below, see M. V. Pauly, "The Economics of Moral Hazard: Comment," *American Economic Review,* June 1968, and references cited.

4. The following borrows from D. R. Cameron, "The Expansion of the Public Economy: A Comparative Analysis," *American Political Science Review,* December 1978, and

Gunnar Myrdal, *Beyond the Welfare State* (New Haven: Yale University Press, 1960). See as well Edwin G. West, "Secular Cost Changes and the Size of Government: Towards a Generalized Theory," *Journal of Public Economics,* vol. 45 (1991), pp. 363–381. Data come from the OECD publication, *Economic Outlook,* July 1995.

5. See West, cited in note 4; D. C. Mueller, *Public Choice* II (Cambridge: Cambridge University Press, 1989), p. 324; W. J. Baumol, "Macroeconomics of Unbalanced Growth: The Anatomy of Urban Crisis," *American Economic Review,* June 1967; Sam Peltzman, "The Growth of Government," *Journal of Law and Economics,* October 1980.

6. Cameron, in "The Expansion of the Public Economy," argues that small open economies also tend to have concentrated industrial sectors that are conducive to the growth of labor movements and left-wing parties.

7. To give an example, the North American Free Trade Agreement (NAFTA) initially raised U.S. exports to Mexico, which then fell sharply when the peso was devalued. The latter caused claims for unemployment compensation to soar in border areas of the United States. (In Laredo, Texas, for example, these tripled over a six-month period starting in October 1994.) These problems may end up being no more than a "speed bump" on the road to prosperity in southern U.S. border regions, as one author claims, but nevertheless they raise the demand for social insurance and retraining in the meantime. See Fiona Sigalla, "Texas' Border: On the Front Line of Change," *The Southwest Economy,* Federal Reserve Bank of Dallas, no. 2, 1995.

8. Ideally, political pressure groups would also be less firmly tied to specific industries than they are in most Western nations. When the power and even the existence of a pressure group are tied to the physical or human capital invested in a declining industry, it is apt to press vigorously for protection and subsidies that delay necessary resource transfers.

9. See, for example, W. Michael Cox and Beverly J. Fox, "What's Happening to Americans' Income?" *The Southwest Economy,* Federal Reserve Bank of Dallas, no. 2, 1995.

10. More generally, while the substitution effect of a higher interest rate acts to increase savings, the wealth effect usually acts to reduce it. The higher rate makes it costlier to consume now rather than to save, but it also makes someone with positive net savings wealthier, because any given volume of savings will buy more future consumption. The wealth effect motivates the individual to consume more *both* in the future and in the present, and therefore to save less.

11. Such restrictions may also make it impossible for households to borrow enough to compensate for government saving on their behalf in the form of obligatory social insurance contributions (usually collected as payroll taxes from employers). However, social insurance plausibly transfers income from households with relatively high savings propensities to those (such as retirees) whose savings propensities are relatively low. Unless the social insurance system is running a substantial surplus, it is therefore unlikely to significantly raise S_p/Y.

12. However, the Japanese government also restricted the supply of foreign currencies, notably via barriers to foreign investment in Japan. Nearly all trading nations subsidize exports and tax or restrict imports to a degree, and it is difficult to know how exchange rates would have behaved in the absence of such (offsetting) policies.

13. Let a firm expand output by 10 percent. With scale economies, the resulting rise in total cost must be lower, say 5 percent. If TC stands for total cost and Q indexes output:

$$\frac{[\Delta Q]}{Q} \div \frac{[\Delta TC]}{TC} = \frac{10\%}{5\%} = 2 = \frac{[TC]}{Q} \div \frac{[\Delta TC]}{\Delta Q}.$$ Average cost is roughly twice as great as marginal cost and must, in general, be greater than marginal cost.

14. A good should be produced, on efficiency grounds, if there is at least one positive output at which total consumer (or user) surplus exceeds the total cost of supplying it to users.

15. See D. K. Benjamin, "The Use of Collateral to Enforce Debt Contracts," *Economic Inquiry,* July 1978, p. 334. Benjamin is the source for the preceding paragraph.

16. See David Lilien, "Sectoral Shifts and Cyclical Unemployment," *Journal of Political Economy,* August 1982.

17. For example, Japanese entry into the United States semiconductor market caused American producers to complain to the U.S. International Trade Commission that Japanese companies had an unfair advantage because they could borrow twenty times as much money overnight and rely on government guarantees of repayment.

Questions for Review, Discussion, Examination

1. In addition to property rights, we can identify basic political rights that are not easily changed by the current government of a given society. What kinds of rights can we identify? Might it be argued that one of these rights is more basic than the others, in the sense that the others are apt to depend on it in practice? Discuss.

2. What problems might be encountered in combining planning with "democracy" in the sense of competing political parties? Do you think that they can be overcome? Discuss briefly. How is the absence of competing political parties related to the ability of a centrally planned economy to control unemployment? Finally, why did a Soviet-type economy potentially provide a better economic basis than a market economy for enduring political control by a single party?

3. Briefly explain what is meant by the "political business cycle."

4. Give one efficiency argument for and one efficiency argument against the financing of health care via social insurance. Explain why expansion of social insurance often leads to large increases in the percentage of national income spent on health care and other insurance-covered benefits.

5.   (a) Give and briefly explain at least four reasons for the dramatic growth of the government sector in every Western economy, as measured by the ratio of government spending to GNP, since World War II.

   (b) In particular, there has been a dramatic growth in social insurance. Why has this occurred? Give at least one benefit and one cost of the expansion of social insurance. Finally, explain why social insurance has been such a rapidly growing expenditure item.

6. What role did Keynesian economics play in the relative expansion of public sectors in Western nations? Why are economists now more skeptical about the ability of government to play the role assigned to it by Keynesian economics?

7. To the extent that the expanding share of GNP accounted for by publicly financed goods and services is a price effect, what indication is there that governments act like suppliers facing inelastic demand? (*Hint:* When demand is inelas-

tic, what happens to the share of income spent on a good as its price goes up?)

8. What two basic views of the nature of the relative expansion of public sectors can we distinguish? Briefly explain each. Which of the two would suggest that suppliers of publicly financed goods and services were able to receive supernormal returns over and above their opportunity costs? Why?

9. Sometimes the area between the supply curve of an input into a specific use or occupation and the price or wage of that input is called its "economic rent." In Figure 3.2, area *WEANS* is the economic rent at wage W = \$25.00 if the supply curve is *SS*, and area *WES'* is the rent if the supply curve is *S'S*. Here economic rent measures the benefit to suppliers of labor of being able to work in this occupation. It is the sum of the difference between the actual wage and the wage at which each worker is willing to supply his or her labor.

   (a) For a given wage, will lobbying pressures to reduce or to nullify any prospective decline in the demand for labor be greater when the economic rent is high or low? Please explain your answer. How can government policy affect the elasticity of labor supply?

   (b) Why might a government subsidize worker training even when job prospects for graduates of such a program are poor?

10. According to the theory of comparative advantage, a nation has a cost advantage in producing those goods and services that make intensive use of the inputs with which that nation is relatively well endowed. Therefore, a resource-rich nation should specialize in industries based on these resources and export part of this output in exchange for imports that make intensive use of inputs with which the country in question is not so well endowed. A land-rich nation with a favorable climate should specialize in farm products, etc.

Given this, why might we expect a successful industrial policy to be one that includes measures to alter a nation's factor (input) endowments? Briefly, how can the latter be done?

11. What are the arguments in favor of systematic government intervention in the economy in the form of market planning (or "industrial policy")? Give at least one counterargument. In answering, indicate the role of experience and scale economies and, more generally, of market failure as a possible motivator of government intervention. Describe the risks involved both in undertaking and not undertaking such a policy.

12. How may it be possible to increase experience economies in firms making use of the same or similar basic technologies? Briefly explain the potential risks inherent in efforts to increase experience economies in this way.

13. What is the problem of collateral? How may it become a source of market failure?

14. Explain how shifts in the composition of demand and supply that give rise to structural change (changes in the assortment of goods and services produced) may lead to recession in market economies.

Chapter 4

Roots of Modern Economic Systems

A Hypothesis of Historical Development

Introduction

The earliest human remains now date to over one million years, while the Earth itself is believed to be at least four billion years old. Thus, if the Earth had lasted ten years, the human race would have but a day of that time, and recorded civilization only the last few minutes of that day. Until the Neolithic Revolution, beginning around 10,000 years ago, most humans roamed the Earth as hunters and gatherers of food. Communal property rights prevailed in land, and socioeconomic organization was next to nonexistent. Then, over the course of a few thousand years, people settled down to become farmers. Private and state property rights developed, along with political organization and socioeconomic differences. In this chapter we look at why this happened as part of an effort to sketch a broad outline of the evolution of economic systems through history down to the present.

First, we shall develop a hypothesis about historical change—undoubtedly, just one of several that could be put forward—that synthesizes the economic theory of history based on Marx and Engels with theories of modern economic historians, notably Douglass North, the 1993 co–Nobel laureate.[1] In the process, this hypothesis tries to be politically neutral. Both approaches are influenced by the thesis of survival of the fittest proposed by the English naturalist Charles Darwin. Therefore, they postulate survival of those systems that are most efficient. As underlying conditions change due to the evolution of basic forces described below, an economic system that was initially efficient loses its comparative advantage and is eventually replaced by a new organizational form that is efficient in the new underlying conditions.

The most inexorable long-run forces in the history of the human race have been population growth and technological change. Population growth suggests diminishing returns to labor vis-à-vis land or other natural resources, and it figured prominently in both the Neolithic Revolution and the demise of human bondage, as we shall see. By contrast, the rise of bondage, in the form of slavery or serfdom, resulted from technological advances that enabled farm labor to produce a surplus over subsistence in conditions in which labor was scarce relative to land. More generally, technological change suggests the Marx-Engels theory of history. Since our theory builds on this, we shall outline it briefly.

The Marx-Engels Theory of History

Marx and Engels held an economic interpretation of history based on production, which they believed to be mankind's basic social activity. According to them, the evolution of the "mode of production"—and, more specifically, of society's "productive forces" (or means of production)—directly and indirectly determines all other change. Therefore, Marx wrote:

> The general conclusion I arrived at—and once reached, it served as the guiding thread in my studies—can be briefly formulated as follows: In the social production of their means of existence, men enter into definite, necessary relationships which correspond to a definite stage of development of their material productive forces. The aggregate of these productive relationships constitutes the economic structure of society, the real basis on which a juridical and political superstructure arises, and to which definite forms of social consciousness correspond. The mode of production of the material means of existence constitutes the whole process of social, political, and intellectual life.[2]

A society's means of production will have both a quantitative and a qualitative dimension. One could speak of an economy's endowments of labor, capital, and natural resources, for example, but also of the technological sophistication of production within it. Over time, society's productive forces will change both qualitatively and quantitatively, but in Marx the emphasis is on the former. At any time and place, there is an optimal set of technologies for production, distribution, and exchange whose evolution ultimately determines all other socioeconomic change. More precisely, Marx and Engels believed that technological progress eventually renders any given socioeconomic organization obsolete as long as scarcity is a fundamental fact of human existence. While decentralized feudalism was once a relatively efficient set of property relations in western Europe, for example—with serfdom constituting, in part, a means of taxing labor to help pay for local defense—this was no longer true by the seventeenth century. Technological breakthroughs had altered the nature of warfare and the possibilities of protecting trade. Other advances had expanded the opportunities for the growth of transportation, communications, and subsequently industry. As a result, the structural relations of feudalism—and especially of serfdom—which tied individuals to a particular area and restrained occupational mobility, became fetters to economic growth. More generally, according to Marx, when established property rights and institutions stop promoting efficiency and become barriers to further progress, the stage is set for class conflict.

At this point, Marx and Engels depart both from conventional economists and from Darwin himself. "Nature Makes No Leaps" was the motto of Lord Alfred Marshall, the father of modern Western economics. Like Darwin, he believed change to be gradual, steady, and evolutionary. But for Marx, nature does take leaps. Stress builds up in a particular society until it finally bursts asunder in revolutionary change, at which time the process begins anew. In this context, Marx and Engels took a dialectical view of historical change. They believed that history moves forward through a clash of opposing forces called "thesis" and "antithesis." For Marx, this clash was essentially socioeconomic class conflict, pitting the established elites—whose power, status, and wealth are rooted in the old organization of society—against those groups that hope to succeed them and to establish a new order. The dominant class constitutes the thesis. Because of technological change, existing property relations and institutions, which were originally compatible with efficiency, eventually begin to stand in the way of progress. The effort by dominant classes to preserve the status quo then creates tensions and divisions in society and leads to a reformist mood among some groups. One or more of these will constitute the antithesis, once their goal has become a fundamental change in property relations and when they have acquired enough power to threaten the system.

While technological progress is the driving force of history, class conflict is the outward sign of major socioeconomic change. In western Europe, capitalism evolved out of feudalism. Under feudalism, we can distinguish at least three socioeconomic classes—the feudal nobility, including the church; the serfs; and the rising commercial classes. The feudal lords (thesis) were the rulers, but as the optimal mode of production evolved, they came into conflict with the rising commercial classes, the upper strata of the peasantry, and the urban craftsmen (antithesis). These forces clashed, and feudalism declined. Under capitalism, private property owners became the new dominant class, which constituted the new thesis. The workers, or proletariat, became the exploited class, or antithesis, according to Marx. Marx expected the labor movement to proceed from reform to revolution, although this has not come to pass.

We may better understand the Marxian view of causation by means of the inverted pyramid in Figure 4.1. We first break Marx's mode of production into two parts—the *productive forces* and the *socioeconomic relations,* which are also property rights or relations. Marx considered these to be class relations, because he believed that the property rights available to an individual depended on his or her socioeconomic class membership. To symbolize the key role played by productive forces, we place them at the base of the inverted pyramid. Their evolution causes everything else to change.[3] Such a material foundation of society implies, for example, that a "work ethic" is the consequence of a high potential productivity of labor at the margin. A society's basic technology of production and its resource endowments ultimately determine its social attitudes.

Property rights occupy the second layer in Figure 4.1. They form the basis of the organization of the economy and give any system its identity. For example,

Figure 4.1 **The Marxian View of Causation**

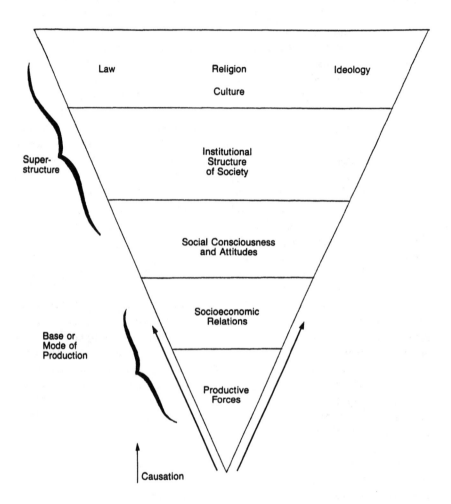

we may speak of the socioeconomic relations corresponding to laissez-faire capitalism, a Soviet-type economy, or west European feudalism. As the base of any society, the mode of production determines its superstructure. More precisely, property relations and productive forces determine social consciousness and attitudes, as well as a society's institutions, and finally its law, religion, ideology, and culture.

The nature of property rights and institutions in any society will also influence the evolution of its productive forces. In modern times, for example, Soviet-type economies had higher rates of saving and investment than Western market economies, but the latter generated higher rates of technological progress. A Japanese-style mixed economy is efficiently designed to adopt basic technologies from abroad and to diffuse them rapidly through the domestic economy while incorporating minor improvements. But it may also generate a low rate of indigenous innovation. However, Marx emphasized causation in the other direction, from changes in productive forces to changes in property rights. In the long run, a set of property rights will always tend to emerge that enables the economy to operate efficiently. In this sense, property relations will adapt to basic changes in productive forces. The nature of efficient property rights depends on the nature of these forces, which is always tending to change (notably, because of technological progress). Eventually, therefore, changes in productive forces will cause basic changes in property relations and institutions.

In the short run, however, changes in productive forces create tension in society, since property rights and institutions are resistant to fundamental change. For Marx and Engels, the reasons behind this resistance are rooted in the class structure of society. Throughout history, in their view, societies have been divided into classes based on economic roles—specifically, on the basis of who has owned the means of production. It has always been true that some classes—constituting a majority of the population—were exploited because they lacked the opportunity to own means of production other than their own labor, while a dominating minority has enjoyed easy access to ownership of capital and natural resources. However, as efficient property relations change, ultimately because of technological progress, the efficient class structure also changes to conform to this, and the dominating classes find their roles being made obsolete by technical progress. (For example, feudal lords have no major role to play under capitalism.)

When this happens, the elite has a vested interest in using its power to preserve the existing property relations from which its privilege derives. However, efficiency requires a new set of property rights, and thus a fundamental change in the economic system. Without such a change, the economy will fall further and further below its potential. As this happens, a new social class or classes will become increasingly aware of gains that they can realize by transforming property rights and institutions. This establishes the preconditions for class conflict, as a result of which a new efficient set of property relations will eventually emerge. In the words of Marx:

> At a certain stage of their development, the material productive forces of society come into contradiction with the existing productive relationships, or, what is but a legal expression for these, with the property relationships [or property rights] within which they had moved before. From forms of development of productive forces, these relationships are transformed into their fetters. Then, an epoch of social revolution opens. With the change in the economic foundation, the whole vast superstructure is more or less rapidly transformed.[4]

Marx and Engels also perceived a simplification of class conflict as history evolved. In *The Communist Manifesto*, they wrote:

> Freeman and slave, patrician and plebeian, lord and serf, guild-master and journeyman, in a word, oppressor and oppressed carried on a constant, now hidden, now open fight, a fight that each time ended, either in a revolutionary reconstitution of society at large, or in the common ruin of the contending classes. . . . Our epoch, the epoch of the bourgeoisie, possesses . . . this distinctive feature: it has simplified class antagonisms. Society . . . is more and more split into two great hostile camps, into two great classes, directly facing each other—bourgeoisie and proletariat.[5]

Thus Marx set out to explore the last great class conflict at a time when, in his view, modern capitalism was growing ever more hostile to an optimal evolution of society's productive forces and was thereby preparing the way for its replacement by socialism. We would add that other theories of institutional change that do not emphasize class conflict nevertheless tend to agree that a fundamental change in property relations not imposed from outside will usually be initiated by a well-organized group expecting to reap major gains from the change.[6] This group is analogous to Marx's antithesis, and it may constitute the vanguard of a new social elite. Resistance will come from groups that perceive the change to be harmful to their interests. Therefore, there is some reason to expect a better chance of success for property rights changes that are efficiency enhancing (i.e., which provide net gains for society as a whole), and this expectation is stronger if the society in question must compete economically with other nations. Changes that reduce efficiency may succeed, however, if their benefits are concentrated on a relatively small number of people and their costs are widely scattered over a larger population or are borne by minority groups with weak bargaining power.

Suppose a society stands to achieve major efficiency gains from basic changes in its property relations and institutions. In the Marx-Engels theory, the dominant classes are too closely identified with the existing institutional superstructure and with its ideology and attitudes to play a leading role in promoting a thorough transformation of society. (Although many feudal lords became successful capitalists, for example, this was the exception.) Therefore, they resist fundamental change. However, they are also presumed to possess "false consciousness." That is, they tend to be shortsighted and to underestimate the potential for systemic change. Because they fail to perceive the long-term consequences of their own actions, they actually set in motion the chain of events that leads to their downfall. They make modest institutional changes (reforms) in the direction of what is optimal, but this induces a process that they cannot control or contain.

We should also note that a society may avoid shifting to a radically different organization or lifestyle without considerable inducement or threat, since the uncertainty involved is a major deterrent. Therefore, even when a basic change in property relations holds the promise of large rewards for a society, the required transformation will not take place automatically. The group of institutional entrepreneurs that brings about change must consist of individuals who not only expect to benefit but are willing to accept the risks involved. Such a change requires both abolition of the old property rights and institution of new ones. The latter step is often the hardest to take. Yet failure to take it means that communal rights will appear, which may make things worse than previously, thereby paving the way for reestablishment of the former property relations.

Modifications to the Prime Movers

As indicated earlier, we shall add population growth to broadly defined technological change to get the prime movers of history. As population or technology changes, society's property rights must eventually change as well in order to be able to continue to promote efficiency. In addition, Marx acknowledged the influence of climate on property relations in preindustrial societies, and we shall do the same. We also accept the inverted pyramid of Figure 4.1, with its expanded base, except that we shall allow for evolutionary, as well as revolutionary change. Historically, use of the term *revolution* to describe major transformations of production or distribution technology (e.g., *Industrial Revolution, Commercial Revolution, Neolithic Revolution*) has suggested a more rapid and disruptive break with past practices than has usually occurred. Changes in property rights have also been less sudden and dramatic, as a rule, than Marx and Engels implied.

Population growth has helped to bring about two basic kinds of changes in property relations. First, by raising the demand for natural resources, it has made these scarce, causing state and private rights to expand into areas in which communal rights previously prevailed. The role of property rights—and especially the role of exclusion—has been crucial in motivating conservation of resources, as well as the discovery or production of substitutes. Property rights with regard to the material means of production and consumption have generally expanded over the past 500 to 600 years. Second, population growth has increased the supply of labor relative to natural resources during the same period and helped to bring bondage to an end. Long before the disappearance of the frontier, diminishing returns to labor in agriculture had appeared in most parts of the world. This helped to end serfdom and other forms of direct human bondage, as we shall see, and led to urbanization of much of the world's population.

At least in the short run, technological progress means increasing output per unit of labor input. Marx believed that it also increases the advantages of specialization in production and the division of labor. "How far the productive forces of a nation are developed is shown most manifestly by the degree to which the division of labor has been carried," he wrote in *German Ideology*.[7] Through most of prehistory, production was directly for use, with no exchange intermediary. However, as scarcity grew general, it became necessary to specialize in production and to exchange in order to maintain and then to raise living standards. Growing specialization led, in turn, to socioeconomic differences based on property relations.

It is by means of the division of labor that the human race reverses its previous domination by nature, and rising technological sophistication requires a socioeconomic organization based on economic roles that grow more and more specialized. Specialization notably increased during the commercial revolution, beginning in the latter Middle Ages, and then accelerated as a consequence of the Industrial Revolution that followed. This increased the value of occupational and geographical mobility and so reinforced the effects of population growth in bringing serfdom and slavery to an end in most relatively developed parts of the world. More generally, while state and private property rights have expanded over time to cover areas of new scarcity, as modern economists have emphasized, some rights have also contracted, as Marx emphasized, when restrictions that had once been compatible with efficiency (notably, human bondage) have become fetters to further progress.

The Role of the State

In chapter 1, we said that government is the ultimate producer and enforcer of property rights, without which massive inefficiency would prevail as long as scarcity is the dominant fact of economic life. More generally, governments provide public goods—notably, internal security, protection from external threat, and public administration—the need for which is created by scarcity in a context in which it is possible to produce a surplus above physical subsistence. We view the emergence of the state primarily as a consequence of growing resource scarcity—which raises the cost of communal property rights—and of competition for scarce resources, as well as of specialization and division of labor, which help to make a surplus possible. In addition, complex forms of government depend on an ability to process and store information that usually requires the availability of a written language.

As a provider of public goods, which are given in exchange for tax revenue and the right to create money, the state has a natural monopoly. But since it is production and enforcement of property rights that allows a society to produce above subsistence, a particular government may be able to use this monopoly power to exploit politically weak groups and capture most of the social surplus for its supporters. In Marx's view, the exploitive nature of presocialist societies is captured in a tendency for property income to constitute an ever-increasing share of national income, causing most of the benefit of economic growth to go to the propertied classes at the expense of labor. Let S denote property income (or "surplus value") and V denote labor income. Then $(S + V)$ equals national income. Marx believed that S/V would tend to rise until the demise of capitalism, although such a tendency does not characterize most capitalist societies during the twentieth century.[8] Marx and Engels also argued that all viable political parties under capitalism would represent the ruling classes against the oppressed.[9] In evaluating their claim, we should take into account the numerous restrictions on voting—notably the requirement to own property and the prohibition of female suffrage—characteristic of their day.

The complete Marx-Engels evolution of systems over the history of the Western world proceeds as follows: primitive communism → ancient slavery → feudalism → capitalism → state socialism → full communism. Each successive stage corresponds to a more advanced range of technologies that produces a higher per capita surplus over subsistence. The nature of the class struggle is also different in each presocialist stage. Marx was especially interested in the evolution of modern capitalism, and he did not insist on the complete universality of this evolutionary chain. However, he did believe that it would always lead through capitalism to state socialism, and that it would end where it began, with communism. Marx thought that, prior to socialism, economic efficiency would be achieved only in a context in which groups that control property exploit others. After the advent of socialism, however, efficiency and equity would begin to go hand in hand.

According to Marx and Engels, each time a new order is established, the new modes of production, institutional superstructure, and so forth become the optimal ones. From then on, a growing divergence between actual and optimal increases the stress on the existing system until it bursts asunder, yielding to another new order. This continues until the final revolution replaces capitalism with state socialism. Then the process ends, and the state eventually begins to wither away. As society heads toward full communism, the exclusion and excess demand associated with state property rights will gradually disappear, and scarcity will vanish. Freed from the scarcity constraint and the myriad conflicts to which it gives rise, the human race can at last go forward to realize its full potential. However, if this vision is utopic, as now appears to be the case, and rising resource scarcity is to be the fate of the human race, efficiency will require an extension, rather than a contraction, of private and state property rights in years to come.

Of course, the basic theory of institutional change that we have set out does not require any specific evolution, but there is wide agreement that what we now call the Neolithic Revolution marked the beginning of the end of prehistory and primitive communism.[10] Consequently, this is where we shall begin our journey through time.

Precapitalist Economies

> Men . . . begin to distinguish themselves from animals as soon as they
> begin to produce their means of subsistence, a step which is conditioned by
> their physical organization.
> —Karl Marx, *German Ideology*

The Neolithic Revolution

Marx and Engels identified five basic economic systems prior to modern capitalism. These are primitive communism, ancient slavery, medieval feudalism (a key element of which was serfdom), oriental despotism, and early capitalism. This list is not exhaustive, and early capitalism becomes modern capitalism when the output of industry exceeds that of agriculture or commerce and over half of industrial output is produced in factories and mines using inorganic power and wage labor. In the next two sections, we shall give the briefest indication of what conditions give rise to different precapitalist systems. Space limitations preclude a more thorough treatment. We shall begin with primitive communism.

For the first twenty-three hours of their day on the Earth, humans led a nomadic existence as hunter-gatherers, usually wandering in bands of fifteen to forty that were held together mainly by kinship ties.[11] As a rule, the socioeconomic class structure and internal organization of the hunter-gatherer society were not well developed. These people felt no overwhelming need to organize permanently for production or for defense—although this changed toward the end of the epoch. Neither did different bands specialize and trade to any significant degree. The earth's population and the technological means of the human race were small, and hunter-gatherers did not renew or re-create the resource base on which they lived—namely, the population of wild animals and plants.

Thus the first humans did not plant crops or assist in any way with the growth of the plants they ate. Neither did they domesticate or control the movements of animals. As hunting became more important, so did specialization and cooperation in killing game and exploiting the kill for food, clothing, and other uses. The development of spoken language and of other means of communication increased the potential gains from such cooperation. It was probably a prerequisite for successful big-game hunting, which gave rise to the first examples of production scale economies and the associated division of labor. This followed the tool-making revolution that began around 40,000 years ago. This period also gave rise to symbolic expression and to the first known works of art, in the form of cave paintings.

Nevertheless, the internal organization and social stratification of the nomadic band remained rudimentary. Not only would a band frequently migrate—responding to climatic change or to the temporary depletion of its habitat, or to follow a pack of animals—it would often break up or merge with other bands. It was in pursuit of game that primitive humans migrated to the far corners of the globe. In such conditions, rights to land, animals, and plants were basically communal. While scarcity might appear in a particular place and or at a particular time, it could usually be overcome by migrating, since the entire resource base was large relative to the demands placed on it. Such an existence forestalled the development of complex cultures. It was not always a bad way of life, although it was often fatal to the old and the very young, who were barriers to mobility. It began to come to an end around 10,000 years ago in the "fertile crescent" of the Middle East, and possibly even earlier in North America, although it also survived in many places into the seventeenth century.

The end of nomadic existence, and ultimately of primitive communism, was caused by population growth and technological progress, which eventually began to deplete animal and plant resources. The latter stages of primitive communism witnessed a tool-making revolution, as noted above. However, given communal property rights, technical advances—in the form of improved organization and methods of hunting, as well as better spears, projectile points, and so on, and the development of the bow and arrow—caused animal resources to be depleted more rapidly. In this respect, the peak of the early big-game-hunting era was a period not unlike the present. It marked the technological high-water mark of the hunter-gatherer era. Living standards were higher than ever before, but they were being sustained by progressive destruction of the resource base.

The hunting and gathering activities of prehistoric men and women thus helped to alter their environment. In North America alone, some fifty large animals became extinct, roughly between 20,000 B.C. and 7,000 B.C., and humans plausibly accounted for the extinction of more than thirty directly, including "camels, horses, bison, mastodons, llamas, ground sloths (including a giant the size of an elephant), mammoths, beavers, short-faced bears, armadillos, several saber-tooth cats (including *Smilodon,* the tiger), shrub oxen, moose, tapirs, antelope, and many more."[12] According to one author, "the North America of 15,000 years ago was [plausibly] comparable to nineteenth-century Africa in terms of the huge strange, 'unlikely' beasts that browsed the forests and brush." The exact role played by early man in the extinction of animal species is in dispute. However, some combination of population growth and improved hunting methods increased the demand for wild animals and plants, until these became scarce. By around 7,000 B.C., in several parts of the world humans could no longer live off nature's resource base without replenishing it. This set the stage for the Neolithic "Revolution," which started mankind along the road to re-creating, controlling, and expanding the resource base that sustained it. In this sense, it was a great divide.

The Neolithic Revolution was an agricultural revolution that replaced hunting and gathering with farming as the major production activity and the major means of survival. The Neolithic Revolution also transformed bands into tribes or chiefdoms (with hereditary inequality) and eventually into states, with socioeconomic class differences and division of labor based on inherited status, age, sex, and skill. Relations among individuals came to depend less on kinship and more on socioeconomic roles. In order to farm efficiently, humans had to end their nomadic existence and settle down in one location. Thus the Neolithic Revolution also increased efforts by villages or tribes to stake out claims to specific territories from which others were excluded or restricted in their access. This was necessary if the effort and investment required by herding, farming, and breeding were to bear fruit. War began as organized attacks by one village on another's territory or as efforts by tribes that were still nomadic to plunder the surpluses of farming communities. But ultimately, most nomads had to settle down, establish property rights in land, and become farmers or herders themselves in order to survive.

Figure 4.2 shows the reason for this transformation. It compares the marginal physical product of labor (MPP_L) in hunting and gathering (the kinked line, HH)

120

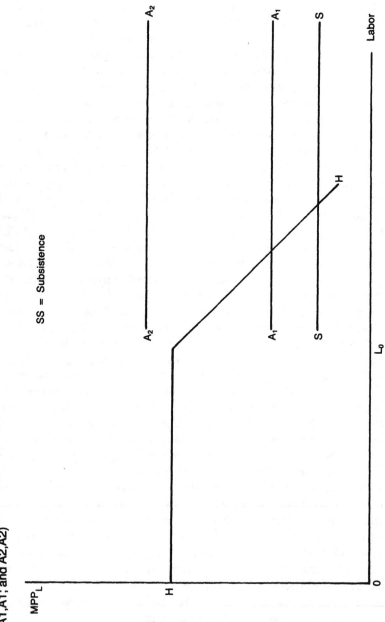

Figure 4.2 The Marginal Product of Primitive Humans in the Hunter-Gatherer versus Agrarian Cultures (SS; A1,A1; and A2,A2)

SS = Subsistence

with that in farming-herding-breeding.[13] *SS* denotes subsistence, here in the sense of physical survival. For a million years or more, the food, shelter, and clothing base was plentiful relative to demand in most places where humans lived, so that substantial diminishing returns did not appear. Labor input into hunting and gathering was to the left of L_0. Eventually, population growth and technological progress caused early man to test the limits of his natural resource base and then led to declining MPP_L in hunting and gathering. At the margin, a given effort resulted in less and less food, clothing, and shelter.[14] Ultimately, the survival of some primitive societies was threatened if they continued to rely solely on hunting and gathering.

By the time of the birth of Christ, the descendants of the North American big-game hunters of more than 10,000 years earlier were growing corn, beans, and squash, as well as hunting and domesticating smaller game. At first, the productivity of labor in agriculture was probably close to subsistence, and for hundreds or even thousands of years, many communities combined hunting or fishing with farming. However, the population-to-land ratio was sufficiently low that, with the technology available, labor served as the main constraint on output expansion, and diminishing returns in agriculture did not become an overriding problem in most regions for centuries.

Moreover, once bands had settled down and established territorial claims, the long-run effect of technological improvements in farming was quite different from what it had been in the hunter-gatherer culture. The ability to exclude outsiders allowed a community to capture the benefits of technical progress in the form of increased wealth for some or all of its inhabitants. There was also a natural learning process about how to raise the productivity of the soil, how to domesticate animals, how to reduce the spread of disease among them, and so forth. Therefore, the marginal product of labor in farming rose over time from *SS* to A_1A_1 to A_2A_2, as shown in Figure 4.2.

The Neolithic Revolution did not always end communal property rights in land within a tribe when it led to exclusion between tribes. But while land was relatively abundant, it was costly to defend and to improve. Therefore, the realm of a given tribe was limited, and private or state property rights in land eventually became necessary to ensure that it would be used efficiently. Even before the Neolithic Revolution, weapons, clothing, and other products of consumption were often private property. Subsequently, movable means of production, such as tools and other implements, became private—and finally so did the land itself—through at least a two-step process. Initially, individual families would receive rights to occupy a plot of land for a growing season and to harvest the resulting crops. But as the long-term need for investment in farm buildings, drainage, protection against soil erosion and exhaustion, and so forth was recognized, these leases expanded until they became permanent.

As the marginal product of labor in farming-breeding-herding rose, tribes acquired the ability to produce a surplus over subsistence. This allowed some people to specialize in nonfarm work and thereby gave rise to the division of labor and to exchange within the community. Different regions were also differently endowed with natural resources, which created potential gains from interregional trade, although in many cases such exchange took a long time to develop. Nevertheless, simple discoveries, such as the wheel, the ability to ride a horse, and later primitive ships, brought tribes more frequently into contact with each other. This also increased the likelihood of merger between tribes, either peacefully or (more frequently) through conquest. Population growth had the same effect. As noted earlier, the development of written languages—or of substitute ways to store and process information—made centralized governments feasible in many areas. Not only plunder but also a desire for protection, for aggrandizement, or for control over fertile farming, hunting, or fishing grounds could motivate the expansion of political units. In this way, the emergence of government above the village or tribal level came about as a direct or indirect consequence of competition for scarce resources.

Frequently the rise of government above the village level also led to slavery. Originally captives were not taken in combat, or were subsequently killed, so they would not have to be fed and looked after. But once it became possible for captives to produce a surplus above their own subsistence, they were more likely to be kept as slaves. As ownership of labor power became more attractive, some tribes even waged war to capture slaves, who also sometimes came from the indigenous population. Due to bad luck, exploitation, or lack of skill, some found bondage the only alternative to starvation or imprisonment, with slavery often resulting from indebtedness.

Slavery and Serfdom

Distinctions Between Slavery, Serfdom, and Wage Labor

To a large degree, slavery was the basis of the glory that was Greece and the grandeur that was Rome. As Engels wrote, "It was slavery that first made possible the specialization in production between agriculture and industry on a considerable scale. . . . At the time of greatest prosperity . . . there were at least 18 slaves to every adult male citizen of ancient Athens. . . . In Corinth, at the height of its power, the number of slaves was 460,000; in Aegina, 470,000. In both cases this was ten times the number of free citizens."[15] The large agricultural estate, or *latifundium*, worked mainly by slaves, became the backbone of the Roman Empire. Ultimately it was synthesized with an ownership form indigenous to the Germanic tribes that overran the northwestern part of the Roman Empire to become the feudal manor of western Europe. The latter was also mainly an agricultural estate—albeit one more diversified and self-sufficient—worked largely by serfs. It became the basic production unit of the medieval period (A.D. 500–1500 in western Europe).

We may distinguish both slavery and serfdom from wage labor by the fact that slaves or serfs cannot collectively or individually hire out their labor of their own free will. In particular, they cannot freely seek out the highest bidders for their services among prospective employers. There is no precise dividing line between slavery and serfdom, although we usually consider the former to be a more complete and servile form of bondage. To distinguish the two forms, we can say somewhat arbitrarily that three conditions must be met before an individual is a slave rather than a serf. First, a slave's basic obligations are defined mainly in terms of specific tasks to be performed, with the implication that he or she will be directly supervised. A serf often had to provide goods as well as labor time to his lord, and the lord also monopolized the supply of essential services, such as the mill, the bake oven, and the wine press. When harvest time came, the serf first had to get in his lord's harvest; only then could he see to his own lands. Thus while he was sometimes supervised directly, he was also supervised indirectly via residual claimancy to his own harvest.

Second, a master directly provides a slave with the bulk of his basic necessities (food, shelter, clothing) rather than with the means of acquiring or producing these essentials. Finally, a slave does not own his own plot of land or other immovable means of production. While slaves can be bought or sold, inherited, or given as gifts apart from other property, serfs usually could not be transferred separately. As well, serfs often had rights of inheritance that were rarely granted to slaves, and the former were better protected from arbitrary changes in the contracts defining their obligations.[16] (Neither slaves nor serfs had anything like what we would consider to be basic human rights, however.) By the end of the medieval era, serfs could buy their freedom, and many did so.[17] A master would have greater direct authority over and more extensive property rights in slaves than serfs.

By the above definition, many Roman slaves were really serfs—especially since the master of a *latifundium* was more likely to be an absentee owner than was a medieval lord—while many medieval serfs were really slaves. The extent of human bondage was less in the last centuries of the Roman Empire than it had been previously, but in some areas it was subsequently restrengthened during feudal times. Therefore, we can identify no violent break between ancient slavery and medieval serfdom. The harshest serfdom, often de facto slavery, occurred in Europe east of the Elbe River, largely in the fifteenth through the eighteenth centuries, when west European feudalism was finished or on its last legs. In medieval Europe, as well as in ancient Rome and Greece, slaves, serfs, and many nominally free men were attached to the land they tilled or to the shops in which they worked. As ownership of an estate was transferred through death, exchange, war, or seizure, its labor force often went along with it.

Marx and Engels were also interested in the opposite side of the master-slave or lord-serf relationship. Whereas the master owed his slaves their food, shelter, and clothing—at least in principle—the feudal lord had only to provide his serfs with certain means of sustenance. Therefore, the lord might supply land, tools, or draft animals, along with protection from attack by external foes, but he usually provided food only in time of famine. In return, a serf had to work three days a week or more on the lord's land, although other family members (normally a grown son) could acquit part of this obligation. In addition, there were taxes, rent, tribute, and military service to be paid.

We may extend this distinction to define a continuum of relations between owners or controllers of the material means of production and their employees, which will take us from slavery to modern capitalism. As we move toward the latter, the direct private property rights of employers in their workers decline. At the same time, the employer's obligation becomes more and more the provision of the means by which his workers try to sustain themselves as opposed to direct upkeep, and it becomes easier for either side to end the employment relationship. More generally, the worker becomes less and less a fixed cost to his or her employer. At the end of this transition, the capitalist can acquit his entire obligation with a money payment, prompting Marx and Engels to declare: "The bourgeoisie . . . has put an end to all feudal, patriarchal, idyllic relations. It has pitilessly torn asunder the motley feudal ties that bound man to his 'natural superiors,' and has left no other bond between man and man than naked self-interest, than callous 'cash payment.' "[18]

Eventually part of the declining responsibilities of employers would be picked up by the state via social welfare and insurance, although this could also be seen as further depersonalization of human relations.[19]

Conditions Under Which Slavery or Serfdom Can Arise

In the final analysis, human bondage is a means of reducing the cost of labor to those who exploit it, although bondage does not always succeed in doing this. To understand when success is most likely, we shall go back to the evolution of property rights in ancient times after technological progress has raised the marginal and average products of labor above physical subsistence (say, to the level of A_2A_2 in Figure 4.2).[20] We shall keep in mind that labor was usually scarce relative to land or capital until the late medieval period—in the sense that shortages of labor constrained the expansion of output.

To help our exposition, Figure 4.3 shows three alternative supply curves of labor drawn under three alternative assumptions about the extent of bondage. Of these, S_LS_L is the usual textbook supply curve, which assumes that work effort can be freely offered and withdrawn as the worker wishes. Its reward is then a wage, paid in money or in kind, whose real value is w/P. (If earnings are paid in money, w is the money wage, and P is a price index of goods workers buy.) By contrast, $S_LS"_L$ is an all-or-none labor supply curve—that is, the supply of labor when workers can choose only between working a set number of hours at given jobs versus not working at all. Therefore, the real wage corresponding to $S_LS"_L$ is

Figure 4.3 The Preconditions for Slavery or Serfdom

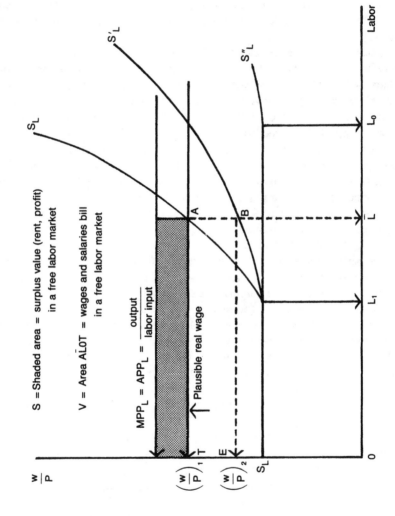

S = Shaded area = surplus value (rent, profit) in a free labor market

V = Area $A\bar{L}OT$ = wages and salaries bill in a free labor market

$MPP_L = APP_L = \dfrac{output}{labor\ input}$

Plausible real wage

the lowest wage that workers can be made to accept and is, in this sense, a subsistence real wage. At such a wage, workers will supply L_0 hours of labor when they can make only all-or-none choices. This corresponds to absolute bondage. On a free labor market, workers would supply just L_1 hours of labor at a subsistence wage and would demand far more before they would work a total of L_0 hours. If the market were not free, but bondage were also incomplete, we would get an intermediate labor supply curve, such as $S_L S'_L$. This case could arise, for example, if there were opportunities to escape bondage by running away.

Because of the relative scarcity of labor, diminishing returns to labor were not very important during most of ancient and medieval times. Land at the margin of tillage was about as good as the average-quality land already under cultivation. Therefore, the marginal product of labor (MPP_L) was roughly constant and equal to labor's average product (APP_L), or output per unit of labor input, as Figure 4.3 shows. Suppose that a free labor market were established under these conditions. Because labor is scarce, competition by employers for workers would drive the real wage up to MPP_L—the demand curve for labor—which is approximately the same as APP_L. Nearly all of income and output would then go as wages, leaving little or nothing as rent or profit (Marx's surplus value).

This is not surprising. When land is relatively abundant, rent will be low, although especially good farmland or land bearing scarce natural resources will yield significant rents. Moreover, competition among employers for labor may not be perfect; the exercise of some monopoly power in hiring labor will drive down the wage rate—for example, to $(w/P)_1$ in Figure 4.3, at which $\overline{L}$ hours of labor will be hired. Here surplus value equal in amount to the shaded area is being generated, but wages and salaries still absorb the area $A\overline{L}T$, which is most of total output. If enough bondage can be maintained to shift out the supply curve to $S_L S'_L$, the effective real wage can be lowered to $(w/P)_2$ when $\overline{L}$ hours of labor input are used. Total real wages will fall by the area of rectangle ABET. However, employers will receive no more than part of this as an increase in surplus value, because the outward shift in labor supply associated with increasing bondage can usually be realized only if employers also incur increases in supervisory costs.

Potential gains to employers from bondage are an increasing function of labor's share of income and output in the event of a free labor market. Therefore, Figure 4.3 shows the conditions most favoring bondage—namely, labor is the relatively scarce factor of production, so that the average and marginal products of labor are constant and equal, and both are significantly above physical subsistence. Under such conditions, we will tend to get some combination of slavery, serfdom, and independent farmers and artisans. Villages featuring the latter have existed at all times since the Neolithic Revolution and were predominant in many places during the centuries following the end of nomadism. They are most likely to exist when the defense of a community or region can efficiently rely on part-time contributions of residents rather than on individuals who specialize as soldiers, who must be supported by taxes and who can also be used to enforce bondage. During the medieval era, and later on in the New World, a relatively free peasantry survived in frontier areas, which also had to offer favorable terms to attract labor. Some of these communities were examples of preindustrial democracy. Within them, small farmers and tradesmen would try to protect themselves from potential bondage or other forms of domination via expansion of suffrage and rights to compete for political office.[21]

Given bondage, the likelihood of slavery versus serfdom depends, in part, on the relative power of central versus local or regional governments. A strong central government is more compatible with slavery, while a weak central government is more compatible with serfdom, for at least two reasons.[22] First, a strong central government representing the interests of employers will help to establish an environment within which labor can be forced to work for a lower reward than it would accept voluntarily. In particular, a strong central authority, not deterred by considerations of human dignity, will promote slavery by promoting a market on which unfree workers can be bought and sold, or else use more direct means of forcibly allocating labor to occupations to which the state wants it to go. Such an authority will also try to abolish other forms of competition for workers, implying that it will help to hunt down and to return runaway slaves while punishing members of the dominant class who entice or harbor runaways. It will also prevent the nobility from warring with one another to obtain labor. These measures will reinforce the monopoly power of the dominant class and increase the likelihood of slavery over serfdom.

Second, a strong central government will permit more regional specialization and trade by protecting against brigands, pirates, marauders, and invading armies. A weak central government will force each region to be more self-sufficient, and therefore to produce a more heterogeneous output mix. This is favorable to serfdom, since slavery usually implies higher supervisory costs, and its supervisory cost disadvantage tends to increase with increasing heterogeneity and complexity of production under the control of each employer. Moreover, in an agrarian society weather variations may produce major year-to-year harvest fluctuations. The higher overhead costs associated with slavery may then make serfdom more attractive to an employer—especially since a serf hardly needs supervision when working for himself—unless the employer can acquire low-cost insurance against fluctuations in the food supply. A strong central government will be able to increase the capacity to store food and to transfer food from surplus to deficit areas, which are the main ways of providing such insurance. It should also be noted that a paucity of smoothly functioning markets for goods plus the absence of a widely used and accepted medium of exchange increase the relative efficiency of taxation in the form of labor dues and specific consumption goods. Thus it raises the attractiveness to a ruling elite of bondage over free labor.

Government was more centralized within the Roman Empire than it was in western Europe during the Middle Ages. The decline of Rome in the fourth and fifth centuries A.D. coincided with a drop in the volume of trade and a regional decentralization of authority, especially in the frontier areas of Europe.[23] This marked the beginning of manorialism (regional government control). Slavery was also declining, serflike obligations were emerging, and the diversity and self-sufficiency of regional production were rising in the final centuries of the western Roman Empire.

Either population growth or labor-saving technological change could bring an end to bondage by reducing the scarcity of labor, and thereby the share of income and output that free labor can command. A rise in the value of occupational or geographical mobility of labor would also create pressures toward a loosening of bondage. The value of a serf to his master depended on the latter's ability to restrict the serf's geographical mobility, which often implied a restriction on occupational mobility as well. The additional supervisory costs required to institute or to increase bondage also allowed some individuals to be spared, even in societies in which bondage was the norm. The more complex or intricate and the less routinized a production process is, the more its successful operation requires skill, care, and independent judgment from the workers involved, and the less familiar it is to the employer, the less likely he is to rely mainly on coercing workers in association with direct supervision of their work. This is why skilled craftsmen, artisans, and artists usually escaped the harsher forms of bondage (and often avoided it entirely) throughout ancient and medieval history. In occupations in which the exercise of independent judgment was important, the value of a slave or even a serf to his master could be much lower than his productive value as a free citizen.

Manorialism

Besides serfdom, two related features of feudalism in western Europe deserve further mention. These are the decentralization of government authority down to the regional or local level—with correspondingly weak central authority—and the medieval scattering of strips of land. The pattern of landholdings owned by individual peasants often seems to modern observers to have been the most inefficient feature of medieval agriculture.[24] A farmer who owned land would almost never have a single parcel in one spot. Instead, his holdings would consist of many long, thin strips—forty was not unusual—separated from one another and scattered throughout the open fields surrounding each village. The shape of these strips resulted from the difficulty of turning a medieval plow and its team of oxen (later horses) around, but their scattering seems inefficient in several ways. More land was required for boundaries and roads, and more time was lost going to, from, and between strips. Boundary disputes were more frequent, and whatever a peasant did on one strip—sowing, drainage, weeding, irrigation, and so forth—inevitably affected his neighbors.

The scattering of strips also resulted from the weakness of central authority and the consequent need for self-sufficiency—since trade routes were frequently blocked or too dangerous to use after Rome's decline—as well as the comparatively low value of land. Since land was plentiful, the loss of land in boundaries and roads was not so serious. Moreover, self-sufficiency obliged each manor to grow several kinds of crops and to divide its land according to crop. The area devoted to wheat was in one place, that sown to oats was in another, that used to grow potatoes or turnips was somewhere else, and so forth. It could take several days to plow, sow, or harvest a given crop, and seasonal patterns varied from crop to crop. In this context, the scattering of strips allowed each peasant landowner to own a strip of land within the area devoted to each crop. As a result, it had the effect of maximizing the amount of time that each peasant landowner spent working for himself rather than for someone else. Many serfs owned little or no land and hired out their labor to peasant landowners. By growing different crops on different kinds of soil in different parts of the manor, a peasant owner could hire the same individuals through the peaks of each harvest and planting season, thereby minimizing the number of different people he had to hire and maximizing the percentage of time they worked for him instead of someone else.

Suppose each peasant owned just one type of land on which he grew one specific crop. Then peasant landowners in a village would have had to work for one another in rotation as the best periods for planting and harvesting each type of crop on each type of soil came and went. Landless serfs would have had to rotate from one employer to another. As a member of a plowing team, a peasant landowner would have had to work a greater percentage of days in which he did not plow any of his own land. In short, the scattering of strips helped to maximize the incentive to work hard with a minimum of supervision, as well as to minimize the costs of necessary transactions between peasants. It also provided insurance against crop failure as well as theft or destruction of crops. A poor crop on one type of soil or in one part of a manor did not necessarily imply the same degree of failure elsewhere, and cropland was usually not enclosed—in part, because of the high cost of capital in medieval Europe. The system of scattered strips survived both serfdom and manorialism in many areas, but it declined with the growth of trade and regional specialization in farming.

Regional decentralization of government authority in western Europe between the disintegration of the Roman Empire during the fifth century A.D. and the rise of the nation-state, beginning in the latter part of the fifteenth century, was made possible by the feasibility of local self-sufficiency in food production. Advances in farming during the early medieval period made self-sufficiency easier to attain by increasing output per hectare and making it possible to grow a wider variety of crops. First, a new plow was invented that was better suited to west European soil. Previously, in the Middle Ages, plows had been adapted from those used since ancient times. The new plow was expensive and heavy, requiring eight oxen or horses to pull, and had to be operated by a team of peasants. Second, beginning in the tenth century, or possibly earlier, a collar and harness were invented that made the horse a more effective draft animal. Finally, the three-field rotation system gradually replaced the traditional two-field system.

Prior to this, decentralization was brought about during the late Roman Empire by successful barbarian incursions and the necessity of shifting defense to local control. By the fourth century, the Roman Empire was threatened on all sides, but especially by barbaric tribes in northern and central Europe. This pressure increasingly disrupted trade. It resulted, in part, from population growth, and perhaps climatic changes outside the empire. Later improved ships and seafaring would turn the Norsemen into feared raiders. Also important was a growing ascendancy of defensive over offensive tactics. Rome had achieved major advances in the latter. But by the second century A.D., she was no longer expanding her empire. Instead she was relying on massive walls as a first line of protection against incursions.

Over time, permanent fortifications, notably the medieval castle in its many forms, evolved and improved in their ability to withstand assault and siege. Given the lack of warning against attack, especially from the sea, and the slowness of transport and communication, defense had to come under local control. By the fourth century, barbarian raids into the empire were frequent, and many tribes were actually welcomed and given land in return for assuming defense burdens. Of course, local authorities in charge of defense could have continued to act mainly in the interests of the empire, but their incentive to do so depended on the emperor's ability to punish anyone who assumed too much power on his own.

The exercise of such authority by a central government vis-à-vis local or regional seats of power grew more expensive as defensive fortifications became harder to overcome during the early medieval period. As well, methods of supplying distant armies remained primitive until near the end of the Middle Ages. An invading army had to live off the land, but it often ate a region bare without subduing it, even when the region was defended by a relatively small and poorly trained force. Seldom has the organization of any society been so heavily influenced by military considerations as was that of medieval western Europe. However, by the mid-fifteenth century, artillery had been invented that was capable of turning medieval fortresses into relics. As the power to subdue local or regional lords increased, central authority reasserted control, and the modern nation-state arose in Europe and in Japan. The invention of artillery was the key technological advance that brought new scale economies to the provision of protection from external threat and the enforcement of internal order. The inventions of printing and of inexpensive paper played a similar role with respect to administering a common-language area.

"Oriental Despotism"[25]

> [In India], irrigated lands . . . pay three times as much in taxes, afford 10 or
> 12 times as much employment, and yield 12 to 15 times as much profit, as
> the same area without irrigation.
> —Karl Marx, "The Future Results of British Rule in India"

From the Neolithic Revolution to the Industrial Revolution, farming was far and
away the main productive activity of the human race. Yet in many parts of the
world, local self-sufficiency in food production and supply was virtually impossible. A given region had to rely on assistance from outside to survive, and
this made it vulnerable to outside political control. On such a basis, centralized
governments—indeed empires—often arose. In particular, once population has
grown beyond a low-density level, irrigation is essential to farming in many
places, even today. The proportion of the world's farmland that can benefit
significantly from some combination of water-control activities—irrigation,
drainage, damming, storage, transportation, and so forth—is well over half. Such
land receives either too much or too little water, or it comes at the wrong time.
Consequently, water control can increase yields by up to ten times.

Given the importance of agriculture, control over the water supply—as well
as over food storage depots plus the transportation network—often became a
source of centralized political control in areas where rainfall farming was inefficient. Irrigation farming uses other inputs—labor, land, tools, seeds, and fertil-
izer—but each of these is divisible and subject to local production and control;
moreover, their effectiveness depends on proper application of water. By contrast, there may be substantial scale economies in supplying water. That is, the
most efficient system of waterworks may be an interdependent network covering
a great expanse of territory and consisting of, for example, rivers, lakes, canals,
dikes, dams, reservoirs, and other drainage and storage facilities. Wittfogel used
the term "hydraulic agriculture" to apply to such economies.[26] This technology
lay behind Marx's Asiatic Mode of Production, also known as "oriental despotism."

When major scale economies existed in water supply and control, whoever
controlled the waterworks had potential monopoly power over the geographical
area in question. Indeed, these scale economies were usually embodied in a
network of rivers and canals, which also served as a backbone of the transport
system. The water network could be used to ship grain into food-deficit regions,
as well as to transport and supply armies. Therefore, control over it, along with
food and water storage facilities, became the foundation of centralized political
power. As the water network expanded and grew more complex—because of
technological progress or in response to population growth and pressure on the
food supply—government also grew more powerful and centralized, usually
through conquest. Marx wrote: "There have been in Asia, generally, from im-
memorial times, but 3 departments of Government: that of finance, or the plunder of the interior; that of war, or the plunder of the exterior; and finally, the

department of Public Works. . . . The prime necessity of an economical and common use of water, which in the Occident, drove private enterprise to voluntary association . . . necessitated in the Orient . . . the interference of the centralizing power of government."[27]

Marx, Wittfogel, and others writing on the subject may have exaggerated this point. Nevertheless, by controlling supplies of water and food, plus the transport system, ancient kingdoms in China, Egypt, Mesopotamia, India, Peru, Mexico, Yemen, and elsewhere—where the alternative was subsistence farming or worse—were able to impose a despotic rule over their subjects. The Roman Empire was partly composed of hydraulic subsections—in North Africa, Egypt, Asia Minor, and elsewhere in the Middle East. The scale economies associated with water supply and control, plus the lack of regional self-sufficiency in food, ultimately explain why government authority could be more centralized in China, India, Persia, ancient Mesopotamia, and Moorish Africa than in medieval Europe, where rainfall farming and local control over water supplies and food storage were the rule.[28]

Wittfogel called these empires hydraulic states. Each was dominated by a bureaucratic elite that was usually able to perpetuate itself through time. As water control was paid for via taxation, one of the tasks of the civil service was to design and administer the tax system. Normally the government could increase its revenues by discriminating in its tax levies, so that those who got more benefit from water control paid more. (This might be approximated by a system of property taxes.) As well, the waterworks had to be constructed and periodically modified, extended, repaired, and maintained. Given the primitive, labor-intensive construction technology then available, the need to build waterworks and to keep them in repair greatly developed the organizational, administrative, and supervisory skills of hydraulic societies. These also evolved new construction technologies, which were lavished on the pyramids and other monuments and put to use in building the Great Wall of China, the "limes" and Hadrian's wall (which protected the northern frontiers of the Roman Empire), and the aqueducts. According to Wittfogel, ". . . hydraulic agriculture taught man to handle all kinds of building materials—earth, stone, timber, etc., and it trained him to manipulate these in an organized way. The builders of canals and dams easily became the builders of trenches, towers, palisades, and external defense walls. . . ."[29]

The rulers of a hydraulic state could also use the organizational skills and knowledge of local conditions—that had been developed to improve the supply of and control over water—to build police and intelligence networks for suppression of internal dissent. Because tax collection is made more effective by regular censuses, census taking became a highly developed art.

Private ownership of land, cattle, and other means of production was often widespread in hydraulic societies. But given the importance of control over water, as well as food stocks and transportation routes, such ownership was generally not a source of power. Moreover, the state limited private property accumulation through such devices as a ban on primogeniture (the right to inherit an estate by the eldest son) and even outright seizure. Also crucial were the isolation and self-sufficiency of village economies. "It was proved before a Committee of the British House of Commons," wrote Marx, "that 'when grain was selling from 6s. to 8s. a quarter at Kandeish [in India], it was sold at 64s. to 70s. at Poonah, where the people were dying in the streets of famine, without the possibility of gaining supplies from Kandeish.' . . . The village isolation produced the absence of roads in India, and the absence of roads perpetuated the village isolation."[30] Isolation of individual communities—or simply control over the main transport routes—was a means by which a despotic ruler prevented countervailing power from arising. In addition, villages were collectively responsible to the central authority for each resident, and the degree of socioeconomic differentiation within a given village was usually low.

The skills and techniques developed by a hydraulic regime to bulwark its power could be transported to a country where hydraulic agriculture did not prevail. A relatively centralized government could even develop when local self-sufficiency in food or in defense was not feasible. For example, in parts of what is now the Soviet Union, centralized power prevailed during the Middle Ages. There climatic conditions were ripe for enforcing the isolation of individual localities. In a given area, food self-sufficiency was difficult or impossible to maintain, or else the raw materials required for building fortress redoubts were unavailable locally. Moreover, in warfare a hydraulic state would often have an advantage over nonhydraulic neighbors, enabling it to expand beyond its natural hydraulic frontiers. Thus the original Roman Republic expanded first to the east and south, eventually absorbing hydraulic states, partly by interfering in domestic quarrels. Then it pushed north and west into western Europe at a time when it had a clear superiority in military technology. But this part of the Roman Empire was generally the least secure and became the first to disintegrate under the pressure of population growth and migration. Nor did it subsequently become part of another large empire, as did the other areas under Roman control.

Marx and Engels were impressed with the permanence and unchanging character of "oriental despotism." Nevertheless, via colonialism they believed that such societies would eventually evolve into capitalism and in this way rejoin the historical evolution Marx had hypothesized. ("The railway system will therefore become, in India, truly the forerunner of modern industry," he wrote.)[31] According to Wittfogel, "Oriental despotism anatomized those nonbureaucratic groups and strata which, in feudal Europe and Japan, spearheaded the rise of a commercial and industrial society."[32] Thus the relative decline of agriculture vis-à-vis commerce and industry, which began in western Europe around the fifteenth century, signaled the relative decline of hydraulic states such as India and China. Eventually many of them became ripe for colonial exploitation. The comparatively decentralized Western countries, which were backwards by Eastern standards in medieval times, leaped ahead after the Renaissance.

As Europe was not stifled by a bureaucratic elite to the extent of India, China, or Japan (where unification of the country did not end feudalism), European industry was much freer to develop, and it soon had the better of Asia in military technology. Wittfogel argues that Soviet-type economies, with their centralized management structures, bureaucratic elites, and control over key productive inputs, were the industrial successors to hydraulic states, although this claim is disputed.

The Emergence of Markets and Nation-States

The Increase in the Size of the State

Many economic historians would agree that some combination of population growth and technological change ultimately caused the fall of feudalism and the rise of early capitalism in western Europe.[33] This transformation included at least four basic changes: (1) the decline of serfdom; (2) the revival of commerce, and eventually of colonialism; (3) the rise of the nation-state, which gained power at the expense of regional government; and (4) the growth of nonagricultural production and of cities. Population growth made serfs less valuable to their masters, while technological advance enabled commerce and industry to expand. The growing potential benefits of specializing and producing for the market, as well as of adjusting to shifting demand patterns, made it more important for labor, capital, and resources to be mobile.[34]

Moreover, since new and more complex methods of production and distribution were becoming available, the importance of entrepreneurship and of management by specialists with a comparative advantage in managing was growing. To exploit scale economies in production and distribution, it eventually became necessary to be able to concentrate large amounts of labor and investment capital. In addition, a need arose for changes in the occupational and geographical distribution of labor. These requirements increased the cost of serfdom and of other feudal restrictions on mobility and on freedom of choice and opportunity. They also increased the cost of concentrating decisions within an elite whose status was by now hereditary and which had no extraordinary endowment of organizational or entrepreneurial talent. At the same time, growing dependence on markets for supplies reduced the value of insurance benefits provided by the village and other medieval collective institutions.

However, the revival of commerce would not have been possible without the rise of strong central governments able to extend their authority over wider areas and to protect trade from pirates and bandits, as well as to enforce an effective contract law. It is not by chance that growth of the modern nation-state coincided with or preceded the rise of early capitalism. In areas where (quasi-) hydraulic states were not feasible, the rise of the nation-state often followed the introduction of artillery as an effective weapon of war. By A.D. 1450 in Europe, the mobile siege cannon had caused medieval fortifications to become obsolete. Now a large army from far away had a better chance of subduing a smaller one fighting for a local lord because the latter's fortress redoubt gave less protection. The cost of effective defense escalated in terms of fortifications, men, training, and matériel. At the same time, improved transport and communications made it easier to supply distant armies. For a lower cost, a central authority could take away a local noble's power to tax and administer his own region. If the latter continued to do this, it was more likely to be at the sufferance of the center. Major battles were waged at Formigny (1450), where the French defeated the English to win the Hundred Years' War and unify their country; Constantinople (1453), whose ancient fortress walls were demolished by Turkish artillery; and Sekigahara (1603), which was also marked by the decisive intervention of artillery copied from Portuguese models, and at which time Japan was unified under the Tokugawa Shogun.

Centralization of government was stimulated in other ways by advances in communications and transportation in late medieval western Europe. Around 1450, Johannes Gutenberg invented printing by utilizing movable type, which more or less coincided with the development of inexpensive paper. Ultimately this led to universal education and to the storage and widespread dissemination of technical information, which would help to make the Industrial Revolution possible. The printing press also ended the role of Latin as the common language of European scholars. In addition, the capacity of governments to make and to enforce rational decisions expanded. Rulers found it easier to issue edicts, to gather and store information about their subjects, and to communicate with them, provided they shared a common language.

The above inventions created new territorial scale economies in government administration and control, although linguistic frontiers tended to constrain the boundaries of nation-states. The economic historians North and Thomas compare the politics of the era 1450 to 1700, in western Europe with the behavior of firms in an industry in which the appearance of new technology has raised the optimal scale of production. Consequently, some companies will be forced out of the industry and possibly into bankruptcy, others will merge in order to survive, and still others will expand and prosper—either by good fortune or by skillfully seizing on opportunities for growth. Such firms may also need new sources of financing, as did expanding governments during the era in question. As feudal lords sought to defend and to enlarge their realms, they collided in open warfare. The period was a time of intrigue, of shifting alliances, and of increasing taxes, growing indebtedness, and frequent failure of nobles to repay loans. It also witnessed the rise of the merchant class (which financed wars and intrigues as well as commercial ventures) and the beginnings of parliamentary democracy. Thus, as North and Thomas have written, "Whether by marriage, purchase, perfidy, intrigue, or military conquest, the nation-state replaced the feudal barony as the seat of coercive power. . . . The grip that each monarch had on his subjects, however, differed drastically from one nation to another."[35]

In England and the Netherlands, legislatures representing mergers of powers outside the throne—feudal lords, the church, merchants, the beginnings of the industrial and agricultural bourgeoisie—arose to check the growing power of the monarchy. Where the threat of external aggression was greatest, as in France and Spain, the power of the king, who controlled or allied himself with the military, was also greatest, and the parliament eventually stopped meeting. But in England, the House of Commons held on to the power to refuse revenues to the throne without receiving freedom and privileges in return. Ultimately, this is why parliamentary democracy and economic growth came to England before they came to France and Spain. In the low countries, a successful revolt against the Spanish king led to a powerful legislature representing local merchants and lords, notably the Dukes of Burgundy. It was here that the economic growth of western Europe began.

The Preconditions for Capitalism

At least three conditions must exist before modern capitalism can develop. First, productivity in farming must be high enough to allow much of the labor force to work in industry and commerce. Second, it must be both possible and profitable to so employ them, meaning that handicrafts, cottage industry, and the rudiments of commerce should already exist, along with the technological know-how to produce on a larger scale. Third, it must also be possible to develop mass markets and to accumulate large amounts of money capital to finance the industrial expansion necessary to supply these markets. From the late medieval period through the Industrial Revolution, the farm surplus and the gains from expanding regional and international trade, as well as the profits from colonial ventures, were the major sources of industrial investment.

Thus, late medieval Europe witnessed the start of the commercial revolution, which was fostered by the Crusades. The early years were symbolized by the voyages of Marco Polo and culminated with the great voyages of discovery of the fifteenth and sixteenth centuries, which opened the Americas and Australia—humanity's last frontier. Throughout this era, trade within western Europe remained more important than trade between Europe and other continents, however, and Holland eventually became the center of the commercial revolution. From 1250 to 1750, the volume of trade expanded manyfold. Its growth was facilitated by technological advances in transportation and communications, including dramatic improvements in seafaring and a steadily increasing knowledge of geography. The growing power of the nation-state also increased the costs to pirates and brigands of preying on trade.

Profits on commercial ventures were high, although there was also considerable risk involved. For example, from 1600 to 1650 the Dutch East India Company paid annual dividends ranging from 12.5 percent to 50 percent, and the British East India Company paid up to 334 percent on single voyages. Many ships and cargoes were lost, but during the sixteenth century profits rose by a third relative to wages, and they remained high throughout most of the seventeenth and eighteenth centuries.[36] Not only did mass markets arise, therefore, but the profits accumulated from many commercial ventures were available for investment in large-scale industry, once the necessary technological progress had occurred. In fact, after a long period of stagnation, a quickening pace of innovation began in the eleventh century—at first in agriculture, and subsequently in industry. In several countries, the savings of rural landowners eventually became another important source of finance for industry.

Population growth, aided by the rising social surplus, was a second feature of the later Middle Ages that increased the ratio of labor to land. At first, good land was abundant. The spread of technological improvements, including three-field in place of two-field crop rotation and the harnessing of the horse, plus gains from increasing specialization and exchange, helped to stave off diminishing returns to labor on land for a time. Eventually the latter began to assert themselves, however, and previously submarginal lands were cleared or drained and farmed. North and Thomas observe:

> In this way, population growth created a frontier movement. . . . Local pockets of diminishing returns seem to have occurred first in France, sending settlers to the clay soils along the banks of the Somme and into the hills of Beaujolais, starting about 950. The draining of the marshes in Flanders, which required a substantial capital investment to reclaim the land, took place in about 1100. . . . Similar population growth occurred in England. During the centuries prior to the Norman invasion, colonization had brought settlement to all the major agricultural areas of the island.[37]

According to North and Thomas, population growth also increased differences in resource endowments among different parts of western Europe. For example, the ratios of labor and capital to land were higher in the older, settled areas than on the frontier. A wider variety of soils also came into cultivation, and technological advances created a greater diversity of capital goods. As a result, potential gains from specialization and trade grew, bringing increased pressure for markets to arise and expand. Eventually the discovery and colonization of the New World—itself a product of the commercial revolution and made possible by technological advances in seafaring—extended this frontier movement, bringing even greater differences in resource endowments into play. By the sixteenth century, the costs of protecting trade and markets were probably lower than they had been in the later Roman Empire. This was largely because of the technical revolution in armaments and improved methods of transport and communications, but population growth and the clearing of land also reduced the safe harbor for bandits who wanted to prey on commerce. Because of technological progress and population growth, the potential benefits from specialization and exchange were high, and there were major transaction scale economies to be realized from expanding trade and market size. For these reasons, the story of the later Middle Ages is one of growing commerce, expanding markets, and greater specialization and division of labor in production.

It was also a time when the bonds of serfdom were loosening. The value to serfs of the protection provided by local lords was falling. Moreover, population growth in the older settled areas of western Europe led to a declining marginal product of labor on land and made each serf less valuable to his master. This reduced the expense that nobles would go to to retain serfs. Often central authorities would not help to track down runaway serfs, since they wished to tax the rising income generated by commerce and industry. In addition, while labor was plentiful in the older agricultural areas, it was often scarce in frontier regions and in the cities, which offered refuge for serfs willing to risk flight. The new agricultural lands offered favorable conditions to attract labor, and freedom was often granted to any serf—originally the property of another lord—who would work there for a year and a day. In fact, serfdom hardly existed in these areas, and the same was generally true of European settlers in the New World (although many served a period as indentured servants).

As protection for commerce grew, along with the role of markets and the use of money, local manors found it more profitable to specialize according to comparative advantage and to produce for the market. In order to do this, the lord of the manor needed a money income to allow him to buy substitutes for goods that had previously been produced on the manor or to cater to newly developed wants. Consequently, he began to convert his serfs' obligations into money payments. This affected feudal relations in a fundamental way, especially where the most enterprising, hardworking, and thrifty serfs were concerned. For a price, many lords were willing to free some of their serfs. Given the reduced marginal product of labor and the rising marginal and average products of land, the nobility could often reap a handsome profit by selling freedom to their serfs, renting the land and some implements out to them, and living off the proceeds. Ownership of land rather than of serfs eventually became the main source of wealth and status, and land came to be considered *the* prudent investment in most of Europe.

Figure 4.4 shows why serfdom (or slavery) was less and less likely to be worthwhile to employers, even as freedom became more valuable to many serfs. As the labor-to-land ratio rises—or as technological change directly and indirectly lowers the least-cost labor-to-land ratio for any given input prices—diminishing returns to labor on land asserts itself more and more. Eventually, therefore, both the average and marginal physical products of labor are falling where the latter intersects the supply curve of labor. Even with perfect competition, a free labor market will set the real wage rate at $\overline{w}/P$, yielding a surplus value of *MORE* and a wages and salaries bill of $0\overline{L}RE$, each in real terms. Under monopolistic hiring, average wages and salaries will be lower still. The extra enforcement costs asso-

Figure 4.4 Diminishing Returns and Bondage

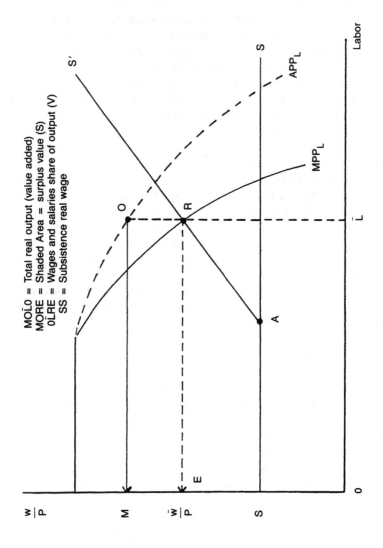

MOL̄O = Total real output (value added)
MQRE = Shaded Area = surplus value (S)
0L̄RE = Wages and salaries share of output (V)
SS = Subsistence real wage

ciated with slavery or serfdom versus hired labor are less likely to pay off for employers.

With the decline of serfdom, more and more work was done by hired labor in western Europe, and during the twelfth through fifteenth centuries, many freed serfs became small farmers (often tenants) or independent craftsmen. Indeed, from at least the end of the fourteenth century, we find serfs in western Europe managing estates, large handicraft and cottage industries, and even a few factories that produced almost entirely for the market and were manned by other serfs. Therefore, as Maurice Dobb has stated, "a main factor in the decline of feudalism . . . was the struggle of small producers to loosen the bonds of feudal exploitation. Particularly conscious of these bonds was the upper stratum of well-to-do peasants, who were in a position to extend cultivation onto new land and to improve it, and who accordingly tended to be the spearpoint of revolt. Such tendencies were both aided by and aided the spread of trade, [capital formation,] and production for the market. . . ."[38]

Many guild masters in the cities and towns also began to employ hired laborers and to emerge as a class of small capitalists. Thus the more prosperous of the small, independent producers were moving into a position from which they could become large capitalists. The revival of commerce and industry in the thirteenth through the fifteenth centuries signaled first the high-water mark of feudalism and then its long decline. In England, the sixteenth century served as the watershed between the two eras. It witnessed a mini-industrial revolution featuring an upsurge of technological advance. Yet real wages fell, owing to a spurt of population growth and a falling marginal product of labor on land plus the dispossession of some of the peasantry.

The Enclosure Movements

According to Marx, one more ingredient was necessary before capitalism could take off. This was a growing mass of people migrating from the countryside to the cities in search of jobs. The newly emerging "industrial reserve army" allowed industry to expand to serve mass markets. Here Marx and Engels emphasized the role of the enclosure movements in Britain and, to a lesser degree, in other parts of Europe. Basically, enclosure was a process of converting state and communal (or ill-defined) property rights in land within manorial villages into private rights of individual landlords and peasants. It allowed greater specialization within agriculture, along with higher output from land that was increasingly scarce, and was often caused by the growth of markets for farm produce. However, it also led to increased social and economic differentiation between peasants and to the eviction of thousands of farm families from lands that had been considered theirs, and which they had farmed for generations, because they were unable to establish firm legal property rights to the soil. By the mid-nineteenth century, half the arable land in Britain was owned by fewer than 2,500 individuals.

In Britain, the enclosure movement began as a response to rapid growth in the European textile industry, itself made possible by trade expansion and technological progress in the manufacture of woolen cloth. Britain enjoyed a strong comparative advantage in the supply of wool when wool prices began rising shortly after 1500. Landowners responded by converting tillage to pasture, expanding and enclosing their holdings, and evicting peasants whose property rights in land were weak. In later centuries, labor-saving technical change lowered the labor-to-land ratio in farming, on the continent as well as in Britain, and enclosure itself facilitated the adoption of new technology and more efficient land use. According to a recent estimate, about 2 percent of England's surface area was enclosed during the sixteenth century, followed by another 24 percent in the seventeenth century, 13 percent in the eighteenth century, and 11 percent in the nineteenth century. There, according to J. R. Wordie, "enclosure appears to have been encouraged by periods of high prices and agricultural prosperity, by the need to convert land to a different use, and by the concentration of land ownership in a few hands. . . . Output gains [from enclosure] in terms of cash value of produce may have been anything between 50 percent and 100 percent, once all technical advantages available to the enclosed farmer had been fully deployed."[39]

According to Marx, most peasants displaced by enclosures found their way into crowded city slums and were forced to accept employment under adverse bargaining conditions. Low wages and a plentiful labor supply then fueled the Industrial Revolution and led to the dominance of modern capitalism in Europe. However, Marx's view of the industrial reserve army needs qualification, especially outside England. In other countries, the rise of early capitalism was slower and not accompanied by such an uprooting of the rural population. Even in England, the process was more gradual than Marx appears to have realized, and feudalism would have given way to capitalism without the enclosure movements. At least by 1800, rising industrial employment was coming mainly from the natural increase of the labor force, and it is plausible that the same thing happened elsewhere in Europe.[40] The ability of industry to absorb a growing share of the labor force relieved population pressure and increased average incomes for those who remained in the villages. However, the strongest force motivating rural-urban migration was probably the pull of city job opportunities rather than the push of enclosure or of labor-saving technological change in agriculture.

Marx divided the capitalist era into two phases. The first, lasting in Britain roughly from the mid-1500s to the mid-1700s, largely preceded the Industrial Revolution, or the second phase, which was based on widespread harnessing of inorganic power. Marx emphasized the importance of the steam engine, although water power also played a major role, and both were eventually dwarfed by electricity. (The first commercial electric power–generating station appeared in 1883, the year of Marx's death.) By 1600, the use of labor-saving machinery would have awed a Rip van Winkle awakening after 400 years of slumber. But it resulted almost entirely from a more efficient harnessing of wind, water, and draft animals. Availability of inorganic power was still minuscule by comparison with what was to come. Otherwise, the main characteristic of the first phase was a growing specialization, division of labor, and exchange. The evolving industrial enterprise made this possible by holding down the increases in transaction costs that would otherwise have been necessary, while helping to maintain a higher volume and quality of product. Even early capitalism realized scale economies requiring large investment outlays by comparison with previous eras, although the biggest gains associated with large-scale factory production awaited the development of interchangeable parts and electric power in the nineteenth century.

By the early 1800s, capitalism was firmly entrenched in much of western Europe and North America, and the second or machine phase was under way in Britain. Subsequently, this came to be known as the modern industry or scientific phase. The combination of scientific and engineering discoveries, expansion of markets, and stronger private claims on returns from investing in innovation increased the application of science to industry, and thereby technological progress and economic growth. In Marx's view, exploitation became more covert and subtle under capitalism, but the fruits of growth went mainly to the expropriators (the capitalists) rather than to the actual producers (or labor).

Notes

1. These modern historians include Robert Paul Thomas and Lance E. Davis, among others. The following are major references:

(a) Karl Marx, *Grundrisse* (Middlesex: Harmondsworth, 1973).

(b) Karl Marx and Friedrich Engels, *The Communist Manifesto* (New York: International, 1948).

(c) Karl Marx, "Preface" to *A Contribution to the Critique of Political Economy;* "Alienation and Social Classes"; *The German Ideology,* Part 1; *The Civil War in France* (with an Introduction by Friedrich Engels); and "Critique of the Gotha Program," all in Robert C. Tucker, ed., *The Marx-Engels Reader* (New York: Norton, 1972).

(d) Friedrich Engels, *The Origin of the Family, Private Property, and the State* (New York: International, 1942).

(e) Lance E. Davis and Douglass C. North, "Institutional Change and American Economic Growth: A First Step Toward a Theory of Institutional Innovation," *Journal of Economic History,* March 1970.

(f) Douglass C. North and Robert Paul Thomas, *The Rise of the Western World* (Cambridge: Cambridge University Press, 1973).

(g) Vernon Smith, "Economics of the Primitive Hunter Culture with Applications to Pleistocene Extinction and the Rise of Agriculture," *Journal of Political Economy,* August 1975.

2. Karl Marx, "Preface" to *A Contribution to the Critique of Political Economy,* in E. Burns, *Handbook of Marxism* (New York: Random, 1935), pp. 371–372. See as well Tucker, *The Marx-Engels Reader,* p. 4.

3. As the capacity to store knowledge grows—and especially after the development of written languages—we can be more and more confident that technology will move inexorably forward, since important discoveries are less and less likely to be lost.

4. Marx, "Preface" to *A Contribution to the Critique of Political Economy,* in Burns, *Handbook of Marxism,* p. 372 (or Tucker, *The Marx-Engels Reader,* pp. 4–5).

5. Karl Marx and Friedrich Engels, *Manifesto of the Communist Party* (New York: International, 1948), p. 9. This can also be found in Tucker, *The Marx-Engels Reader,* pp. 335–336.

6. See Davis and North, "Institutional Change."

7. Tucker, *The Marx-Engels Reader,* p. 114.

8. Marx further believed that the real wage of an unskilled worker would remain near a psychological "subsistence" level, which would tend to rise as a result of economic growth. (On the latter point, see Marx, *Grundrisse,* p. 641.)

9. Marx and Engels, *The Communist Manifesto,* p. 11.

10. This term was first used by V. Gordon Childe in *What Happened in History* (London: Harmondsworth, 1942).

11. The discussion below borrows from Smith, "Economics of the Primitive Hunter Culture," and D. C. North and R. P. Thomas, "The First Economic Revolution," *Economic History Review,* May 1977. For an alternative view and a summary of other opinions and positions, see R. J. Wenke, *Patterns in Prehistory* (New York: Oxford University Press, 1980).

12. Smith, "Economics of the Primitive Hunter Culture," p. 729. The next quote comes from Smith, p. 730.

13. The discussion below essentially follows North and Thomas, "The First Economic Revolution." That of Smith, "Economics of the Primitive Hunter Culture," is far more complex.

14. Technological progress, in the form of improved organization, methods, and weapons for hunting, would make prehistoric big-game hunters better off for a time but would eventually be offset by the depletion of larger, more edible, and easier-to-kill species.

15. The first quote is from Friedrich Engels, *Anti-Dühring* (New York: International, 1939), pp. 199–200. The second is from Engels, *The Origin of the Family, Private Property, and the State,* pp. 107, 153.

16. North and Thomas distinguish between slavery and serfdom as follows:

The Western European serf, while born to a contract specifying the kind and extent of his obligations, which he could not change without the lord's permission, was in fact also generally protected from arbitrary changes in the terms of the contract by the lord, as a consequence of the customs of the manor. This is clearly different from the case of a North American slave or the eventual position of the East European serf [who had no such contractual protection]. . . . Thus, while our definition of serfdom involves a special kind of contractual relation which could be changed only by both parties, a slave . . . has no *legal* control over decision-making with respect either to his labor or to his income stream.

Yet slaves did sometimes have contractual protection against arbitrary acts by their masters, making this distinction again a matter of degree. See D. C. North and R. P. Thomas, "The Rise and Fall of the Manorial System: A Theoretical Model," *Journal of Economic History,* December 1971, quote pp. 778–779.

17. Many Roman slaves were also emancipated. However, a number of these or their descendants found it impossible to remain free in a climate of heavy tax obligations and stiff competition from *latifundia* and large workshops that were owned by the wealthiest citizens and virtually exempt from taxation. Freedmen became tied to their plots of land or to their workshops, often as a consequence of indebtedness, and were effectively transformed into serfs during the final three centuries of the western Roman Empire.

18. Marx and Engels, *The Communist Manifesto,* p. 11.

19. Ibid. The rise of modern social insurance came mostly after the deaths of Marx and Engels. To be fair and impartial, the administration of such insurance must be depersonalized to a degree. That is, it must apply the relevant rules and regulations uniformly to everyone.

20. The following borrows from North and Thomas, "The Rise and Fall of the Manorial System," pp. 778–780.

21. We may find here some roots of democracy in the United States. Historically, the United States is unique because of the relatively small role played by labor unions and labor-oriented political parties in expanding the franchise. With the major exceptions of the slave population and the native peoples, universal male suffrage was achieved well before the expansion of large-scale industry during the second half of the nineteenth century, and well before its achievement in most of Europe. It was successfully promoted in the late eighteenth and early nineteenth centuries by the Republican Party of the day (the "Democratic-Republicans"), founded by Thomas Jefferson, whose supporters were mainly small "farmers, mechanics, and tradesmen." They sought to protect themselves from domination by large landowners, merchants, and industrial capitalists. The hypothesis that economies in which land is plentiful and labor is scarce will also be economies in which labor takes the form of slavery, serfdom, and/or independent farmers and artisans is due to Evsey Domar. See "The Causes of Slavery or Serfdom: An Hypothesis," *Journal of Economic History*, March 1970.

22. See North and Thomas, "The Rise and Fall of the Manorial System."

23. See A. H. M. Jones, *The Later Roman Empire, 284–602 A.D.* (Norman: University of Oklahoma Press, 1964), esp. vol. 2, and Gerald Gunderson, "Economic Change and the Demise of the Roman Empire," *Explorations in Economic History*, January 1976.

24. The following borrows mainly from Stefano Fenoaltea, "Risk, Transactions Costs, and the Organization of Medieval Agriculture," *Explorations in Economic History*, April 1976. See as well D. N. McCloskey, "English Open Fields as Behaviour Toward Risk," *Research in Economic History*, vol. 1, 1976, and Gregory Clark, "The Cost of Capital and Medieval Agricultural Technique," *Explorations in Economic History*, July 1988.

25. The references for this section are to Marx's "On Imperialism in India" and to Engels's "On Social Relations in Russia," in Tucker, *The Marx-Engels Reader*, and to Marx's *Grundrisse*, pp. 471–514, "Forms which precede capitalist accumulation," as well as to Karl Wittfogel, *Oriental Despotism* (New Haven: Yale University Press, 1957).

26. Wittfogel, *Oriental Despotism*, chap. 1.

27. Marx, "On Imperialism in India," p. 579. See as well R. L. Carneiro, "A Theory of the Origin of the State," *Science*, August 21, 1970, esp. note 7, p. 738. For criticisms of Wittfogel, see B. Hindess and P. Q. Hirst, *Pre-Capitalist Modes of Production* (London: Routledge and Kegan Paul, 1975), pp. 207–220, and Wolfram Eberhard, *Conquerors and Rulers: Social Forces in Medieval China* (Leiden: E. E. Brill, 1970).

28. The precondition for hydraulic agriculture, as Wittfogel uses this term, is state "control" over the water supply network, but this control may be direct or indirect and does not require state agencies to operate the network on a day-to-day basis.

29. Wittfogel, *Oriental Despotism*, p. 34.

30. Marx, "On Imperialism in India," pp. 584–585.

31. Marx, "On Imperialism in India," p. 586. This article is the main source for the preceding paragraph.

32. Wittfogel, *Oriental Despotism*, p. 8.

33. The discussion below borrows from North and Thomas, *The Rise of the Western World*. See as well J. U. Nef, "The Progress of Technology and the Growth of Large-Scale Industry in Great Britain, 1540–1640," *Economic History Review*, October 1934; E. H. Phelps-Brown and Sheila Hopkins, "Builders' Wage Rates, Prices, and Population:

Some Further Evidence," *Economica,* February 1959; and Ben Baack, "The Economy of Sixteenth Century England," *Economy and History,* 1, 1978.

34. There were scale economies to be realized in expanding markets, as well as in expanding production. See, for example, Clyde Reed, "Transactions Costs and Differential Growth in Seventeenth Century Western Europe," *Journal of Economic History,* March 1973.

35. North and Thomas, *The Rise of the Western World,* p. 82.

36. L. M. Hacker, *The Triumph of American Capitalism* (New York: Columbia University Press, 1947), p. 59.

37. North and Thomas, *The Rise of the Western World,* p. 36.

38. Maurice Dobb, "The Transition from Feudalism to Capitalism," lecture delivered to the Institute of Statistics at the University of Bologna, Bologna, Italy, March 24, 1962.

39. J. R. Wordie, "The Chronology of English Enclosure, 1500–1914," *Economic History Review,* November 1983, quote from pp. 503, 505. Estimates of enclosure by century are on p. 502.

40. See J. D. Chambers, "Enclosure and Labour Supply in the Industrial Revolution," *Economic History Review,* April 1953, and references cited. See as well B. R. Mitchell and Phyllis Deane, *Abstract of British Historical Statistics* (Cambridge: Cambridge University Press, 1971).

Questions for Review, Discussion, Examination

1. In what way is the Marxian theory of historical evolution of economic systems, as well as the approach of many modern economists, influenced by Darwin's "survival of the fittest" thesis? In what way does the Marxian theory depart from Darwin's thesis? Explain briefly.

2. Outline the Marxian theory of historical evolution of economic systems, paying attention to the roles of property rights, class conflict, and changes in the forces of production.

3. What is the specific evolution of economic systems foreseen by Marx? Has this evolution been realized in practice—in particular, since the Industrial Revolution? Explain briefly.

4. What two basic kinds of changes in property rights has population growth helped to cause? Are these favorable to the eventual emergence of full communism? Explain briefly.

5. What was the Neolithic "Revolution"? Why did it occur, what basic changes in property rights did it cause, and why is it sometimes referred to as a "great divide"?

6. In 1970, the economic historian Evsey Domar said that it would be impossible to have at one and the same time "free" land, "free" labor, and a landowning aristocracy. If "free" land means land that is in superabundant supply relative to demand and "free" labor means labor that is free of bondage, explain why Domar would put forward such a proposition.

7. If land is "free," in the sense of question 6, what three basic organizations of a predominantly agricultural economy are available? What factors determine which of the three will prevail?

8. What do we mean by the medieval "scattering of strips"? Why was this method of landholding chosen? (Or why were strips belonging to one household not consolidated into a single holding in one location, as they would be today?)

9. What is a hydraulic state ("oriental despotism")? By what means does the ruling elite of such a state maintain centralized control? Can the same means be used in areas where a basic hydraulic network is absent? Discuss briefly. What common denominator does it share with a Soviet-type economy?

10. Why did the nation-state replace the smaller feudal barony as the center of government in western Europe during the period between the mid-fifteenth and eighteenth centuries A.D.? (Or why did government centralize, usually around a common-language area, during this epoch?)

11. How can population growth lead to the demise of human bondage? How might technological change reinforce this demise? Is the result necessarily to make labor better off? Discuss briefly.

12. What were the enclosure movements? Why did Marx believe they were essential to the establishment of modern capitalism? Do you feel he was right in this respect? Discuss.

Chapter 5

Two Views of the Evolution of Modern Capitalism: Capitalism as a "Pressure" Economy

Marx on the Evolution of Modern Capitalism

Basic Theory

With the advent of modern capitalism and the widespread harnessing of inorganic power, industry assumed primacy over agriculture and the basic factors of production became labor and capital rather than labor and land, which had been the basic factors in previous agrarian societies. The latter point is crucial both in grasping Marx's theory of the evolution of capitalism and in understanding why he foresaw a future classless society within which scarcity would have been eliminated. Since capital is reproducible, the possibility exists of expanding it until it is no longer scarce. Moreover, capital is a carrier of technology. As it increases in quantity and improves in quality, the average product of labor rises. By comparison with the systems of previous epochs, modern capitalism has an enormous power to expand production. But its key contradiction, according to Marx, is that it is eventually unable to expand the demand for goods and services at the same pace. Therein lie the seeds of its destruction.

In this context, Marx believed that technological progress under modern capitalism is strongly labor saving. Its crucial feature is that it increases the average product of labor by more than labor's marginal product (or the productivity of a worker at the margin), causing the gap between the two to widen over time. This prevents labor from becoming scarce—indeed, it helps to create unemployment—and no scarcity emerges that could serve as the foundation of a future class-based society. As we shall see, labor-saving technical change also increases the ratio of property income to wages and salaries (Marx's rate of exploitation). In the process, it becomes the main cause of the tendency for aggregate demand to lag behind the economy's ability to produce.

To grasp the outline of Marx's theory, let us recall that national income net of depreciation (analogous to net national product) is defined as the sum of wages and salaries (V) and property income or surplus value (S).[1] National income gross of depreciation (analogous to gross national product) is defined as $C + V + S$, where C is depreciation, viewed as an increasing function of the size of the capital stock, K. Finally, Marx defined the rate of exploitation, E, as S/V, and the rate of profit, π, as $S/C + V$ (or the ratio of property income to wages and salaries plus depreciation). Both terms may be defined for the whole economy or for a particular industry, region, or firm.

A recurring theme in discussions of the evolution of capitalism is the "falling rate of profit." According to both Marx and modern Western economists, the "capitalist" firm invests mainly for profit. If the expected profitability of investment falls, so will the incentive to invest, causing a crisis or depression unless government can intervene to prevent this. A long-run tendency for the rate of profit to fall will lead to secular stagnation, and, according to Marx, a worsening sequence of crises, culminating in the overthrow of capitalism and its replacement by state socialism. This is inevitable, in Marx's view, because of the sluggish nature of aggregate demand and also because of a rising capital-to-labor ratio, which is in part another consequence of labor-saving technological change. The falling rate of profit can be seen against the backdrop of the labor theory of value, which argues that only living labor can create value, or it can be derived without reference to this theory, which will be the approach taken here. The rising capital intensity of production leads to a rising ratio of C to V or to a rising $q = C/C + V$, where q is the "organic composition of capital." Increases in q, brought about by capitalists' own investments, ultimately cause the rate of profit to fall.

To understand why the rate of profit falls, note first that π, E, and q are related by the formula $\pi = E(1 - q)$.[2] Therefore, as q rises, for any given E, π will fall. However, labor-saving technological progress will also cause E to rise under capitalism by throwing some workers out of jobs and by forcing others to accept low wages. Marx believed that the average real wage would remain close to a culturally determined subsistence level. Therefore, if π is to fall, E must not rise so fast as to offset the rising tendency of q. A further complication is that π, as defined by Marx, is not the best measure of the incentive to invest. A better measure would be the yield or rate of return on investment. Therefore, we shall modify Marx and adopt this yield as our measure of the rate of profit in the discussion below. Marx also assumed that technological progress increases both the minimum efficient scale of production and the optimal division of labor.

In these conditions, capitalism goes through a worsening sequence of crises and ultimately crumbles because it cannot maintain *both* a tolerable level of employment and a tolerable level of wages. Let us first try to understand the basic long-run evolution of capitalism and then indicate how cyclical fluctuations are superimposed on this. At any point in time, employment will depend on the short-run demand for labor. Therefore, consider Figure 5.1, where the supply of labor to a particular industry is given by the curve TSS', and $T0 = SL$ is the

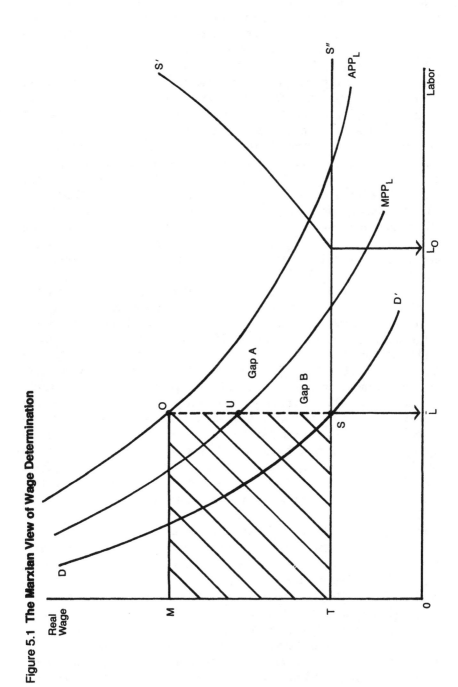

Figure 5.1 The Marxian View of Wage Determination

culturally determined subsistence real wage. The short-run average product of labor (value added per unit of labor input) is APP_L, which slopes downward, because of the law of diminishing returns. Therefore, MPP_L, which measures the marginal product of labor, lies below APP_L, and it also slopes downward.

If the management of each enterprise is certain of being able to sell whatever it produces at present prices, a competitive industry's short-run demand curve for labor will be approximately MPP_L.[3] But since demand tends to lag behind production capacity, firms will often be unable to do this. Instead they face the risk of accumulating inventories that can be sold only at a loss, either because prices must be cut or because goods remain too long in stock. As capitalists are assumed to be risk averse, they will produce less and demand less labor, at any given real wage, than MPP_L indicates. Therefore DD', the industry's short-run demand for labor, will lie below MPP_L. The vertical distance between the two will be larger, the greater the uncertainty (risk) associated with future selling prices, the more pessimistic the business outlook—in the sense that maintenance of present production levels and prices would create an expected excess supply on the market—and the greater the concentration of selling power within the industry.[4]

The intersection of demand, DD', with supply, TSS', gives an employment of $\bar{L}$ workers at real wage, $T0 = S\bar{L}$, the cultural subsistence level. Total real value created in the industry is given by area $MO\bar{L}0$, of which $TS\bar{L}0$ is paid as wages and salaries, and the shaded area, MOST, goes as surplus value to property owners and managers. The ratio of surplus value to wages (S to V) is therefore the ratio, MT to $T0$ or OS to $S\bar{L}$, and we may view the distance, OS, as a sum of two gaps—gap A between APP_L and MPP_L and gap B between MPP_L and DD'. Competition between workers for jobs depresses the real wage to its minimum "acceptable" level. Because he expected an excess supply of labor at this minimum real wage, Marx believed that such competition would replace feudal bondage as the force depressing the earnings of labor. Since L_0 workers want jobs in this industry at a real wage of $T0$, there is an excess supply of $(L_0 - \bar{L})$—a condition viewed as typical throughout the economy. If these people cannot get jobs elsewhere, they become part of the reserve army of unemployed.

The original reserve army was created when peasants were evicted from the land, notably by enclosure, and forced to seek industrial employment. Marx believed that, as capitalism evolves, labor-saving technological change directly and indirectly renews and enlarges this army. The direct effect of a labor-saving innovation, together with the investment it generates, is to increase the average product of labor. Because workers have better technology and capital to work with, a given number of them can produce more output. But once the industry has found a new equilibrium after the innovation, the marginal product of labor (productivity of a worker at the margin) will at best not have risen by much. The labor-saving nature of technical progress strictly limits the ability of the industry to absorb additional workers, and it may even have to discharge some. Since

APP_L shifts up more rapidly than MPP_L over time, gap A expands, causing S/V to rise as well.

The indirect effect of labor-saving innovation stems from this redistribution. In essence, Marx believed that the working class as a whole has a marginal propensity to consume of one. Each additional unit of wage and salary income will be spent on consumption as long as labor incomes remain close to cultural subsistence. By contrast, capitalists save substantial proportions of their incomes, even when the real return on savings is quite low. They have a marginal propensity to consume of much less than one. As capitalism evolves, they are assumed to receive larger and larger shares of national income, so that the ratio of savings to national income rises, while the ratio of consumption demand to national income falls. In this scenario, the people with the money will not spend it, and the people who would spend it do not have the money. Over time, the economy's ability to produce goods will expand more rapidly than the demand for these goods—unless the rising share of national income that is saved also can be absorbed by an investment demand that grows more rapidly than total output.

But the profitability of investment is ultimately tied to expanding the demand for the additional consumer goods and services that this investment allows to be produced. Therefore, the declining propensity to consume will restrict the volume of profitable investment opportunities further and further below what is needed to achieve full employment, unless capitalists accept lower and lower returns on their investments. To maintain both full employment and roughly constant investment yields (in real terms) over the long run requires consumption demand to grow at about the same percentage rate as national income. Then investment can also grow at that rate. But if consumption demand grows more slowly, either investment must grow more rapidly—which will force investment yields to fall—or unemployment must rise.

Over the long run, Marx expected a combination of these two tendencies. He felt that unemployment would rise owing to a growing deficiency of aggregate demand, and that the rate of profit or yield on investment would fall. Consider Figure 5.2. There the interest rate, r, on investment loans is plotted on the vertical axis, while intended saving (SA) and investment plus government spending ($I + G$) are measured along the horizontal. For now we shall treat G as a passive component of aggregate demand, although we shall comment on this below. We also think of r as the "real" interest rate—that is, as the nominal rate minus the rate of inflation. In equilibrium, r will equal the real yield on investment, and for any given spread between rates paid on savings deposits and rates charged on loans, r also indexes the real return on voluntary saving. For simplicity, we ignore the foreign sector and include all income not spent on consumption in SA. Then aggregate demand equals aggregate supply when SA just matches ($I + G$), and is less or greater than aggregate supply as ($I + G$) is less or greater than SA.

For any given r, ($I + G$) depends on expected future consumption demand,

Figure 5.2 **A Deflationary Gap Caused by Rising Exploitation**

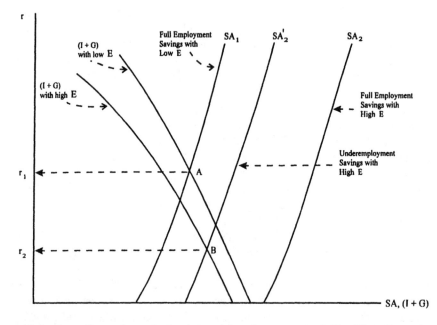

which plays the major role in determining investment yields. Therefore, the lower the rate of exploitation and the higher the expected future national income, the greater the number of investment projects that will pay off and the higher investment demand will be. An increase in the rate of exploitation therefore shifts $(I + G)$ inward, since the implied redistribution from workers to capitalists raises savings and lowers consumption. As a result, it also shifts the savings schedule outward. For any given E, a rise in national income raises savings. It may also raise $(I + G)$, but for simplicity, we treat $(I + G)$ as independent of current income.

Over time, the rising rate of exploitation shifts the savings schedule corresponding to full employment outward and the $(I + G)$ schedule inward. In the early days of capitalism, these schedules may intersect at A, giving interest rate and yield on investment of r_1 and a full employment level of aggregate demand and demand for labor. However, rising E shifts these curves apart until they no longer intersect.

Then a deflationary gap appears, which is also a deficiency of aggregate demand below full employment aggregate supply. In order to reach equilibrium, a fall in national income below the full employment level is necessary. This lowers profits as well as wages, and sends some firms into bankruptcy. Thus it lowers the savings schedule for any given rate of exploitation, until an equilibrium such as B is found, with interest rate r_2, which is below r_1. We can think of

r_2 as a minimum acceptable return on investment or on lending, even when the real return on savings deposits is zero (so that the nominal interest rate on deposits equals the rate of inflation). The fall in national income also pushes the demand for labor below its full employment level, as shown in Figure 5.1. As this demand falls, either real wages will drop below psychological subsistence, which serves as a flash point for revolution, or unemployment will increase until it threatens to become a flash point for revolution. If the subsistence level serves as a floor on real wages, this second flash point will eventually ignite.

The long-run tendencies for unemployment to rise and the rate of profit to fall are counterpointed against a series of cyclical fluctuations in which output and the rate of profit rise and the number of jobless falls in periods of prosperity, only to be reversed during subsequent crises or depressions. To see how a "typical" business cycle may unfold, suppose that one firm in an industry makes a labor-saving innovation. Consequently, it has lower costs and begins to earn a higher rate of profit than its competitors. Attracted by the prospect of greater profitability, rival companies then invest to exploit this innovation. If several industries go through such a process at more or less the same time, the economy will thrive temporarily. However, the lead firm's increased profitability was partly due to its being ahead of everyone else. When rivals switch to the new technology, competition will force down product prices relative to unit costs. Not only will the initial profit increase disappear, but the enthusiastic investment response—plus the larger scale economies that Marx associated with more modern technology plus an assumed low (inelastic) response of product demand to price cuts—will lead to excess capacity in the industry and to a glut of its output on the market. As a rule, the latter will force one or more firms out of business. The industry will then have fewer companies plus a higher capital-to-labor ratio and a higher average product of labor. However, most of the latter increase will go to capitalists as surplus value because of the labor-saving nature of technical progress. While total profits will have risen, the capital stock will have risen by even more (owing to overinvestment), and the *rate* of profit will have fallen.

If collusion against the introduction of new products or production processes is not feasible, most firms would be individually rational to introduce the new technology, for otherwise they would face higher costs. Moreover, collusion to suppress new technology often fails, because the successfully innovating firm gains a significant and more than momentary advantage over its competitors. Yet Marx believed the end result would be a lower rate of profit, although the assumptions of rising scale economies and low product-demand elasticity are crucial to this conclusion.

After the collapse of the rate of profit in several key industries due to over-investment—resulting in excess capacity, followed by layoffs and bankruptcies (or exit of firms from these industries)—the rate of investment falls. Planned saving exceeds planned investment, so that aggregate demand for goods and services is too low to sustain the existing level of income and output. The latter consequently falls further as the crisis spreads.[5] Each crisis or depression leads to additional layoffs, bankruptcies, and unemployment, as big capitalists drive out little ones and take over the latter's capital at low prices. Yet this is not generally the end of capitalism. Normally a recovery will occur—which is to say that the business cycle will continue from depression to expansion to cyclical peak, and then begin to slide down again into depression. Until the last crisis, there will always be a turnaround that temporarily raises the rate of profit part way back up to its precrisis level, for some combination of the following reasons:

1. New advances in technology may set off another expansion, although this will again end in a crisis of overproduction.

2. New colonial markets and sources of supply will also help a revival, and colonies constitute a profitable avenue for investment—according to Marx, because of their low organic composition of capital and susceptibility to exploitation. Marx considered such "imperialism" to be an important temporary offset to the falling rate of domestic profit in developed countries.

3. As capital becomes more and more concentrated in a few hands, the "big, firmly placed capitalists" may be willing to accept lower yields on their investments, being compensated by the greater sums they invest. In Figure 5.2, the interest rate can then fall below r_2, although it presumably could not fall below zero. In this context, *finance capitalism,* or the close association of banks, each with a group of firms—as in Japan and Germany—is viewed as a way of concentrating investment capital.

4. In the previous discussion, we viewed the state as passive. However, government, viewed as an extension of the bourgeois class and as its instrument, could adopt an activist role to fight depressions. Therefore, it may lower taxes on property income, raise subsidies to business firms, and raise government spending to offset any fall in private demand. It may also "bribe" the workers with social welfare payments to keep them from rising up to destroy the system. But the state can only prop up the bourgeoisie for so long in these ways, owing to the budget deficits that they cause. Ultimately it will have to change its policies or face bankruptcy itself. Marxians would view today's record public sector budget deficits in this light.

5. Input prices tend to fall because of the low level of demand. Even the real wage of labor temporarily drops below subsistence as the industrial reserve army reaches its cyclical peak. The cost of raw materials also declines, and some capital is expropriated by the big capitalists at less than its original cost of production. This increases the rate of profit obtainable on it. In addition, capacity is withdrawn from production, as a result of expropriation and liquidation. At the same time, inventories run down, and depreciation of existing capital may exceed new investment, causing a further decrease in production capacity. The above reductions in costs, inventories, and capacity increase the profitability of expanding production.

Eventually each expansion leads to excessive capital formation in the form of excess capacity and excess inventories that can be sold only at a loss. This restarts the downturn, following which layoffs and bankruptcies again cut into aggregate demand, making matters worse. After each crisis, the recovery of the rate of profit is only partial, and it plummets to new historic lows during each succeeding business cycle trough. Depressions therefore grow increasingly severe and recoveries ever more feeble. The bourgeois class dwindles even as property income is rising, both absolutely and relative to labor income. The working class grows in numbers and in self-assurance—or in what Marxians call "social consciousness"—as small capitalists are competed out of business and forced to sell their assets at bankruptcy prices. Power therefore concentrates in the hands of a smaller and smaller elite until the pit of the last great depression arrives. Then the working class finds itself strong enough to launch the social revolution, seize the reins of power, and establish a dictatorship of the proletariat.

Criticisms

With hindsight, we can say that both Marx and many conventional Western economists were overly optimistic about the ability of capital accumulation to solve the basic problem of scarcity. The Industrial Revolution and the technological breakthroughs that surrounded and followed it owed their success to an efficient, rapid exploitation of basic natural resources—most of which are nonrenewable—to a greater extent than was generally understood until recently. Again with the aid of hindsight, we can find other flaws in Marx's forecasts. The most basic of these require that technological progress be strongly labor saving in the sense that the ratio of the average to the marginal product of labor progressively rises over time. However, there is little evidence of this in the twentieth century, during most of which the ratio of S to V has tended to remain steady or even to fall.[6] Economists disagree over whether the rate of profit has had a long-run tendency to fall. While firms have grown larger owing to scale economies, market size has expanded as well. This has held down increases in industrial concentration. (However, national or international oligopolies have, in many instances, supplanted regional and local ones.)

On balance, the relation between economic development and inequality appears to follow a pattern described by the Kuznets curve, an example of which appears in Figure 5.3.[7] There we plot a measure of inequality on the vertical axis and the level of development, as measured by income per capita, on the horizontal. Economic development first raises, then lowers, inequality, resulting in a "typical" Kuznets curve that is umbrella shaped. Labor-saving technological change plausibly accounted for the rising portion of the curve, at least in Britain and the United States, although this worked in more complex ways than Marx appears to have had in mind.[8]

In Britain, inequality began rising around 1760 and continued to increase for

Figure 5.3 **The Kuznets Curve**

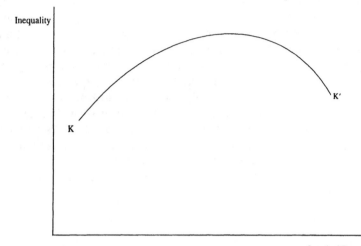

over 100 years. The peak of the Kuznets curve was reached just prior to 1870. Thus Marx (who died in 1883) observed the rising portion of this curve and projected existing trends forward to the end of capitalism, a fairly common approach to forecasting among statisticians and economists. As a result, he completely missed the reduction of inequality over the century following 1870. In the United States, inequality began rising around 1830, and the peak of the curve was reached about 100 years later. Since the mid- to late 1970s, inequality has begun to increase again in both Europe and America, on which more shortly.

Also on shaky ground is Marx's doctrine of the increasing severity of crises, since the worst depression to date (the Great Depression) reached its trough in 1932. Moreover, the heroic time of colonial adventure was precisely the time of early and immature capitalism—when the rate of profit and the labor-to-capital ratio should have been high at home, according to Marxian theory, and when barriers to exploitation of domestic labor were still low. (Nor does the *average* rate of profit obtainable on colonial ventures appear to have been much above that on investments in Europe.) Neither is finance capitalism an advanced state of decay of the capitalist order. Countries utilizing this system have been latecomers to industrial development, needing a way to mobilize the savings of many small savers and to combine these with entrepreneurship to generate growth, since would-be industrial managers were usually not wealthy enough to do the job with their own capital.

The ownership of physical capital has become more concentrated over the last 50 to 100 years. Yet an array of small firms has survived in nearly every Western country, and in some (e.g., Germany, the United States, and Japan) they account for 40 percent or more of employment. Small firms are especially common in farming and services, but they do all manner of work where independent judgment is important or products are specialized (nonstandardized) so that scale economies are low.

Finally, the middle class has not vanished in most Western countries, but has grown and includes many workers. In this context, more and more people have invested in their own skills and abilities, or in "human capital," whose ownership has grown more widespread and which has become a major source of income. Without this, the scientific revolution in production technology could not have proceeded. Investment in human capital tends to increase wages and salaries, and thus to lower S/V. It has played a major role in generating the falling portion of the Kuznets curve. It also helps to make the notion of class conflict more complex under capitalism and to throw doubt on the historical simplification of this problem postulated by Marx and Engels in *The Communist Manifesto*. Access to acquisition of human capital is greater for some than for others, and is consequently another potential basis for exploitation.

To relate this to our earlier discussion of inequality and growth, we note that inequality has again been rising in Western nations since the mid- to late 1970s.[9] In part, this results from technological change that has increased the return to some types of human capital (and thus to education), notably those linked to the new information technologies. However, it is also a result of falling trade barriers and the tendency to group countries with vastly different capital intensities and returns to labor within free trade zones, such as NAFTA (the North American Free Trade Agreement) and the expanded European Economic Community. This may well increase per capita incomes in affected countries, but it also alters distribution. The rewards to any productive input, including labor, will have some tendency to equalize within a free trade zone, which usually means downward pressure on earnings in countries where these are relatively high. Here employers find themselves with greater bargaining power, since they can more credibly threaten to move production to low-wage areas and then export back to the high-wage country. One result is to decrease the share of national income going to unskilled labor or to labor with skills that are relatively abundant within the free trade zone, and to increase the shares going to physical and to relatively scarce types of human capital.[10] Access to one or both types of capital has become more crucial to raising a household's living standard, as product markets have become global owing to falling trade barriers and an ongoing communications revolution.

Within any given country, the result of this expansion of markets is to increase the demand for some types of skills and to decrease the demand for others. In the short to medium run, before supply can fully adjust to the shifts in demand, this causes higher earnings in occupations in which demand has risen and lower earnings or layoffs in occupations in which demand has fallen. Over the long run, however, supply can more readily (or elastically) expand or contract in response to changes in demand, and subsidized education and training programs may speed up these supply adjustments. Their effect is to reduce or even eliminate (when long-run supply is perfectly elastic) many of the initial changes in occupational earnings that result from the shifts in demand. The more elastic long-run supply, the greater the changes in relative numbers of workers in each occupation and the smaller the changes in relative earnings per worker in response to shifts in demand.

Only in cases in which long-run supply is inelastic or restricted in some way will these shifts cause large permanent changes in relative earnings among different skills. Inelastic supply applies in particular to individuals with supernormal ability that cannot be reproduced through education, training, and/or experience alone. Therefore, one aspect of the increased inequality resulting from the globalization of markets is an increase in earnings differences within individual occupations between those with perceived supernormal talent or ability and those with average skill, whose supply can be made more elastic. More generally, inequality has risen within the workforce between those with relatively high wages or salaries and those whose earnings are relatively low. This increase in inequality has been pronounced in the United States and United Kingdom during a period (the mid-1970s to mid-1990s) of falling trade barriers and expansion of world trade. In time, supply adjustments may eliminate part of the increase, but probably not all.

In continental Western Europe, by contrast, the increase in inequality among workers has been less, but the rise in unemployment has been much greater. This is usually attributed to greater downward rigidity of real wages there than in the United States or United Kingdom. To explain this rigidity, we note that it is possible to prop up the earnings of individual workers by restricting the supply of labor into a particular occupation or by excluding part of this supply from wage bargaining. For example, within any given unionized industry or profession—or in any situation with collective bargaining or the threat of collective job action—there is often differentiation between workers on the basis of seniority. Primarily, this is differentiation in terms of job rights, and we sometimes apply the term "insiders" to those whose job rights and influence within a collective bargaining or work unit are relatively high. "Outsiders" are workers whose seniority, influence, and job rights are relatively low.[11] Workers with the least seniority are the first to be laid off and the last to be rehired or promoted. They do the least desirable work and suffer some discrimination in wages and benefits vis-à-vis high-seniority workers. Seniority-based discrimination is not necessarily worse than viable alternatives. The individual whose job rights, working conditions, and earnings are relatively poor in his or her youth may still look forward to better things later on.

But some people may find it harder than others to build up seniority or to gain access to jobs or to education or training that will put them on track for relatively attractive occupations. Instead they tend to remain outsiders, performing undesirable work with low earnings and poor job rights. Barriers to entry into many occupations (or into training programs that prepare for these)—erected by professional associations and unions seeking to stabilize members' incomes and to support them by restricting supply—are one cause of this, as are a variety of other barriers that trap individuals and their families in poverty.

The Excess Supply of Labor Under Capitalism[12]

The excess supply of labor is a key feature of Marx's capitalist system that contrasts with the excess labor demand that existed in most socialist countries. In this context, Marx's complaint was that capitalism could not provide full employment at "acceptable" or "reasonable" wages—not simply that it could not provide full employment. What is considered a reasonable or fair wage for any type of work may be quite different from a wage that has the technical property of balancing the supply of and demand for labor, especially in times of downward pressure on demand. Above-equilibrium wages lead to unemployment, because they motivate firms to move production sites to lower-wage areas, to economize on labor by choosing more capital-intensive production methods, and/or to reduce output. These factors help to make the demand for labor downward sloping and to determine its elasticity.

Above-equilibrium wages arise because suppliers of labor are able to organize to bargain and lobby effectively, with bargaining strength ultimately based on the threat of collective job action or withdrawal of labor services. A prerequisite for the success of union organizers has been their ability to solve the free-rider problem by effectively taxing those who benefit from union activities to get the funds used to pay organizational, bargaining, and lobbying costs. Moreover, some economists argue that unions and other representatives of labor bargain mainly on behalf of insiders, seeking the largest earnings consistent with a high probability of job retention for these people. The excess supply of labor—consisting mostly of outsiders—has a relatively weak bargaining voice, according to this view. Excess supply, therefore, fails to push down earnings in the manner suggested by supply and demand analysis, allowing above-equilibrium wages to persist. To put it another way, above-equilibrium wages potentially lead to congestion among suppliers of labor, just as below-equilibrium prices potentially lead to congestion among buyers. In those sectors in which it exists, the insider-outsider dichotomy acts like a quota system, paring supply down to demand, but concentrating most of the costs of excess supply (lower job security, unemployment, job search, etc.) in the ranks of outsiders.

Labor has also lobbied for government policies to expand the aggregate demand for goods and services over the short run. During the Great Depression, much unemployment plausibly resulted from a fall in aggregate demand—triggered, according to some, by a decline in innovation-associated investment, and according to others (Monetarists) by a fall in the money supply. Between 1929 and 1933, for example, U.S. prices fell by over 22 percent, while unemployment soared from 3.2 percent to 24.9 percent. In several countries, the downward rigidity of real wages helped to turn the fall in aggregate demand for goods and services into a loss of jobs. Real wages actually rose in some cases, even when unemployment was at or near record levels. Since World War II, by contrast, unemployment has often gone hand in hand with rising prices and a strong aggregate demand for goods and services. Maintaining the latter has not ensured full employment.

To see why, we first note that unemployment is partly frictional—consisting of workers between jobs—while another part is seasonal, and a third part is structural. Some workers have the wrong skills or are in the wrong locations relative to demand. During the 1980s and early 1990s, structural unemployment is believed to have·been high, since Western economies were undergoing major changes in production technologies and output assortments. Moreover, several declining industries of the 1970s and early 1980s paid relatively high wages, which made their laid-off workers more reluctant to look for jobs elsewhere, and government subsidy policies sometimes delayed structural adjustment by propping up these industries at the expense of sectors with growth potential. Some economists also argue that a fourth part of measured unemployment is a moral hazard consequence of unemployment compensation (see chapter 3). That is, the greater and more widespread is insurance against unemployment, the more attractive it will be to some people to take advantage of the system by working only part of the time in order to qualify for benefits while they are idle. Unemployment insurance may also subsidize job search, during which time individuals are classified as unemployed.

Finally, a major part of unemployment is excess supply of labor, which results because labor costs—wages and salaries plus fringe benefits—are above levels that would balance supply and demand. Economists advance two basic reasons for this. First, periods of rising prices and prosperity condition suppliers of labor to expect more of the same, and therefore to bargain for higher wages in multi-year employment contracts. When such expectations are later thwarted by falling inflation or growth, unemployment rises. For example, we might attribute part of the high unemployment of the early 1980s to inflationary expectations built up during the late 1960s and 1970s, which Western governments were unable, for political reasons, to sustain. At first, expansionary fiscal or monetary policy may increase both employment and inflation. But the employment gain is based not so much on a rise in the real demand for labor as on the fact that suppliers of labor overestimate their real wages because they underestimate future inflation. After their inflationary expectations have risen, the employment increase is eventually more than reversed because of the political need to reduce inflation below expected levels. Thus over a complete business cycle, expansionary policy does not necessarily increase average employment and output.

Second, collective bargaining and the threat of collective job action have been used to obtain relatively high and stable earnings for insiders, in combination

Figure 5.4 **The Tendency for the Burden of Unemployment to Fall on Outsiders**

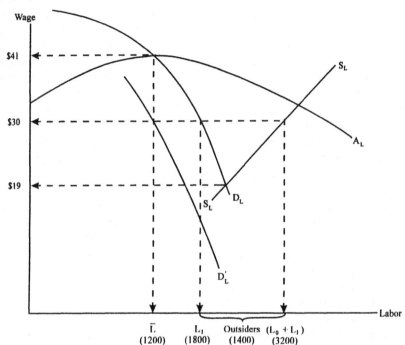

with relatively strong job rights. The former are supported by rationing jobs or training vacancies so that part of the potential supply of labor (consisting mainly of outsiders) is excluded. Insiders protect themselves by making job rights a function of seniority and by insisting on a narrow range of pay rates for each job, regardless of who holds it. This leads to higher wages for many less well-organized or low-seniority workers than they could get from bargaining on their own, but weaker job rights, and thus a higher probability of layoff or dismissal, as well as higher search and other costs of obtaining jobs. Strength of job rights is correlated with seniority or influence within a bargaining unit.

As a rule, labor demand curves are believed to be downward sloping. Within limits, therefore, the upward bargaining pressure that labor representatives can bring to bear on wages will be a decreasing function of the number of insiders in a given labor market. The greater the number of insiders, the greater the number of jobs that must be provided and the smaller the maximum wage that will ensure demand (and thus employment) for all insiders.

Figure 5.4 represents an attempt to capture the basic idea. There the (money) wage obtained by a collective bargaining unit appears on the vertical axis, and the number of workers is measured along the horizontal. D_L gives the demand for labor supplied by this unit, and S_L is the total labor supply to this enterprise, industry, or region; these curves will also depend on product prices. A_L measures the average productivity of labor, as well as the wage-paying ability of employers. Specifically, it is total revenue, minus nonlabor costs, divided by the number of workers. It rises as L increases from zero to $\overline{L} = 1,200$, and then falls. In the short run, the rising portion results from a spreading of fixed costs over more output and employment, as L increases and nonwage costs per worker decrease. In the long run, the rising portion results from increasing returns to scale at low rates of output and employment. Beyond $\overline{L}$, falling A_L results from downward-sloping product demand plus diminishing returns to labor in the short run or decreasing returns to scale in the long run.

In these conditions, production can be profitable only if employment is at least as great as $\overline{L}$, which maximizes the average product of labor and gives the highest possible wage. Neither employers nor employees would want a smaller value of L. Beyond $\overline{L}$, D_L gives the wage that employers will pay at each level of employment, and a wage of $19 will therefore just balance supply and demand. However, the wage bargained for by representatives of labor will be the highest at which all insiders have jobs. The number of insiders will depend on the past history of this firm, industry, or region, but a typical number in Figure 5.4 would be one greater than $\overline{L}$, say $L_I = 1,800$. Labor's representatives would then hold out for a wage of $30, at which 3,200 workers would be willing to supply labor, but 1,400 are unable to obtain jobs. These are outsiders, who must get jobs elsewhere, remain jobless, or perhaps work only part of the time.

The wage that labor representatives will hold out for depends on their perception of the demand for labor. Suppose that an unforeseen decrease in labor demand were to occur, such as that caused by the Great Depression of the 1930s or the energy crises of the 1970s. Both of these shocks put many people out of work. After a spell of unemployment, those who were insiders would start to lose their influence and bargaining power and eventually become outsiders. The reduced number of insiders would put upward pressure on the wage, which would at least partly offset the effect of the fall in demand. As seen in Figure 5.4, an unforeseen fall in labor demand to D'_L could reduce the number of insiders to 1,200. If so, labor representatives would still request a wage of $30 (or, more precisely, a wage with this purchasing power, should prices change). Therefore, real wages will tend to be rigid, and unemployment may rise and then persist at the higher level. It does not necessarily fall back to levels common before the shock occurred. Similarly, an unforeseen increase in labor demand will increase both employment and the number of insiders, which tends to offset the upward pressure on real wages of the demand increase.

By contrast, changes in labor demand that are foreseen do not alter the number of insiders. Therefore, they affect mainly prices and nominal earnings rather than employment. In particular, unemployment may endure and real wages remain rigid in the face of expansionary macroeconomic policy, as long as this policy is anticipated by suppliers of labor. Its main effect will be rising wages, which will lead to rising prices via upward pressure on the costs of production. As indicated above, the insider-outsider explanation of unemployment and rigid real wages is believed to be more applicable to Western Europe than to the United States over the period since 1975. In the United States, unions have had less control over the wage-setting process and the supply of labor.

Schumpeter's Theory of Capitalist Development

Basic Theory

An alternative view to Marx's capitalist evolution—one that also forecasts a falling rate of profit leading to the demise of capitalism—comes from the Austrian economist, J. A. Schumpeter. He traced the decline of capitalism to the disappearance of entrepreneurship, which he viewed as the engine of innovation and of economic growth. Schumpeter agreed with Marx as to the dynamic nature of capitalism and criticized conventional economic theory on this point. "The problem that is usually being visualized," wrote Schumpeter of contemporary economists, "is how capitalism administers existing structures, whereas the relevant problem is how it creates and destroys them. . . . Capitalism is, by nature, a form or method of economic change and not only never is, but never can be stationary. . . ."[13]

However, Schumpeter refused to accept Marx's characterization of the fundamental nature of class conflict under capitalism. For Schumpeter, this was between "productive" and "unproductive" classes, and he insisted on allying the proletariat with many capitalists in the former. Indeed, what made a capitalist system progress, according to his doctrine, was the drive by entrepreneur-innovators to introduce and to exploit new products and methods of production and distribution. These effectively "destroyed" old ways of doing things by rendering them obsolete and replacing them with something new and better. Schumpeter called this process "creative destruction." He wrote:

> In capitalist reality as distinguished from its textbook picture, it is not ["static"] competition which counts, but competition from the new commodity, the new technology, the new source of supply, [and] the new type of organization . . . competition which commands a decisive cost or quality advantage and which strikes, not at the margins of profits and the outputs of existing firms, but at their foundations and their very lives. . . . [This is] the powerful lever that in the long run expands output and brings down prices. . . . The process of Creative Destruction is the essential fact about Capitalism.[14]

Creative destruction is investment that "revolutionizes" existing products and methods. The first assembly line was a creative destruction project, as was the airplane, the automobile, the electronic computer, the electric light bulb, the steam engine, the first fully automated production process, and subsequent major improvements in these. By undertaking creative destruction projects, Marx's social parasites become Schumpeter's dynamic entrepreneurs, who are the mainspring of progress. It was largely with this transformation that Schumpeter turned Marx's flaming indictment of capitalism into an eloquent defense.

Figure 5.5 shows the effect of creative destruction on product users and producers. Suppose Firm X develops a new tire capable of significantly reducing automobile fuel consumption. When marketed, the new Brand X tires will hurt producers of older types, while making consumers better off. The value of the resulting increase in consumer welfare will exceed the value of producers' losses, as Figure 5.5 shows. Suppose the industry is perfectly competitive before Brand X tires come along, with price, P_B, and quantity, Q_B, given by the intersection of supply, S_B, with demand, D. For simplicity, Q will index consumption of tire services rather than of tires per se. As a result of the innovation, Firm X and companies licensed by it can supply tire services more cheaply than the rest of the industry by supplying better tires. Therefore, the industry supply curve shifts out to S_A. If it remains competitive, price will fall to P_A, and quantity will rise to Q_A, of which Q'_B comes from the older type of tire and $(Q_A - Q'_B)$ from the new Brand X tires. (Eventually, all tire manufacturers may have to adopt the new technology to produce the new kind of tire, but it may take some time for this to happen.)

Schumpeter also believed that the ability to innovate was the major cause of the growth of firm size and of market power. Therefore, suppose that the innovation gives Firm X some market power, enabling it to set price, P_E, higher than P_A, which reduces quantity demanded to Q_E. Even so, it creates additional consumer surplus of approximately area P_BBEP_E, while destroying producer surplus equal to area P_BBCP_E, for a net gain of BEC to society, over and above the gain to the innovating firm.

From this dynamic perspective, the innovation benefits society as a whole. If we take a more conventional static approach, however, the opposite appears to be true. A standard economic evaluation of the tire industry before the innovation would find it efficient, since it is competitive and price is set equal to marginal cost, which is the basic pricing rule for efficiency in product markets. After the innovation, the same evaluation would find this industry to be less efficient. Firm X's market power leads it to maximize profit by setting price above marginal cost, resulting in a "deadweight" efficiency loss approximately equal to area EAT. With good reason, Schumpeter believed that much of conventional microeconomic theory suffered from this static perspective. Because the capitalism it describes is divorced from reality, he considered it to be ". . . like *Hamlet*, without the Danish prince."[15]

In Schumpeter's view, the advantage of capitalism, in its heyday, is that it is the best system to promote innovation, since it embodies the four conditions noted in chapter 2 that are favorable to entrepreneurship. Thus, investment decisions are made by enterprise owners and managers rather than by higher-level political authorities, and the former have strong claims to profits and losses.

Figure 5.5 Creative Destruction

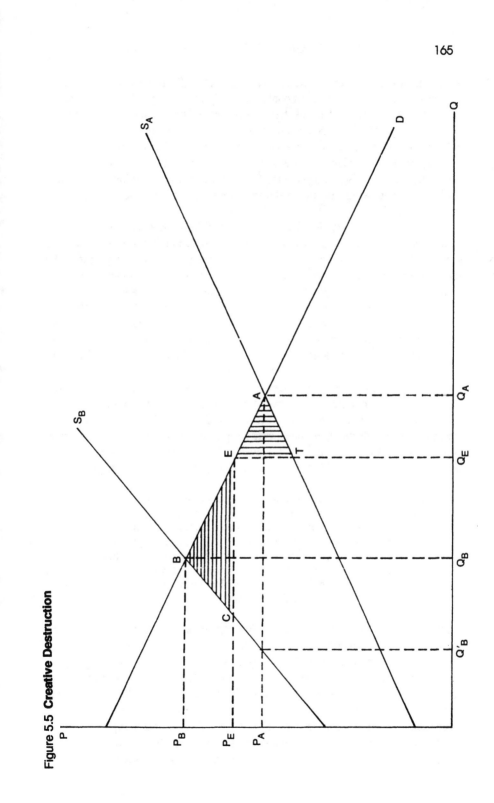

Where most products are concerned, at least several firms actively compete for market share, and suppliers must continually improve their products and production methods just to hold on to their customers.[16] Finally, success depends on product acceptance by users. Schumpeter believed that the dominant form of industrial organization under capitalism would sooner or later come to be oligopoly, and he acknowledged that departures from static efficiency would then be inevitable. But he also believed that firms in perfect competition would have neither the financial resources nor the short-term security necessary for successful innovation.[17]

Such men as Henry Ford and Thomas Edison are superstars of the Schumpeterian entrepreneurial class, and they are cited mainly for their ability to successfully market new products or to introduce new ways of doing things. The successful entrepreneur, according to Schumpeter, is more an industrious businessman with keen foresight and a perceptive grasp of what goods and services the market will accept than a successful inventor. He must also be a gambler.

If we look at a payoff profile for a "typical" creative destruction investment project, its most important feature is that it is nearly impossible to quantify. No one could say with confidence that the yield on the first commercial airliner to cross the English Channel would be x percent or higher with 95, 75, or 50 percent probability. In fact, this venture went bankrupt, as do most would-be creative destruction projects, and around 90 percent of all new products fail. The second most important feature of such a payoff profile is a small chance of earning a very high yield, coupled with a high probability of losses. Therefore, while some entrepreneur-innovators eventually become rich, many more go broke and drop out. As a class, they are a bargain, according to Schumpeter:

> In some cases [creative destruction] is so successful as to yield profits far above what is necessary in order to induce the corresponding investment. These cases then provide the baits that lure capital on to untried trails. Their presence explains in part how it is possible for so large a section of the capitalist world to work for nothing: in the midst of the prosperous 1920s, just about half of the business corporations in the United States were run at a loss, at zero profits, or at profits which, if they had been foreseen, would have been inadequate to call forth the effort involved.[18]

"Profits" are therefore viewed by Schumpeter as a reward for innovation involving risk, particularly nonquantifiable risk. As such they are also the earnings of entrepreneurship as a factor of production. However, most property income cannot be classified as profit by this definition, and Schumpeterian entrepreneurs are the cream of the business world, both in skill and in daring. Entrepreneurial profits are necessary to call forth entrepreneurial effort. The entrepreneurial drive stems, in part, from the satisfaction of creating or introducing something new and of building an industrial empire. But it also derives from the enormous payoff that one can earn from success. Therefore, if rewards are attractive enough, would-be innovators will undergo incalculable frustration and endure physical hardship, if necessary, in gambling against enormous odds. Schumpeter believed that egalitarian constraints directed against earning and keeping large profits, including taxation and some types of regulation, would decrease entrepreneurship and innovation. Eventually this would help to bring about the downfall of capitalism.

For Schumpeter, business cycles result from the ebb and flow of innovation over time. An unforeseen and unexpected wave of innovations stimulates investment to exploit the new opportunities that these innovations create. The result is a boom, as during the early 1920s, that will sustain itself for a while. But after the investment opportunities created by the new products and processes have been exploited and have spread through the economy, creating jobs and generating income, a comparative dearth of fresh innovations sets in. Since the demand being generated by the old ones is now largely confined to replacement, investment will fall, causing a recession or depression. Later, a new wave of innovations will stimulate investment, leading to renewed expansion and growth.[19]

In contrast to Marx, however, Schumpeter did not expect a sequence of increasingly severe cycles to culminate in the destruction of capitalism. Opportunistic elements could take advantage of chaos, indecision, or a weakening of government caused by a severe depression to seize power and establish a "socialist" government. But Schumpeter believed that capitalism was doomed to die a mature death from natural causes even if this did not occur.[20] In the latter case, as the long-run power of creative destruction rises, so does the amplitude of accompanying business cycles. Then, after creative destruction has passed its zenith as a "revolutionizing force" and begun its inevitable descent, the severity of business cycles will also become less and less. The Schumpeterian profit share of property income will begin its long-run decline, and the supply of capable, dynamic innovators will start to dwindle.

Capitalism itself, then, proceeds downhill, until one day the government replaces all corporate securities and other ownership certificates with government bonds. By then, an important distinction between managerial and property incomes, on one hand, and "ordinary" wage and salary incomes, on the other, will have become blurred. We recall that managers and owners are viewed as residual claimants to the earnings of an enterprise after its debts, including its wage and salary bill, have been paid. This makes their incomes riskier and contingent upon the efficient operation of enterprises under their control. It thereby disciplines them to strive for efficiency and innovation.

But for reasons to be given, the managerial function comes to be more and more the province of salaried personnel whose incomes depend less and less upon the residual earnings of the organizations for which they work. These residuals also become more certain with the decline of innovation, since established market positions are in less and less danger. Production becomes more bureaucratized, and government subsidies to rescue firms in trouble may also become more frequent. By the time complete nationalization arrives, little difference will remain between the streams of earnings yielded by government bonds and those of private certificates and securities. Consequently, widespread resistance to the exchange does not arise. Capitalism ends not with a bang, but with a whimper, after much of the real transformation has already been accomplished.

Two factors combine to bring this result to pass, both arising out of what Schumpeter called "the civilization of capitalism." Whereas decision making in precapitalist societies generally involved magic or mystery, at least in part, and often spurned logic, capitalism must by its nature encourage a "rational attitude." A calculating, critical mentality is part of this, but so is an inquiring mind that makes every idea, individual, social institution, product, or technology justify itself according to a performance standard. Along with this goes a tolerance for new ideas and the necessary freedom to try them out. Without freedom to enquire and to innovate, there would have been no Industrial Revolution and no modern economic growth, but also no Age of Enlightenment. A legacy of greater industrial freedom is a generally high level of social tolerance by historical standards. Here Schumpeter parts company with many Western intellectuals:

> Radicals may insist that the masses are crying for salvation from intolerable sufferings and rattling their chains in darkness and despair, but of course there never was so much personal freedom of mind and body *for all*, never so much readiness to bear with and even to finance the mortal enemies of the leading class, never so much sympathy with real or faked sufferings.[21]

When creative destruction is in its heyday, existing firms must constantly scramble to keep their positions in the market from being cut out from underneath them. Managers must continually improve their product lines and production methods just to stand still (hold on to their market shares) in the face of dynamic competition. This, plus the rewards awaiting the first enterprise to introduce a successful innovation, puts a premium on the rational attitude and also on the freedom to innovate and to collect the rewards therefrom. In Schumpeter's view, a capitalist society cannot afford to crush the freedom of which it disapproves without risking to crush the freedom on which it depends at the same time.

What could be more rational in these conditions than to Taylorize innovation itself by reducing it to a "scientific," impersonal routine based on cost-benefit analysis? To Schumpeter, it seemed that:

> Technological progress is increasingly becoming the business of teams of trained specialists who turn out what is required and make it work in predictable ways. The romance of earlier commercial adventure is rapidly wearing away, because so many more things can be strictly calculated that had, of old, to be visualized in a flash of genius. ... [Consequently] economic progress tends to [become] depersonalized and automatized. Bureau and committee work tends to replace individual action. ... The leading man no longer has an

opportunity to fling himself into the fray. He is becoming just another office worker—and one who is not always difficult to replace."[22]

The entrepreneur who first employed cost-benefit analysis to aid his investment decision making has let a genie out of its bottle. An entire industry of research and development laboratories, think tanks, engineering and management consulting firms, and the like evolves to take over the entrepreneurial function. The individual entrepreneur finds himself in his own museum, alongside the horseless carriage, the hand loom, the silent movie projector, the horse-drawn plow, the blacksmith's shop, and the megabit chip—his role having been made obsolete.

To routinize and automate investment decision making is inevitably to bureaucratize it to a degree. Bureaucratization comes with the rise of the modern corporation, whose growth is spurred by innovation. While most innovation arguably comes from small and medium-sized firms, the latter often grow to become corporate giants by exploiting the investment opportunities to which their innovations give rise. Within these bureaucracies, nonconformists (as entrepreneurial types are wont to be) are not promoted, and large firms increasingly tend to suppress competition from smaller rivals because of greater efficiency or access to financial resources, as well as the ability to erect barriers to such competition. Thus within large corporations, entrepreneurial types tend to be squeezed out, and increasingly the option of successfully starting one's own small firm is closed off.

Bureaucratization of the entrepreneurial function is by no means always desirable. A cost-benefit calculus is helpless when the payoff profile of a proposed investment can scarcely be quantified, and those benefits not subject to quantification will tend to be ignored. Consequently, cost-benefit analysis can often tell the management of a farm-machinery corporation which types of tractors to market under different geographical and economic conditions and how far to go in mechanizing or automating a particular tractor plant. It would have been far less useful to the entrepreneur who first tried to market a tractor. If he had been an element in a bureaucracy, the idea might not have occurred to him, or it might have been rejected by a superior as involving unacceptable risk. (The cost of a failed innovation is likely to be more evident than the cost of failing to make an innovation.) If pushed too far, therefore, the gains from cost-benefit analysis are not worth the cost.

At the same time that the individual entrepreneur is being squeezed out, the business elite comes under mounting attack from the "unproductive" sector. To Schumpeter, unproductive individuals are those who have no direct responsibility for practical affairs. In addition to intellectuals, more narrowly defined, this classification embraces malcontents and hangers-on of a variety of shades and hues, and others, notably many journalists, who make their living from social commentary. As a capitalist, the entrepreneur encounters more than his share of growing hostility—in the form of egalitarian constraints, controls on his behavior, increasing regulation, and social disapproval. As creative destruction gives way to the industry of invention, these attacks gather force. And, as the resulting controls and constraints become more numerous and intense, they hasten the decline of creative destruction.

Because capitalism fosters innovation, it gives rise to an economic surplus, which is immense by the standards of precapitalist economic systems. For the first time since the dawn of history, the great mass of society does not have to preoccupy itself with the everyday tasks of production and distribution just to survive. Consequently, a large class of intellectuals arises and grows with the social surplus.

Spending on higher education eventually grows faster than the gross national product. In part, this may be because its demand is elastic with respect to income (it may be a luxury good, in other words). In addition, it benefits from substantial subsidies, as well as a sympathetic attitude. Higher education becomes a large industry with significant power, which eventually turns out a surplus of graduates for occupations that require university-level training. The college diploma then becomes a kind of union card, and college graduates feed the growing public sector, likewise spawned by the economic surplus. Neither higher education nor the public sector in general is subject to the market test of user acceptance at prices that cover its cost of supply.

According to Schumpeter, the intelligentsia foments class conflict. Intellectuals court the laboring "masses" and embrace a variety of left-wing causes. The workers sometimes use the intelligentsia as a cutting edge in their drive for better wages and working conditions. But workers also have a vested interest in the existing system, which, far from leaving them at subsistence, has brought them the greatest gains in wages and working conditions in history. Therefore, the working class is not likely to become revolutionary unless intellectuals are successful in egging it on.

The ultimate reason for the intellectual's dissent, in Schumpeter's view, is that such an individual is always in danger of not having enough useful things to do. This includes a risk of losing status, of lacking a sufficient challenge or creative outlet, and of being "unceremoniously told to mind his own business." The classical economists had been worried that a society confronted by a niggardly nature would not be able to support a large service sector from the surplus earned in manufacturing and in agriculture. But now this surplus is too "large," in the sense that it supports too many intellectuals to allow each to be usefully occupied. Intellectuals try to solve this problem by adopting for themselves the role of social critic. At its worst, this leads them to "flatter, promise, and incite left wings and scowling minorities, sponsor doubtful or submarginal causes, [and] appeal to fringe ends. . . ."[23] In the competition to criticize society, a tendency emerges to compare the existing system with an absolute ideal, instead of with a feasible alternative.

In a society with a high propensity to engage in social criticism, the business elite finds itself the obvious target. Because intellectuals are essentially onlookers, without the firsthand knowledge of practical affairs that only experience can give, Schumpeter believed that they would fail to perceive the importance of the entrepreneurial role. Therefore, although the wealth and faults of entrepreneurs are evident, their contribution is not well understood. Moreover, in achieving wealth and passing it on to heirs, the entrepreneur may well violate some moral code. Therefore, it is easy for the intellectual to ignore those would-be innovators who fall by the wayside or who barely survive one crisis in time to confront another and to rationalize away the contributions of those who succeed. Moreover, while the entrepreneurial role is essentially one of individual leadership, it is also unromantic and antiheroic in nature, according to Schumpeter.

The business world, and with it the entrepreneurial elite, therefore finds itself the prime target of the intelligentsia, which exercises influence beyond its numbers and responsibilities. The public becomes increasingly suspicious of private industry in general and more and more favorable toward a growing body of constraints, restrictions, and regulations applied by a public sector whose expansion mirrors the progressive socialization of the economy. This expansion includes both nationalization of a growing number of enterprises and greater control over the remaining private sector. Finally, a point is reached at which the state finds it feasible and desirable to nationalize all remaining private industry, save possibly for small firms.

To summarize, in the view of Schumpeter, as well as Marx, the growth of firm size under capitalism is due to innovation and technological progress spurred by the drive for profit. In contrast to Marx, Schumpeter thought that technological change is not necessarily labor-saving, but that it does tend to routinize and depersonalize production, as well as to result in new and better goods and services. In addition, opportunities for further specialization and cooperation in production continually arise, leading to larger and larger scale economies and firm size. Internally, firms grow more bureaucratic and cautious. Decision making becomes more collectivized, and decisions increasingly depend on numerical calculations. Ultimately, entrepreneurship itself is replaced by routine calculations in the form of cost-benefit analysis. This occurs amid growing hostility toward the bourgeois class, especially on the part of intellectuals, and growing regulation of business by the state.

The superstructures of Western democracies grow less and less protective of private property rights and more and more supportive of redistribution and restrictions on those rights. In a climate of rising affluence, financial security, and redistribution, individuals also grow less willing to take major investment risks and less willing to work long hours with no certain reward. Vanishing entrepreneurship seals the fate of capitalism, although we could argue, as in chapter 2, that routinization of innovation is inefficient because it will suppress the most important potential technological advances. It is not necessarily optimal in a social sense when the "calculable result" replaces the "vision." Table 5.1 gives a more complete summary of Schumpeter's theory of capitalist development.

Table 5.1

Schumpeter's Theory of Capitalist Development

1. *Nature of Class Conflict:*

    Productive versus unproductive. The focus of class conflict is on the intelligentsia versus enterprise managers and owners.

    The *productive* class consists largely of entrepreneurs, other managers or entrepreneurs and workers with a "direct responsibility for practical affairs." Their efforts are market-oriented. However, the workers are passive, for the most part, in any class conflict, except where this can win them better wages and working conditions.

    The *unproductive* class consists of intellectuals and others, including journalists, who do not have a direct responsibility for practical affairs. They are largely onlookers, and often are not market-oriented or dependent upon acceptance by buyers of the product they produce. The intellectuals are the active perpetrators of class conflict.

    Note: In contrast to Marx, class identification is subdued and does not play a principal role in the evolution and eventual demise of capitalism.

2. *Changing Nature of Mode of Production:*

    Increasing automation and technical sophistication of production, improving product quality, widening range of products—all brought about by "creative destruction." The expanding social surplus permits mass higher education, which produces a large class of intellectuals.

    Ultimately, creative destruction also leads to increasing use of routine numerical calculations, in the form of cost-benefit analysis, as a tool of managerial decision making. The managerial function itself becomes increasingly standardized, routinized, automated, and bureaucratized. In particular, it is depersonalized and "Taylorized," as was factory production during the nineteenth and early twentieth centuries.

3. *Profit Viewed as:*

    A reward for innovation requiring the bearing of risk, particularly when this risk cannot be quantified. An "entrepreneur" is someone who innovates, when this requires the bearing of nonquantifiable risk.

4. *Forces Working to Destroy Capitalism:*

    (a) "Creative destruction" continually makes the economy more productive by rationalizing the process of production. Eventually, innovation begins to routinize, standardize, automate, and ultimately to bureaucratize the entrepreneurial function itself. The entrepreneur becomes obsolete and eventually becomes extinct on that account.

(continued)

Table 5.1 *(continued)*

(b)   Capitalists turn upon and destroy or wear away institutions that sometimes fetter innovative efforts, but which could also protect the enterpreneurial class from hostile elements. "Capitalism creates a critical frame of mind, which after having destroyed the moral authority of so many other institutions, in the end turns against its own; the bourgeois finds . . . that the rationalist attitude does not stop at the credentials of popes and kings but goes on to attack private property and the whole scheme of bourgeois values."

(c)   Capitalism also creates mass higher education, from which entrepreneurs derive some short-term benefits but which likewise expands far "beyond the point determined by cost-[benefit] considerations." Thus capitalism breeds the class of intellectuals that will ultimately destroy it.

(d)   Because intellectuals are essentially onlookers, without the firsthand knowledge of practical affairs that only experience can give, they fail to perceive the importance of the entrepreneurial role. Thus, although the wealth and the faults of entrepreneurs are evident, their contribution, as the engine of progress, is not well understood.

5.   *The Rate of Profit Falls Because:*

As the entrepreneurial function gives way to standardization, bureaucratization, and cost-benefit analysis, risk bearing that cannot be quantified tends to be avoided. Consequently, the expected rate of return on more and more potential "creative destruction" projects is understated, and the probability that such a project will be undertaken becomes less and less. It is in this sense that the rate of profit "falls."

6.   *The Cause of Business Cycles:*

Business cycles result from alternating and unforeseeable floods and droughts of creative destruction—motivated investment spending. However, the ebb and flow of creative destruction can be controlled only by eliminating creative destruction as an innovating force. According to Schumpeter's theory, business cycles do not become increasingly severe as capitalism falters. Cycles ultimately start to dampen as creative destruction dies out. Nevertheless, recessions and depressions do generate hostility toward private business and may lead to revolution before capitalism reaches the point at which a peaceful evolution is both possible and desirable to a prospective socialist leadership.

7.   *The Depletion of the Entrepreneurial Class:*

(a)   As the entrepreneurial function becomes routinized, depersonalized, and subject to mounting controls, its attraction to aspirants diminishes. To complement this, risk avoidance increases with rising incomes. Individuals become more willing to trade a certain income with a relatively low expected annual value for an uncertain stream with a higher expected annual value. These individuals may still join the managerial class, but they are no longer "hungry" would-be entrepreneurs in the sense defined above.

(continued)

Table 5.1 *(continued)*

    (b)   In addition to and reinforcing the above, as capitalism becomes increasingly productive, it supports a larger and larger intelligentsia for at least two reasons. First, the demand for higher education rises relative to the demand for other goods. (It is a "luxury" good.) Second, successful entrepreneurship requires an atmosphere of comparative tolerance, and this extends to intellectual ferment, even when directed against the "system."

            Under capitalism, intellectuals are often reasonably well-off in material terms. Higher education itself becomes a large-scale industry and is helped along by a favorable public attitude, in combination with the fact that it need not meet a market test. (It is highly subsidized.)

            All this plus a rising hostility toward the managerial class, implies that more and more potential managers may opt to do other things. Some will join the intelligentsia to put their critical minds to work there.

            The net result of (a) and (b) is a dwindling supply of entrepreneurs, because the function is depersonalized, because of growing hostility and disaffection, and because of a willingness to pay a higher price to avoid risk.

    (c)   The drive to standardize and to automate entrepreneurial decision making ends up by bureaucratizing it as well. Thus a falling demand for the services of entrepreneurship complements the dwindling supply.

8.   *Growing Hostility and the Demise of Capitalism:*

    (a)   Capitalism may end violently with some combination of a foreign invasion and revolution, perhaps following a severe depression or some other state of chaos in the organization of production. This would have to be combined with disaffection toward a still strong and influential bourgeois class. For Schumpeter, this would be a "premature" ending. Barring this, capitalism would wither away naturally, and a revolution would become unnecessary.

    (b)   In the hands of the managerial class, the rational critical attitude that capitalism encourages is productive, possibly except insofar as it mechanizes progress and ultimately replaces the entrepreneur with the industry of invention. But in the hands of the intelligentsia, the critical attitude becomes destructive. The intelligentsia must find some activity to occupy itself and to justify its existence. Therefore, it engages in "social criticism," whose brunt is borne by businesspeople for reasons already outlined. Working through the political process, this ultimately results in a rising number of restrictions and regulations that hamper entrepreneurs and reduce their potential rewards (through "wealth redistribution"). The obsolescence of the entrepreneurial function is thereby speeded up.

            Because of rising hostility, controls, regulations, taxes, automation of decision making, and a dwindling supply of entrepreneurs, the role of creative destruction eventually vanishes. Risks that cannot be quantified and diversified are no longer taken. Stocks and corporate bonds become more and more like government bonds. The actual demise comes to pass when the government issues bonds to replace all securities of private firms, but by then capitalism is already a hollow shell of its former self.

Criticisms

Because the private sector will have become a hollow shell of its former self by the final nationalization, Schumpeter felt that the emerging socialist economy would outperform its immediate predecessor. Not only would it be free of cyclical fluctuations and class frictions, but it would be able to combine satisfactory growth, albeit along relatively unchanging product lines, with a more egalitarian income distribution. Schumpeter also believed that a socialist society "should embark upon its career . . . as richly endowed as possible by its capitalist predecessor—with experience and techniques as well as with resources—and also after the latter has sown its wild oats, done its work and is approaching a stationary state. . . ."[24] Of the various socialist blueprints, Schumpeter preferred the Soviet-type economy, believing that it would become a kind of computopia, an extension of the large (and bureaucratized) corporation under capitalism.[25]

But this is a socialism that never was and quite possibly never could be. Contradicting Schumpeter's forecast, it was socialism that gave way to capitalism, in Russia and in Eastern and Central Europe—as well, one might argue, as in China—although the latter nation remains under the political control of its Communist Party. These Soviet-type economies had low rates of innovation, but they were also characterized by atrocious allocation and use of investment resources—far from the rational calculation expected by Schumpeter. In chapter 1, we saw that even a socialist market economy would have to suppress secondary stock and bond markets and put other restrictions on capital markets in order to be "socialist" in more than name. As a result, the value of producing enterprises remains unknown, making it difficult or impossible to carry out the rational cost-benefit calculus that Schumpeter believed would characterize management decision making under socialism. (It is efficient for a firm to make an investment if and only if this will increase the value of the enterprise to society.)

At the same time, the socialist state's control over income rights of capital and natural resources makes it an inevitable target of lobbying pressures aimed at protecting returns on past investments in human and physical capital whenever these are threatened by economic change. Such rent seeking is prominent under capitalism, of course, but the socialist state's greater control over income rights, plus its difficulties in making rational investment choices, means that would-be rent seekers have more to gain or to lose. Rent seeking would therefore be expected to use up more resources. In such conditions, political, ideological, and administrative criteria can easily crowd out economic criteria in determining resource allocation. Socialist economies, including Yugoslavia (sometimes cited as an example of market socialism), were characterized by considerable waste, including environmental degradation. In addition, these societies were not necessarily seen as egalitarian by those who lived in them. The perceived illegitimacy of the state under Communist Party control was a factor in the collapse of these regimes after 1989.[26]

Schumpeter would also be surprised at the survival of a large sector of small firms in developed capitalist economies. Like Marx, he expected technological progress to keep increasing the minimum efficient size of an enterprise in any given industry. However, the emergence of "postindustrial" societies with large service sectors and more flexible approaches to manufacturing, design, and marketing has reinforced the advantages of small firms, which continue to play the entrepreneurial role that Schumpeter admired. Self-employment continues to attract some of society's most capable individuals, despite the fact that average earnings for given skills, experience, and educational levels are lower than in dependent employment.[27] High-technology sectors contain many small and mid-sized enterprises that take advantage of their abilities to innovate and to respond flexibly to changing market conditions. Within these firms, employees are often called on to exercise independent judgment, which would make it costly to subordinate them within large bureaucratic structures. Large firms that are unable to innovate or to respond flexibly to innovations by competitors—as was arguably the case with IBM after the invention of the microprocessor—find their survival threatened and are forced to downsize and lose market share.

One might argue more generally that capitalism proved far more adaptable than the Soviet-type economy to the technological changes that created the information- and service-intensive economies of the latter twentieth century. These changes hastened the fall of bureaucratic socialism. Moreover, while governments of developed market economies have expanded to absorb far larger shares of gross domestic product than in Schumpeter's day, they now face budget deficits plus strong citizen resistance to higher taxes. They, too, are likely to have to downsize, although they will probably remain much larger than before World War II. The wave of deregulation and privatization—in some cases of firms that had previously been nationalized—since the 1970s likewise runs counter to the trend foreseen by Schumpeter. Some observers now argue that the evolution of economic systems down through history comes to an end with the combination of capitalism and political party democracy, although this view may also prove to be shortsighted.[28]

Finally, while the opposition of many intellectuals to capitalism remains firm, they have been unable to recruit enough allies in Western countries to bring about the major systemic changes they have desired. This is because the combination of capitalism and political party democracy is now believed to combine freedom with prosperity (although hardly for everyone) at levels far above those associated with the kinds of socialism that have been tried. For many citizens of former Soviet-type economies, however, this prosperity is still a dream. Their lives have worsened since the transition to a market economy began, and we may wonder what they would have done in 1989 and 1990 had they realized what was to follow.

We shall explore transition problems in chapter 7. First, however, we want to follow up our discussion of Schumpeter by viewing exchange within a capitalist market economy as a kind of mirror image of exchange in a Soviet-type economy. This perspective is in some ways consistent with that of Schumpeter—and yields results that conflict with standard microeconomic theory—but is suggested more precisely by the work of Kornai, which focuses on the symmetry between the two systems.[29]

On the Symmetry Between Soviet-type and "Free Market" Economies

As indicated, some economists believe there is a symmetrical relationship between Soviet-type economies, on one hand, and "free market" economies, on the other, in which firms compete for customers and claims within the enterprise to profits and losses are comparatively strong. Whereas excess demand for goods and services characterizes Soviet-type economies—at least in the "first" or official economy—free market systems are characterized by overall excess supply, according to this view. While households and firms in a Soviet-type economy find it comparatively costly to transform money into goods, Western firms find it relatively costly to transform goods into money (or to sell goods), and Western households sometimes find it hard to transform their labor into money. This would lead to excess capacity, surplus inventories, and unemployment. We examined the excess supply of labor under capitalism earlier in this chapter.

In addition, according to conventional theories of imperfect competition, there is a kind of limited excess supply in product markets of capitalist economies. Such theories predict that firms will maximize profit by setting product prices above marginal costs, since marginal revenue is less than price when the demand facing the firm is downward sloping. As a result, firms want to make additional sales at existing prices, and there is excess supply in this sense. If P is the price and MC is the marginal cost of such a product, $(P - MC)$ is the profit on an additional unit produced and sold, if this unit can be sold without lowering P. Such would be the case, for example, if the firm's forecast of demand was too pessimistic and its demand curve turned out to be DD, in Figure 5.6, rather than $D'D'$.

In this context, firms in capitalist market economies actively seek to shift out their product demand curves by taking customers away from competitors and by enlarging the markets for the goods and services they supply. Efforts to shift demand include advertising, but also service and quality improvements, innovation, and various forms of customer assistance (or activities designed to make products and product information more accessible to buyers). In fact, firms compete along many dimensions other than price, and economists such as Schumpeter and Kornai have considered nonprice competition to be more important, even to constitute the essence of capitalism. One reason for this is that a successful advertising campaign or change in the nature of a firm's products or product-related services may give it a larger and longer-lasting increase in sales than would a cut in prices. Unless they are kept secret, price cuts can be quickly

Figure 5.6 **Price and Output (P_B and q_B) in a "Pressure" Economy**

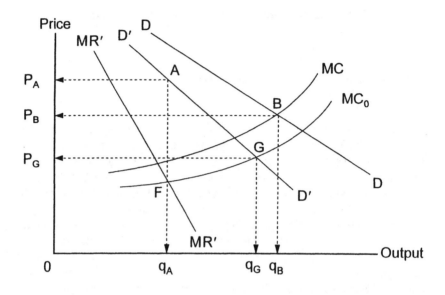

matched, but this is not always true of an innovation or successful ad. If nonprice competition is favorable to customers, firms will have to continually improve their products or lower their costs just to keep their market shares. However, fraudulent claims, high-pressure sales efforts, misleading advertising, and other devices that cause buyers to act against their own best interests are also elements of nonprice competition, whose net welfare effects are therefore uncertain.

Following Kornai, we can view enterprise efforts to sell goods in a market economy as the counterpart of buyers' efforts to obtain goods in a Soviet-type economy, which is in particular a shortage economy. Within the latter, buyers use up resources—notably their own time and energy—competing for access to goods at below-equilibrium prices, which leads to the waste analyzed in chapter 1. Although producer goods are usually allocated via a system of quotas (or formal rationing), in practice this system often fails to deliver enough inputs to firms to enable them to meet their plan targets. Therefore, enterprises short of key raw materials, intermediate goods, or fixed capital send out "pushers" or "procurers" (in Russian, *tolkachi*) to obtain these items, often with the aid of gifts or bribes. The exchanges in question are outside the framework of the state plan, and thus of the official or first economy, and are often illegal. Historically, they were part of the unofficial or second economy that grew up in each of these systems.

The counterparts of the *tolkachi* in market economies are salespeople, whose task is to try to expand demand—if possible, without lowering prices. (In economic terms, the job of a salesperson is to increase the demand facing his or her employer.) Following Kornai, we can say that there is "pressure" on the market when there is tension between the sales aspirations and realizations of suppliers, with the result that sellers find it profitable to use nonprice methods to shift their demand curves or to increase the demand for their products at given prices. An enterprise operating under perfect competition would have no perceptible effect on the market demand for its products unless it is able to differentiate them from the products of rivals. But then perfect competition would no longer prevail. A pressure economy is therefore characterized mainly by imperfect competition, as are most modern capitalist systems.

Is this good or bad? A central thesis of mainstream economic theory is that perfect competition leads to an efficient allocation and use of resources for two basic reasons. First, free entry into and exit from any market ensures that low-cost suppliers are the ones able to survive. Second, a perfect competitor maximizes profit by setting each output where the good's price equals its marginal cost, which is also the pricing rule for economic efficiency. However, the superiority of perfect competition rests on rather strong assumptions that are unlikely to apply in practice. For example, if perfect competitors are too small to realize scale or experience economies, they will not be low-cost producers, and least-cost production could occur only under conditions of oligopoly or monopoly. As well, if the small size of perfect competitors limits their access to financing (because they lack good collateral or security), they may on that account be unable to produce at least cost.

Perfect competition requires that there be "many" firms supplying a market, none of which has a "large" market share. The larger and more numerous the markets supplied by each firm, therefore, the larger average firm size can be without violating this constraint. Even when markets are large and numerous, however, perfect competition can exist only when there is no product differentiation among enterprises. The products supplied by one firm must be perfect substitutes for those supplied by each of many independent competitors. Suppressing product differentiation may suppress differences among goods and services that are "frivolous" or even "imaginary." But such efforts may also suppress innovation, which usually results in products that are new in the sense of not being perfect substitutes for existing goods or services. This alone can more than offset any advantages of perfect over imperfect competition, as we saw in the previous section. Indeed, economists who would argue the theoretical merits of perfect competition would often be reluctant to recommend to policy makers that the conditions necessary for perfect competition be established and enforced in the real world.

Two key elements of the case against imperfect competition are that it leads firms to follow the "wrong" pricing rule and that barriers to entry and exit, including import restrictions, may keep low-cost suppliers out of the market, allowing high-cost producers to survive.[30] The barriers-to-entry argument has merit, although with two qualifications already noted in chapters 1 and 2. First, if there is good reason to expect that domestic suppliers will benefit from significant scale or experience economies (more generally, *Kaizen*), temporary protection for these firms may be justified, along with carrots and sticks to ensure that the gains in question actually are realized. This is an extension of the traditional "infant industry" argument. Protection may also be justified on noneconomic grounds, such as the possibility of "excessive" dependence on foreign and possibly unreliable suppliers in the event of emergency. As a rule, this sort of argument is overused.

Second, as barriers to world trade fall, there are potential gains in real income for all nations involved. However, we argued earlier in this chapter that there would also be redistribution, since earnings of any given productive input will show some tendency to equalize across trading partners. In particular, differences in wages and benefits between countries for workers with similar skills and abilities will tend to decline. In nations with relatively high labor earnings to begin with, the resulting downward pressure on labor demand may lead to efforts to prevent decreases in incomes and living standards by unions and professional associations that bargain on behalf of labor. The result is often to cushion the fall in real earnings, but at the cost of higher unemployment (mainly of outsiders), which would offset efficiency gains from international trade.

Firms operating under imperfect competition are said to follow the "wrong" pricing rule from society's point of view, because they face limited and downward-sloping demand. According to conventional analysis, such an enterprise increases sales by moving down its demand curve and lowering price. This price cut applies not only to additional output but also to units of output it was already able to sell at the higher price. Therefore, its marginal revenue is less than its price, and its marginal revenue curve, such as MR' in Figure 5.6, lies below its demand curve, $D'D'$. Whereas the price measures the benefit to a user of an additional unit of output, the smaller marginal revenue measures the benefit to a producer, who therefore supplies too little of the product and charges a price that is too high. The conventional profit-maximizing solution is at A in Figure 5.6, where MR' equals marginal cost, MC_O. At A, price P_A is above marginal cost, giving rise to a deadweight loss equal to the area of triangle AGF. This is the net social gain (benefit minus cost) of expanding output to the conventional efficient solution at G, where $D'D'$ intersects MC_O.

The above analysis is basic. However, we can still ask whether a firm selling in a market on which there is "pressure" in the sense described above will set price greater than marginal cost and produce less than the efficient rate of output. The question arises because such a firm may try to increase sales not solely or even primarily by reducing prices but also by expanding demand at given prices. By applying "pressure" on the market, such a firm would try to shift its demand curve outward—for instance, from $D'D'$ to DD in Figure 5.6—although we should keep in mind that demand-shifting efforts of different firms will partly cancel across an industry. This perspective, yielded by viewing a capitalist market economy as a mirror image of a Soviet-type economy, suggests a different view of pricing under imperfect competition.

Suppose that, by spending an additional $2 on service or quality improvements or on advertising, a firm can increase its quantity demanded by one unit without changing price. At price P, the firm's revenue gain from this additional unit is P, while its increase in cost is $2 plus the marginal production cost, MC_O, of expanding output by one unit. When profit is maximized, the increase in profit caused by such an expansion will be zero. Therefore, $P = \$2 + MC_O$, where $2 is the marginal cost to the firm of shifting demand outward by one unit. Adding this to MC_O gives the full marginal cost to the firm of a unit increase in output. Let $MC = MC_O + \$2$ be this full marginal cost. Then in order to maximize profit, the firm must set $P = MC$, and in this sense engages in marginal-cost pricing, producing at B in Figure 5.6.

From an efficiency standpoint, is B better or worse than G, which would be the outcome if the firm followed the pricing rule associated with perfect competition? The answer to this question depends on the nature of the expenditures used to shift demand. At G, price also equals marginal cost, in the sense that $P = MC_O$. However, the firm is making no effort to shift demand outward, as a result of which it has a lower demand ($D'D'$ instead of DD for given demand-shifting efforts by competitors) but also a lower marginal cost (MC_O rather than MC). This is because the demand-increasing expenditures will also differentiate the firm's products from those of competitors, in most cases, and are therefore incompatible with perfect competition.

Therefore, the gain or loss to society of going from G to B depends on the social value of these expenditures. If they increase demand by offering better values to buyers in the form of better quality and service or better information about products and prices, they are socially worthwhile and it would be inefficient to suppress them. Customers are better off, even if the expenditures of rival firms largely cancel across an industry, in the sense of leaving each seller with about the same market share that it would have if none of them tried to shift demand (keeping in mind that each raises its own demand, to some degree, by reducing the demand facing competitors).

When demand-shifting efforts increase demand by increasing the value of products to users, B is preferable to G. The pricing rule associated with imperfect competition in a pressure economy yields a more efficient outcome than the pricing rule associated with perfect competition. This is true even if the imperfect competition in question turns out to be monopolistic competition, a much-abused form in microeconomics texts because it allegedly leads to firms that are too small to realize economies of scale and that operate with excess capacity. In fact, neither of these criticisms is true in a pressure economy.[31]

However, the freedom to shift demand by offering better products to buyers may also be the freedom to deceive them, whether by inducing them to pay prices that are too high or to purchase goods they do not really want or need or that are harmful. Schumpeter notwithstanding, government has a responsibility to try to restrict the latter freedom while promoting the former.[32] Moreover, firms may find it harder to profit from false or misleading claims if they face active competition, giving buyers several alternatives, and if entry barriers are low enough to allow new competitors to enter when existing suppliers become inefficient.

Firms may also be able to increase demand by lobbying government through political pressure groups to suppress competition, subsidize their prices, buy more of their output, and/or to force other buyers to do this. History yields an unending stream of such examples in which governments try to benefit suppliers at the expense of product users. A major reason is that the supply side of a product market is usually easier to organize for purposes of political action than is the demand side. Specialization in production and diversity in consumption mean that there are generally far fewer sellers than buyers of any given type of product and that individual suppliers have far more to lose or to gain from changes in the prices of the products they sell.[33]

However, economic growth comes from technological progress, realization of scale and experience economies, and continuing increases in product quality and variety. Growth results when producers expand their markets by overcoming barriers, by improving old products and introducing new ones, or by lowering prices. The challenge for government policy is to make this the most attractive option to domestic producers rather than obtaining protection or subsidies that allow them to increase profit or to survive at the expense of their customers.

Therefore, the discussion of this section does not justify monopoly, or even barriers to entry that permanently increase marginal costs of supply by excluding potential low-cost producers.[34] This being said, the theoretical advantage of perfect over workable but imperfect competition disappears when we view a market system as a pressure economy. Product differentiation among firms is not necessarily bad, and it must occur if innovation is to flourish.

Notes

1. To get Marx's theory of the evolution of modern capitalism from Marx himself is difficult, but potentially rewarding. Aside from *Capital*, I would recommend *Wage-Labour and Capital* (London: Lawrence and Wishart, 1933); *Value, Price and Profit* (New York: International, 1935); and the *Grundrisse*, esp. pp. 239–471. For the reader who is starting out and wants to be selective in reading *Capital*, I would recommend chaps. 1–4, 7, 10, 12–16, 23–27, and 32 from vol. 1. Most of this material is reprinted in Tucker, *The Marx-Engels Reader*, part 2. From vol. 2 of *Capital*, I would recommend part 1 and chaps. 15–16, and from vol. 3 I would recommend parts 1 and 3. Two excellent short guides to Marx are Ben Fine, *Marx's Capital* (London: Macmillan, 1975) and A. Balinky, *Marx's Economics: Origin and Development* (Lexington, Mass.: D. C. Heath, 1970).

2. To derive this formula, note that

$$(1-q) = 1 - \frac{C}{C+V} = \frac{C+V-C}{C+V} = \frac{V}{C+V}$$

Therefore, $E(1-q) = \frac{S}{V} \frac{V}{C+V} = \frac{S}{C+V} = \pi$

3. This would only be true as a rough average across the entire economy.

4. Regarding the risk factor, see A. Sandmo, "On the Theory of the Competitive Firm Under Price Uncertainty," *American Economic Review*, March 1971, and H. E. Leland, "Theory of the Firm Facing Uncertain Demand," *American Economic Review*, June 1972.

5. Therefore, the crisis follows the end of an investment boom. Business cycles could be said to result from expansions and contractions of investment demand.

6. For evidence on the nature of technological change, see C. Kennedy and A. P. Thirlwall, "Technical Progress," in Royal Economic Society, ed., *Surveys of Applied Economics*, vol. 1 (London: Macmillan, 1973); Murray Brown, *On the Theory and Measurement of Technological Change* (Cambridge: Cambridge University Press, 1966), part 3; and M. Brown and J. Popkin, "A Measure of Technological Change and Returns to Scale," *Review of Economics and Statistics*, November 1962. See as well Simon Kuznets, *Modern Economic Growth* (New Haven: Yale University Press, 1966), chap. 4, and R. M. Solow, "Technical Change and the Aggregate Production Function," *Review of Economics and Statistics*, August 1957. Finally, the major source for the statistical relation between inequality and growth is Jeffrey G. Williamson, *Inequality, Poverty, and History* (Oxford: Basil Blackwell, 1991).

7. Simon Kuznets, a pioneer developer of national income accounting and a Nobel laureate in 1971, first proposed the Kuznets curve in his 1954 presidential address to the American Economic Association. The major contemporary source is Williamson, op. cit. See as well the references cited by Williamson.

8. Marx tended to confine his analysis to the effects of labor-saving technology within single factories or workplaces. By contrast, see Williamson, op. cit., chap. 1, esp. pp. 21 ff.

9. See, for example, Peter Gottschalk, "Changes in Inequality of Family Income in Seven Industrialized Countries," *American Economic Review*, May 1993, and references cited. See as well Richard B. Freeman and Lawrence F. Katz, eds., *Differences and Changes in Wage Structures* (Chicago: University of Chicago Press, 1995). Finally, see Jeffrey Sachs and Howard Shatz, "U.S. Trade with Developing Countries and Wage Inequality," *American Economic Review*, May 1996, and references cited.

10. Ibid. and W. Michael Cox and Beverly J. Fox, op. cit.

11. In general, there are many reasons for differentiating workers on the basis of seniority, but we shall be interested in this chapter in cases in which collective action (or the threat of same) by insiders has a strong influence on earnings, while the influence of outsiders is weak to nonexistent. See O. J. Blanchard and L. H. Summers, "Hysteresis and the European Unemployment Problem," Harvard Institute of Economic Research, Discussion Paper no. 1240 (Cambridge, Mass.: Harvard University, May 1986); Assar Lindbeck and D. J. Snower, "Efficiency Wages versus Insiders and Outsiders," *European Economic Review*, February/March 1987; and R. Carson, "Involuntary Layoffs and Rigid Wages," *Journal of Economics and Business*, February 1982.

12. The discussion that follows relies on the references in note 11 plus the following: A. W. Phillips, "The Relation Between Unemployment and the Rate of Change of Money Wages in the United Kingdom, 1861–1957," *Economica*, November 1958; M. Friedman, "The Role of Monetary Policy," *American Economic Review*, March 1968; M. Friedman

and A. J. Schwartz, *A Monetary History of the United States* (Princeton, N.J.: Princeton University Press, 1963), esp. chaps. 6–7; W. H. Branson, *Macroeconomic Theory and Policy,* 2nd ed. (New York: Harper and Row, 1979), chaps. 6–8, 17–18; R. E. Hall, "Is Unemployment a Macroeconomic Problem?" *American Economic Review,* May 1983; H. G. Grubel, M. A. Walker, eds., *Unemployment Insurance: Global Evidence of Its Effects on Unemployment* (Vancouver: The Fraser Institute, 1978); and M. Olsen, Jr., *The Logic of Collective Action* (New York: Schocken, 1968), esp. chaps. 1–3.

13. J. A. Schumpeter, *Capitalism, Socialism, and Democracy* (New York: Harper and Row, 1950), pp. 84, 82. The discussion that follows is based mainly on part 2.

Schumpeter was a modern economist. He died on January 8, 1950, several days after delivering an address, "The March into Socialism," to the American Economic Association in New York. This is reprinted at the end of *Capitalism, Socialism, and Democracy* and in the *American Economic Review,* May 1950.

14. Schumpeter, *Capitalism, Socialism, and Democracy,* pp. 84–85; 83.

15. Ibid., p. 86.

16. This recalls *Kaizen,* or "continuing improvement," from chap. 1 and is sometimes called the "Red Queen" effect after the Red Queen of Lewis Carroll's *Through the Looking Glass,* chap. 2, who had to keep running in order to avoid going backward.

17. Strictly speaking, moreover, perfect competition requires each firm's products to be perfect substitutes for those of competitors. Since innovation usually results in new products that are imperfect substitutes for those of competitors, innovation requires product differentiation among firms, and in this way is incompatible with perfect competition.

18. Schumpeter, *Capitalism, Socialism, and Democracy,* p. 90. Schumpeterian profits are long-run disequilibrium profits. They are earned between the time an industry is shocked out of long-run equilibrium by an innovation and the time it returns to equilibrium. During this period, the innovator should have a better cost-price margin than his competitors or than he himself can hope to have when equilibrium is restored. Schumpeter believed these profits were much more important than long-run monopoly rents.

19. Just as a sequence of random numbers will move up and down in cyclical fashion, so will the stream of creative destruction projects ebb and flow in at least a partly random manner.

20. See Schumpeter, *Capitalism, Socialism, and Democracy,* chaps. 11 and 12.

21. Ibid., p. 126.

22. Ibid., pp. 132–133.

23. Ibid., p. 154.

24. Ibid., p. 178.

25. Ibid., chaps. 16–18.

26. See Francis Fukuyama, "Capitalism and Democracy: The Missing Link, *Journal of Democracy,* July 1992. Fukuyama adds (p. 103): "The certainties of enterprise managers in actual socialist societies turned out to be symptoms of their inability to innovate or to seek out new markets effectively."

27. See B. H. Hamilton, "Does Entrepreneurship Pay? An Empirical Analysis of the Returns to Self-Employment," McGill University, Department of Economics, Working Paper no. 17–93, Montreal, April 1993.

28. For example, a view along these lines (albeit much more complex and qualified) is given in Francis Fukuyama, *The End of History and the Last Man* (New York: Free Press, 1992).

29. See *Anti-Equilibrium,* op. cit., part 3. In part the approach below can also be traced to Robert Dorfman and Peter O. Steiner, "Optimal Advertising and Optimal Quality," *American Economic Review,* December 1954.

30. It may be useful to indicate how different kinds of industrial organization are classified. We first divide all industries into those characterized by *perfect competition*, on one hand, and imperfect competition, on the other. Perfect competition requires that firms be small relative to market size and that each firm's products be perfect substitutes for those of many competitors. As a result, each firm is a price taker (cannot influence price by changing quantity supplied on its own), which is the reason for marginal-cost pricing. There must also be free entry and exit, as a result of which price equals average cost in long-run equilibrium. Imperfect competition covers all cases in which at least one of the above conditions is violated. It includes (a) *monopoly*, or single seller in an industry; (b) *oligopoly*, or "competition between the few," in which firms' pricing decisions are interdependent and there may or may not be barriers to entry and/or product differentiation; and (c) *monopolistic competition*, with many small sellers, no barriers to entry, and product differentiation.

31. See note 30. In long-run equilibrium, a monopolistic competitor is said to operate where its downward-sloping demand curve (owing to product differentiation) is tangent to the downward-sloping portions of its long- and short-run average cost curves (because of free entry and the envelope theorem). This conclusion does not take into account the firm's ability to shift its demand curve, which is a bit surprising since it can often do so via its choice of location, and location is often cited as a factor in product differentiation.

In long-run equilibrium, a monopolistic competitor makes zero economic profit because of free entry. Its profit is $Pq - TC$, where P is the price, q is the quantity of its output, and TC is its total cost. TC will depend on q and also on an index, E, of its effort to shift demand. However, at each given q we can select the value of E that maximizes profit for that value of q. When this is done, TC depends only on output, q, and the same is therefore true of average cost, AC. In long-run equilibrium, $P = AC$ because of free entry, and since $P = MC$ also holds, we have $AC = MC$. The firm operates at the bottom of its long- and short-run average cost curves, realizing economies of scale and optimal use of capacity.

32. This can be done with restrictions, such as a truth-in-advertising law, but also by easing the way for organizations (such as a consumers' union) that test products and survive on their reputations for accuracy, honesty, and promptness.

33. A government may also find it attractive to tax incomes received in sectors that benefit from restrictions on competition (which raises incomes in these industries), and this may make it more willing to provide such protection.

34. In order to profitably shift its demand outward—e.g., from $D'D'$ to DD in Figure 5.6—a firm may have to capture sales from competitors (firms supplying substitute products) instead of only from suppliers of unrelated goods. If so, a pressure economy cannot be one dominated by monopolies. More generally, it cannot be characterized either by too little market power or by too much.

Questions for Review, Discussion, Examination

1. What is the crucial feature of technological change under modern capitalism, according to Marx? What is the key contradiction of modern capitalism? How does the first lead to the second? Explain. How does this technological feature cause recessions, and ultimately the destruction of capitalism?

2. According to Marx, capitalism goes through a worsening series of business cycles that culminates in its destruction.

(a) One problem is the falling rate of profit. Why is the rate of profit important under capitalism, and what causes its long-run tendency to fall?

(b) What happens to income distribution as a capitalist economy evolves over time? Why? How is this related to the long-run tendency for aggregate demand to fall behind aggregate supply?

(c) Do actual changes in income distribution as a capitalist economy grows match those foreseen by Marx? Explain how this relates to the Kuznets curve.

3. Give three or four reasons why a capitalist economy will recover from all recessions (or "crises") save the last. How can modern budget deficits in capitalist market economies be fitted into this framework?

4. Discuss two basic criticisms of Marx's view of the evolution of modern capitalism. What is the "Kuznets curve," and what role would it play in such a criticism?

5. How has inequality changed in the United States and in several other Western countries since the mid-1970s? What has happened to the return on human capital? What may account for this?

6. Some economists view Soviet-type economies as systems characterized by shortages or "excess demand" and capitalist economies as systems characterized by "excess supply," especially in labor markets in which excess supply takes the form of unemployment. What features specific to labor markets in Western countries may produce excess supply? In particular, how may the tendency for wages to be set or bargained for by labor "insiders" cause real wages to be rigid in the face of excess labor supply?

7. How may the tendency for wages to be set or bargained for by labor "insiders" reinforce and prolong the negative effects of unemployment on an unforeseen shock to the economy, such as the Great Depression or the energy crises? How may this tendency also prolong the full employment resulting from an unforeseen expansion of demand or an unforeseen reduction in (the growth of) labor supply? (The West German economic miracle and the building of the Berlin Wall, which shut off the flow of refugees from East to West Germany, may be examples of the latter.)

8. Along what main lines does Schumpeter's theory of the evolution of modern capitalism diverge from Marx's theory? How does the end of capitalism differ in the two theories? What is "creative destruction," and why did Schumpeter believe that this was the essential feature of capitalism?

9. What role does routinization of the entrepreneurial function play in the demise of capitalism, according to Schumpeter? Why may routinization of this function cause it to be performed poorly?

10. What role do intellectuals play in the demise of capitalism, according to Schumpeter? In recent years, returns to education appear to be at or near an all-time high in North America. Is this consistent with Schumpeter's view? Explain briefly.

11. Has modern socialism conformed in practice to Schumpeter's expectations? Explain in what way(s) it has or has not.

12. What do we mean by a "pressure" economy (or by a market on which there is "pressure")? Why might we describe it as the opposite or mirror image of a Soviet-type economy?

13. How are prices set in a market on which there is "pressure"? How does this differ from conventional price setting under imperfect competition, as portrayed in microeconomics textbooks? What does this have to do with nonprice competition?

14. Are prices and outputs efficient in markets on which there is pressure? On what considerations does your answer depend?

15. When is point B in Figure 5.6 preferable to point G? When is the reverse true? Why is G usually said to be preferable to A? What has this to do with the "deadweight loss" triangle in Figure 5.6?

16. How does freedom on the part of suppliers to compete for market share via nonprice competition embody both potential advantages and potential dangers of capitalism? What factors can reduce the dangers? Discuss briefly.

Chapter 6

Varieties of Socialism and Pretransition Efforts to Reform Soviet-type Economies

> The workers, having conquered political power, will smash the old bureaucratic apparatus; they will shatter it to its very foundations; they will destroy it to the very roots; and they will replace it by a new one, consisting of the very same workers and office employees *against* whose transformation into bureaucrats the measures will at once be taken which were specified in detail by Marx and Engels: (1) not only election, but recall at any time; (2) pay not exceeding that of a workman; (3) immediate introduction of control and supervision by *all*, so that *all* shall become "bureaucrats" for a time and that therefore *nobody* may be able to become a "bureaucrat."
>
> —Lenin: *State and Revolution*

> Vital work we do is sinking in a dead sea of paperwork. We get sucked in by a foul bureaucratic swamp.
>
> —Lenin (after the revolution)

> He did truly marvelous things, but only found out later what they were.
> —An adviser to Mikhail Gorbachev

The Socialist System Envisaged by Marx and Engels[1]

What concrete institutional details can we give about the socialist system fore-seen by Marx and Engels? Its task was to carry the masses forward from the poverty and misery they associated with capitalism toward full communism. Along the way, the social consciousness of society's members was to develop and expand, through education and experience, and the state was eventually supposed to wither away, as scarcity vanished. Marx did not leave exact blue-prints for his future socialist system, however, which is why economies as di-verse as the former Yugoslavia (for many years, the only socialist market economy) and the former Soviet Union could profess to be its embodiment.

The key requirement of a Marxian socialist state would be a change in the form of labor relations. These were viewed as exploitive and alienating under capitalism because capitalists bar workers from ownership of the means of production and from the fruits of their labor. Thus Marx emphasized the importance under socialism of collective ownership of these means by all members of society, as well as the need for free occupational choice, workers' control over their conditions of work, democratic relations within the workplace, and the absence of a class structure in society. Factories were to be manned by "free associations of workers." The management of each firm would be responsive to elected representatives of its employees. The workers would also have some direct control over working conditions, notably over safety and health standards, and over the pace of work.

Initially, a socialist economy would rely on team spirit, social pressures within the workforce, growing social consciousness, and profit sharing to motivate efficiency within each enterprise. Over time, as social consciousness developed, it would become possible to share profits and losses more widely across society as a whole. Development of team spirit and intrinsic motivation would also allow for reductions in the number of managers and supervisors. It could be argued, in fact, that management of firms by state administrative agencies merely substitutes for the dictatorial control by private managers and owners under capitalism to which Marx and Engels were objecting. This substitution does not eliminate class differentiation, and some Marxians went so far as to call the Soviet economy an example of "state capitalism."

However, Marx was also emphatic in contrasting the anarchy of the market with the scientific, disciplined, and purposeful division of labor and vertical organization within the enterprise. He apparently did not understand how the efficiency of such an organization depends on the ability to routinize production, to concentrate it in time and space, and to utilize indivisible plant and equipment. Under socialism, he wanted to extend this organization to the entire producing sector. He therefore favored an economywide plan to govern production, as well as a linking of producers' (or workers') associations, which would be in charge of each firm, into one giant union embracing the entire producing sector. If we combine all recommendations of Marx and Engels, we appear to come out with a worker-managed Soviet-type economy—a contradiction in terms, inasmuch as workers' management implies enterprise autonomy and therefore market relations. We must either choose or compromise between management of a firm by its workers and management by higher-level authorities.

To see what sort of compromise Marx and Engels had in mind, we note that both lavished praise on the Paris Commune, the organization set up by the workers of Paris who seized and temporarily held the city from February through most of May 1871. Both approved of the organization of the French economy foreseen by commune leaders that might have been implemented had the latter been successful. Here we find factories directed by elected worker representatives and manned by free associations of workers, with all associations joined into one large union. Each firm was to be governed by an economywide plan.

However, the central government was also to be weak vis-à-vis local (or communal) governments, and plan construction was to be a bottom-up affair, with the center simply aggregating the plans of individual enterprises or communes and adjusting these to ensure consistency. (The center would play largely a coordinating and procurement role, in other words.)

How firms were to determine their output targets and input needs is not concretely specified, nor are investment financing or incentives dealt with. Indications are that Marx wanted factories to supply products to meet mainly local or regional needs, measured in an unknown way following the abolition of the market. Both specialization and division of labor would be reduced, compared to a modern capitalist economy, since Marx viewed these as alienating and dehumanizing. However, Marx and Engels did not object to the subdivision of production processes into minute, repetitive tasks per se as much as they did to the resulting "imprisonment" of workers within particular "spheres of activity." In *The German Ideology,* Marx and Engels wrote:

> For as soon as the division of labor comes into being, each man has a particular, exclusive sphere of activity which is forced upon him and from which he cannot escape. He is a hunter, a fisherman, a shepherd, a critical critic, and must remain so if he does not want to lose his means of livelihood; while in communist society, where nobody has one exclusive sphere of activity, but each can become accomplished in any branch he wishes, society regulates the general production and thus makes it possible for me to do one thing today and another tomorrow, to hunt in the morning, fish in the afternoon, run cattle in the evening, criticize after dinner, just as I have a mind, without ever becoming hunter, fisherman, shepherd, or critic.[2]

Thus a socialist society would retain some specialization and division of labor—in the sense of subdivision of production processes—even into full communism. But it would also practice extensive work rotation, including worker participation in management and management participation in blue-collar labor, so that no one would be imprisoned in a job. (In particular, everyone was to do both manual and mental labor.) As noted above, regional specialization and trade would be restricted, so consumers would live in the same region as producers of most of the products they consumed. Marx considered it essential for users to identify goods and services with their producers, and for producers and users to be in direct personal contact. This would make producers responsible for their products, but also it would allow them to realize their need for self-expression through the creation of goods and services that users value. In turn, this would reduce the alienation of producers from the production process, which Marx believed to be a characteristic of modern capitalism.

In France, the commune was to be the form of government of every community, down to the smallest, and Marx believed that power would reside there, although rural producers were to be "under the intellectual lead" of the central towns of their districts. The center was to be merely a "free federation" of all communes with Paris. Each commune was to be controlled by municipal councillors elected via universal suffrage and subject to recall by the populace at any time. The commune was to be both an executive and a legislative body to which the police and national guard would be responsible. There would be no professional standing army, this being replaced by the national guard, in which all working men (and possibly women) were to be automatically enrolled. Officials and judges were also to be elected and subject to recall; their pay was not to exceed that of an ordinary laborer. The emphasis was on impermanence and revocability of authorities' rights. Marx and Engels foresaw a rotation procedure through which a large proportion of society would serve as officials, generally for short periods. This would be an extension of general work rotation.[3]

The workability of such a system is by no means assured. We may wonder whether the extent of freedom of occupational choice envisaged by Marx and Engels is compatible with any practical organization of production. Moreover, rotation and the constant threat of recall would impose short time horizons on officials. With low pay, authorities might become corruptible, and with constant rotation they might not be able or motivated to acquire the expertise needed to run the economy well. It would not be surprising to see a more permanent leadership and bureaucracy emerge, with the ability to accumulate power, although they might remain nominally under officials subject to election and recall. Lenin's notion of a "vanguard" elite (the Communist Party) leading the revolution and guiding society through all aspects of the struggle to achieve communism was a logical addition to Marx's system. But it raised the possibility that the party, rather than the proletariat, could become dictator.

We may also wonder whether the system would remain as administratively decentralized as Marx and Engels hoped. State agencies would have the task of ensuring that plans are consistent, meaning that they must physically balance the supply of and demand for most goods. The power to make plans consistent is the power to order increases in the outputs of some goods, along with decreases in the outputs of others. It is thus the power to overrule lower-level requests and to issue commands, which must rise to a level above the enterprise. Otherwise, communal property rights would prevail over goods and resources, which are still scarce under socialism. This scarcity would find concrete reflection in the nearly certain tendency for widespread shortages to be embedded in the targets and quotas proposed by individual firms. Unless the government moved to assert its control, markets and quasi-private property rights would be likely to reemerge as a result of efforts by producers and consumers to avoid the losses associated with communal rights. It would also be possible to make plans consistent in many different ways. Each would reflect a different set of adjustments to the original output and input target proposals, and thus a different set of priorities. The power to make plans consistent is therefore the power to determine priorities. The state's obligation to maintain a high rate of investment would enhance this power by giving the government strong leverage over the allocation of capital goods.

We recall that centrally set priorities in the Soviet Union and in most East European countries were backed up by central control over supplies of key inputs and investment credits. This is where the system foreseen by Marx and Engels would have to enforce partial decentralization. To accord with reduced regional specialization and trade, the supply of and demand for most goods would have had to be balanced separately in each region, where supplies are also controlled. The resulting decrease in specialization and division of labor would reduce income and output, although it might also reduce alienation. The economy would still be state managed, albeit mainly by regional and local government agencies. Unfortunately, the latter can be just as authoritarian and just as wasteful of resources as central government agencies.

Finally, present-day socialism did not succeed mature capitalism, as Marx had forecast. Instead, most socialist governments came to power in countries where capitalism had not yet reached maturity. This was, in part, the secret of their success in achieving rapid economic growth and in competing with more developed capitalist nations for a time. They inherited relatively plentiful supplies of labor—and, in the case of the Soviet Union, an abundance of natural resources—in combination with a poverty of capital. Thus, by mobilizing savings and accumulating capital rapidly while transferring labor from agriculture to industry and exploiting or importing large quantities of natural resources, they were able to achieve record rates of industrial expansion. By and large, this was done wastefully, and without the benefit of a high rate of technical progress from indigenous sources. As a result, the marginal productivity of domestically produced capital fell dramatically after the 1950s in Soviet-type economies, which relied more and more on technology imports from the West to generate lower and lower rates of growth.

Basic Forms of Socialism

> What is and what is not socialism is not so clear to me today as when
> I was young.
>
> —Milovan Djilas (author of *The New Class*), 1982.

Introduction

Table 6.1 summarizes the three basic forms of socialism from the standpoint of plan and market. Of these, the centralized administrative or "Soviet-type" economy was by far the most dominant in practice, successfully resisting efforts to decentralize it for many years. The decentralized administrative form is the socialist system envisaged by Marx and Engels. Most socialist economies con-

Table 6.1

Basic Forms of Socialism from the Standpoint of Plan and Market

Type of System	Characteristics
Centralized administrative (command)	State management of production and inter-enterprise exchange, which are coordinated via an economy wide plan. Also, widespread state property rights and excess demand. The latter leads to an important market sector (the second economy), based to some extent on barter, which fills gaps in the supply network.
Decentralized administrative (Marxian system)	Worker control of enterprise management. However, there is little or no coordination of firms through a legally sanctioned system of markets. Instead, co-ordination takes place through an economy wide plan, as in the command system. But here the plan for the whole country is supposed to be no more than an aggregation of the plans of individual firms and communes, adjusted by a weak central government to ensure consistency.
Market socialism	Although the state legally own the material means of production, firms and households are largely coordinated by a system of markets, We can identify two basic types of market socialism. In Type A, enterprise management is responsible to public authorities outside the firm (e.g., to ministerial or to local government officials). In Type B, enterprise management is responsible to its employees (workers' management), as in the decentralized administrative system. Under market socialism, government planning would have to rely on guidance rather than command.

tained some elements of this system. Over the long run, it would probably prove unworkable, however, and would therefore evolve into a combination of centralized control, market socialism, and regional self-sufficiency. Its major defect is the absence of a mechanism for balancing supply and demand and thus for allocating goods and resources. In consequence, one could argue that it is not really a system.

If production is coordinated via the targets and quotas of economywide planning rather than through the market, the central planners will sooner or later have to take responsibility for ensuring that plans of different regions, industries, and enterprises are consistent. To do this, they must have the power to set final, binding production targets and to control financial flows, as necessary, to back these up. This is essentially a Soviet-type economy. If regional self-sufficiency is unacceptable, permanent decentralization requires flexible prices to coordinate production and exchange, plus incentives that will make supplies of different goods respond elastically to changes in their prices (so that prices, although flexible, remain relatively stable). As long as individuals are self-interested, the latter requires competition among firms, plus stronger enterprise claims to profits and losses than has been usual under command planning. Moreover, unless price rationing expands to fill gaps left by the retreat of targets and quotas following decentralization, shortages and bottlenecks will eventually become disruptive. Absence of flexible prices was a major cause of failure of efforts to reform Soviet-type economies.

Our discussion in chapter 3 suggested that political democracy, in the sense of universal suffrage and competing political parties, would be incompatible with a Soviet-type economy. Therefore, "democratic" socialism would also have to be market socialism, one form of which would combine political with "industrial" democracy in the sense that the management of each producing enterprise would be elected by its employees and responsible to them. This would be market socialism of type B—or possibly a combination of market socialism and command planning. Historically, the most prominent example of such a combination—which did not incorporate political or industrial democracy—was the New Economic Policy Era (1921–28) in the Soviet Union. It featured central management of the "commanding heights" of the economy (heavy industry, defense, banking and finance, energy, transport, and foreign trade), along with market coordination of other sectors.

The Lange-Lerner Model

The best-known theoretical model of market socialism is the Lange-Lerner system, a form of market socialism, type A.[4] It was the brainchild in 1936 of Oskar Lange, then a professor at the University of Chicago and subsequently an official of the Polish State Committee of Science and Technology until his death in 1964.[5] Lange's model has a simulated market, with the central planners setting all product prices and adjusting these on a trial-and-error basis in an effort to keep supply and demand in balance for each good and service. When a shortage of any product appears, the planners are supposed to raise its price. When a surplus appears, they lower its price. They also set and adjust interest rates to match the supply of savings with the demand for loanable funds. Production and investment are controlled by enterprise and industry managers, who are appointed by the state.

Enterprise managers take responsibility for short-run decisions regarding the use of a given production capacity, while industry managers take responsibility for long-run investment decisions that determine the nature and level of production capacity in each industry. These managers are instructed to minimize the total cost of supplying any given assortment of outputs and to set each positive output where the product's price equals its marginal cost, since this is the pricing rule for economic efficiency. A good or service should be supplied if and only if its total benefit to users (or consumer surplus) is greater than the cost to society of supplying it. In this context, industry managers are told to increase any type of production capacity when the return on the required investment exceeds the interest cost of borrowed funds from the state bank and to decrease capacity (by not replacing it as it wears out) when the return falls below this interest cost. These actions of industry and enterprise managers determine the supply of each product and the demand for each productive input. However, there is no discussion of managerial motivation or remuneration, and it is unclear what happens when a firm defaults on a loan or becomes technically bankrupt. Concrete criteria for rewarding, replacing, promoting, and demoting managers are never spelled out.

Lange wanted to show that "democratic" socialism was theoretically possible, and in particular to reply to right-wing critics (Von Mises and Hayek).[6] The latter had argued that a socialist economy could never have rational prices, and in particular could never have real stock and bond markets or markets for capital goods and natural resources. On the theoretical level, Lange's reply was effective to a degree. He showed that most markets could be simulated and that most rules for setting efficient prices could be followed in a socialist society. However, capital and resource markets must be restricted under socialism, as we argued in chapter 1. As a result, the value of most producing enterprises will be unknown. Since an investment is worthwhile over the long run if and only if it raises the value to society of the firm making the outlay, it is far from clear that Lange's system would generate enough information to allow an efficient allocation and use of investment funds, even if the central planners succeeded in keeping prices and interest rates close to levels that would balance supply and demand.

On a practical level, the Lange-Lerner system has further difficulties. The central planning authorities have an almost infinite number of prices to set. There is no mathematical guarantee that simultaneous trial-and-error adjustment of many different prices will ever converge to form a set that leaves all markets in equilibrium where supply equals demand. The result of such adjustment could be chaotic disequilibrium. Alternatively, the bureaucratic nature of centralized pricing could cause prices to remain fixed over long periods in the face of supply and demand shifts because they are costly to change. Either way, shortages and surpluses will abound, and the information content of prices will be low. The pricing of new products is apt to be especially difficult. If this is slow and comes to involve much red tape, the result will be to discourage innovation.

Questions also arise about the probable behavior of industry and enterprise managers, since the former have monopoly positions. In practice, a simple instruction to set prices equal to marginal costs is unlikely to be effective. To arouse their enthusiasm, the pay and promotion prospects of managers will have to depend on "success indicators," at least one of which is profit. Since managers will be able to figure out what rules govern price setting, they can use their market power to increase their profit by inducing the central authorities to set monopoly rather than competitive prices. To do this, they need only restrict supplies to monopoly output levels, causing shortages until monopoly price levels are reached. On balance, market socialism with decentralized pricing is likely to work better, but it is still subject to the problems outlined in chapter 1.

Workers' Management

A worker-managed firm is an enterprise whose professional management is responsible to elected representatives of its employees, much as it would be responsible to shareholder representatives of a conventional private enterprise. These elected representatives form a workers' council or board of directors that makes or at least ratifies the most basic decisions relating to production, investment, pricing, and distribution of profits. Except in small firms, these representatives hire professional managers to run the enterprise on a day-to-day basis. They do not try to manage directly, any more than they try to get along without other kinds of skilled and professional labor. The workers share in the firm's profits and losses and may or may not own shares in the enterprise. If they do, share prices must be fixed under socialism.

By giving employees control over the firm's destiny and by letting them share in its profits or losses, workers' management may stimulate their enthusiasm for work and take full advantage of the potential efficiency gains discussed in chapter 2. Proponents of industrial democracy sometimes contrast the initiative that it allows enterprises to take with the dependence of firms in a Soviet-type economy on their planning superiors. In addition, employees may be in a better position to supervise enterprise management than outside shareholders. Advocates of workers' management also argue that such a system makes major strides toward the age-old dream of a classless society by blurring traditional class distinctions among owners, managers, and workers. In giving employees more control over their conditions of work and over the nature of their products, advocates would hope to make work a more meaningful and creative extension of individual workers' lives and thus to reduce the alienation of the worker from production. Finally, socialist authors have often considered "democracy" in the management of firms by their employees to be a natural extension of political democracy. The same authors would generally not consider this to be true of "shareholder democracy," inasmuch as most shareholders wield little power and ownership of equity is highly concentrated in most capitalist economies.

Figure 6.1 **Wage Setting in a Worker-Managed Firm**

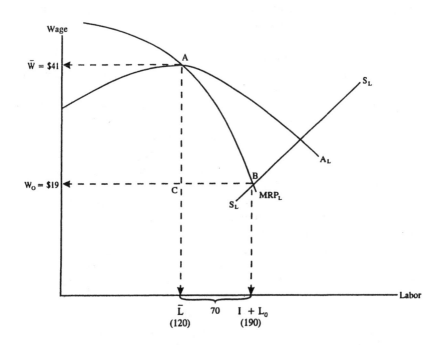

Offsetting these prospective gains, however, are potential efficiency losses resulting from employees' inability under socialism to claim future profits after leaving or retiring from the firm. The right to share profits from the current use of capital, but not to keep the proceeds from its sale, imposes a shortened time horizon, as in other kinds of socialist economies.[7] To overcome this, a labor-managed firm would have to offer long-term employment, a close identification between employees and their enterprise, and the expectation that their own and their families' prospects will depend on present and future evaluation of their contributions to company success. A second potential source of inefficiency arises from the tendency of such a firm to maximize profits per employee rather than total profits (since the employees will share profits and losses), while a third arises from the inability to specialize in risk bearing.

When a worker-managed firm maximizes profits per employee, it will seek a solution at A in Figure 6.1, which is similar to Figure 5.4.[8] In both figures, A_L gives the average net revenue product of labor, or the firm's total revenue minus nonlabor costs, divided by the number of workers. A_L therefore indexes the average productivity of labor and the wage-paying ability of the firm. As workers share profits and losses, A_L is the curve linking the wage that is paid to employment. The wage is maximized at A, regardless of whether the supply curve of labor to the firm is $S_L S_L$ or any other supply curve consistent with at least 120 workers being available at a compensation of $41. It follows that an economy filled with worker-managed firms may have widespread unemployment, since the wage is set without reference to labor supply, provided only that enough workers are available to reach the top of A_L.

In this context, when a firm is able to earn positive economic profit over and above its opportunity cost, it is more reluctant to expand by adding labor when it is maximizing profit per worker than when it is maximizing profit. In the latter case, it adds an employee whenever he or she can increase profit by any amount. However, a worker-managed firm will add an employee only when he or she can increase (or at least not decrease) the previous average profit per employee, and therefore only when the new worker adds an amount to profit at least as great as this previous average. Such a firm will therefore be more capital intensive and produce less output with less labor than a capitalist firm facing similar cost and demand conditions. By contrast, with free entry and exit—and therefore zero economic profit in long-run equilibrium—the two firms will supply the same output with the same labor force. In this case, the worker-managed firm would still operate at A in Figure 6.1, but A_L would be lower and tangent to a horizontal supply curve of labor at A. (Greater competition means a lower maximum wage, and the supply curve of labor must not pass below or entirely above A_L if economic profit is zero.)

Efficiency of workers' management therefore depends on competition and efficient financial markets that channel savings into the best investment alternatives available. These are necessary to ensure low unemployment and efficient output levels, as well as to guard against variations in profitability from firm to firm that are unrelated to variations in enterprise efficiency. There is also a danger of inelastic (or nearly vertical) product supply curves, and even of supply curves that are backward bending. Suppose the product demand curve facing the enterprise in Figure 6.1 shifts upward. In response, the firm may simply raise prices and wages, and it could even cut output and employment in the short run. While the A_L curve shifts upward, its peak (initially at A) does not necessarily shift forward, and it could just as easily remain above $L = 120$ or move backward.[9] Over the long run, the firm will respond to a permanent upward shift in demand by adding capital, and possibly labor, but it will still make larger increases in prices and wages and smaller increases in output than would a profit-maximizing firm facing the same conditions. The reason, once again, is that it is more reluctant to expand employment when it can earn positive economic profit.

All this makes it doubly important to have efficient financial markets, together with free entry and exit, as the primary means of ensuring output expansion and contraction in response to shifts in demand, as well as low unemployment and efficient output levels. By the same token, a failure to build such markets or to keep entry barriers low, for reasons outlined in chapter 1, would impose costs that would be potentially high. In Yugoslavia, the only socialist market economy in practice, investment decisions were not very responsive to rate-of-return criteria, and the antimonopoly law was never enforced. One way to obtain further expansion of employment and output would be to allow wage discrimination based on seniority, although this would risk creating two categories of workers analogous to insiders and outsiders. The reason for not expanding from $L = 120$ to $L = 190$ in Figure 6.1—where the marginal revenue product curve cuts $S_L S_L$—is that this would require the firm to spread its net revenue over more workers, thereby lowering the wage of each.

The firm can overcome this by setting two wages—$19 for low-seniority workers and a higher wage for high-seniority employees. If the MRP_L curve gives the addition to the firm's total net revenue of each additional worker, the firm can increase its total net revenue by the area under this curve between A and B if it expands its workforce from 120 to 190. After paying $19 in wages to each new hire, the enterprise has an amount left over equal to area ABC. By sharing this, high-seniority workers can increase their wage above $41.00.[10] In this way, the flexibility afforded by wage discrimination can eliminate unemployment and any tendency to produce less than a profit-maximizing firm, but we now have two categories of workers. If qualified low-seniority employees always move up the seniority ladder to higher wages later on, there is no obvious conflict with the notion of a classless society. But if some employees found this climb to be unduly difficult or impossible, a permanent underclass could result, leading to a class distinction reminiscent of capitalism, since both higher earnings and control over the enterprise would go to the high-seniority employees (or insiders).

In this context, a worker-managed firm is by its nature an enforced risk-sharing agreement among its employees, whose pay depends on its profits and losses because of profit sharing. Each worker automatically absorbs part of the risk of its business operations, no matter how risk averse he or she may be. It is not possible, as under private ownership, for some individuals (the owners) to specialize in risk bearing by agreeing to be residual claimants to enterprise income, while others work for wages that are largely independent of profitability. Neither is it possible for employees to diversify away part of this risk, since their claims to profits and losses are not transferable. Reluctance to share risk internally could lead to external risk sharing between the firm and the rest of society via the soft budget constraint, as was the case in Yugoslavia. It could also reinforce the distinction between insiders and outsiders and/or make the distinctions in this system more like class distinctions under capitalism.

A potential problem with any socialist society is that it may discourage entrepreneurship, inasmuch as venture capital is apt to be in short supply and there will be constraints on the ability to earn profits from a new venture. Under workers' management, the entrepreneur has to persuade the firm's more risk-averse employees to go along with his or her investment proposals, which may require a greater sharing of profits than of losses. This lowers the return on entrepreneurship. Efforts to get around this by reducing the circle of profit sharing from among the firm's employees and/or by expanding it to include suppliers of risk capital who are not employees would alter the nature of workers' management and make it more like capitalism.[11]

Finally, workers' management may lead to greater equality than many types of capitalism. However, a source of inequality in both systems is the probable dispersion of profitability from one firm to another (unless the soft budget constraint operates under workers' management). Some enterprises will succeed spectacularly, many more will fail, and most will fall at various points between these extremes. A major consideration in gaining a good trade-off between efficiency and equity is that capital markets should allocate savings to the best investment opportunities available. If some firms are saturated with capital, while others are starved for funds, and still others fail to get started because of entry barriers or lack of access to start-up capital, we will have neither efficiency nor equity, since income per worker tends to increase with capital per worker. Unfortunately, capital markets are not likely to work well under the constraints of socialism, and experience in Yugoslavia also suggests that eliminating class distinctions will not be easy. There representatives of blue-collar workers took little interest in the details of management, accounting, finance, or engineering, which continued to be the province of specialists. Instead labor representatives concentrated on traditional blue-collar issues of wages, benefits, and working conditions.[12]

Against these criticisms of workers' management, we have the potential advantages indicated at the outset of our discussion of this topic. But these now seem to be more an argument for laws that allow workers' management to exist, and perhaps that encourage it, than for laws that ban other forms of enterprise organization and ownership. Workers' management is no cure for society's basic economic ills, but there may well be types of economic activity in which it has a comparative advantage. The same is true of other cooperatives, notably credit unions and retail consumer co-ops, that are found in nearly all market economies.

Efforts to Reform Soviet-type Economies

As of the mid-1980s, communist parties controlled the governments of seventeen countries—the Soviet Union, China, Cambodia, Vietnam, Laos, North Korea, Cuba, Yugoslavia, Albania, Mongolia, Hungary, Bulgaria, Romania, Poland, Czechoslovakia, the German Democratic Republic, and Afghanistan—with about a third of the world's population. Of these, only Yugoslavia was not basically a Soviet-type economy where her industrial sector was concerned, although China had already carried out a successful decollectivization of agriculture (and would be followed by Vietnam), and Hungary had taken several steps toward a market economy. By the mid-1990s, only Cuba and North Korea remained Soviet-type economies, this even though the Communist Party continued to rule in China and Vietnam. The Soviet Union and Yugoslavia had split along ethnic seams, and Afghanistan was still torn by civil war, but with the Communist Party no longer a serious contender for power.

The revolutionary changes of 1989–90 could almost make us forget that efforts to reform Soviet-type economies had begun nearly thirty years earlier. In the Soviet Union itself, official interest in reform sparked a famous article in *Pravda,* the Communist Party newspaper, by Yevsei Liberman as early as September 9, 1962.[13] Entitled "The Plan, Profits, and Bonuses," it called for decentralization of some decisions down to the level of the enterprise, as well as more prominent use of profitability as a success indicator and an end to the "petty tutelage" of firms by their ministries. Liberman also advocated making goods acceptable to users before allowing them to count toward plan fulfillment. Despite charges in the West that he was "borrowing from capitalism," his primary goal was to improve state planning and management. Liberman wanted to base managerial bonuses on profitability. However, he would award no bonuses unless a firm achieved specific output targets—determined, as before, by its planning superiors, although with the "active participation" of the enterprise—and delivered its goods on schedule to users or to the state wholesale network.

In this way, the center would keep control of the "main levers" of planning and continue to chart the basic direction of economic growth. It would also retain financial control and control over major investments. Firms would become responsible for many lesser investments and would receive greater freedom to determine labor and materials inputs. Indeed, the enterprise was to set *all* its own targets—relating to inputs, investment, costs, productivity, and new technology, in addition to profits—with the exception of its output plan.

The idea was to motivate firms to become enthusiastic, reliable participants in plan formation and to do away with their tendency to "meet with fixed bayonets" all suggestions that their plan targets be "improved." Firms would no longer hoard, conceal, or waste scarce inputs, Liberman reasoned, or refuse to introduce new technology, because profitability would suffer. To motivate firms to set realistic profit targets, he proposed that, if an enterprise failed to reach its target, it should receive a bonus geared to actual profitability. However, if it overfulfilled its target, it would receive a bonus geared to the average of its actual and target profit rates. For example, if a firm were to achieve 15 percent profitability when its target was 10 percent, it would receive an incentive payment based on 12.5 percent. If its actual rate of profit were 8 percent, it would get a bonus based on 8 percent.

If we pursue Liberman's proposals to their logical conclusion, they suggest a mixture of plan and market. Every firm's first obligation is to the state, but its output targets should normally be within its capacity to produce. Above-plan production is to be guided by profitability, although it is unclear just how much freedom of choice the enterprise would have. If its planning superiors were sufficiently favorable toward reform, an official system of markets would arise on which above-plan production would be bought and sold. At least limited competition would exist here, along with some right to choose buyers and suppliers. These markets would ideally give free rein to the initiative of the enterprises, bring all their hidden reserves into production, and fill gaps in the official supply network.

In short, official markets would do everything that the second economy did and more, since they would operate in the open. But whether they could actually play this role would depend on the attitude of the planners toward reform, as Liberman realized. Two dangers are that prices would continue to be rigid and that output targets would continue to be raised aggressively on the basis of current performance. The unofficial nature of the second economy meant that most transactions there went unrecorded by state authorities. The threat that planners would begin to record them and then tighten enterprise plan targets in consequence would probably have been enough to dry up much of the second economy supply.

Within the ranks of East European economists urging reform in the 1960s, Liberman occupied a middle ground. On one side was a group advocating market socialism, and on the other a group that wished to centralize economic decisions by programming the economy on a phalanx of computers. The latter included L.V. Kantorovich, inventor of linear programming and co-Nobel laureate in economics for 1975. In this crowd, Liberman was no radical, and some of his proposals were adopted in the context of the Chinese reforms many years later. At the time, however, they met the same fate as would many other reform proposals in the two decades to follow. The official Soviet reforms, announced by Premier Alexei Kosygin in September 1965, did not go as far as Liberman had recommended, and even most of these were rolled back without fanfare in subsequent years. By 1985, it is not clear that directors of state firms in the Soviet Union had any more independence in practice than they had already achieved before the Kosygin reforms.[14] A 1970 cartoon in *Krokodil,* the Soviet humor magazine, showed office workers fleeing while their desks, chairs, lamps, wastebaskets, and telephones were being swept away by a tidal wave of "valued instructions of our ministry."[15]

Reasons for Reform Efforts and Reform Failure

Pressures to decentralize Soviet-type economies were rooted in the inefficiencies of such a system, described above in chapters 1 and 2, and in political struggles within the various communist parties. Given the desire of these governments for rapid economic growth, a critical weakness of command planning was its inability to generate intensive growth and its consequent reliance on increases in inputs, mainly capital after 1960, to generate increases in output.

Returning to Figure 2.3, suppose again that a Soviet-type economy is moving upward along path T_1 because it is able to expand its stock of industrial capital more rapidly than its industrial labor force. (A major reason for this was the disappearance of the transferable farm labor surplus.) The slope of this path is a measure of the yield on investment—specifically, the average increase in output resulting from a given net investment or increase in the capital stock. As the economy moves up T_1, the yield on investment, so defined, eventually begins to fall (in the vicinity of A) owing to the law of diminishing returns. Since Soviet-type economies also followed energy- and resource-intensive strategies of growth, rising costs of fuel or of basic raw materials will reinforce this decline. In the vicinity of B, the curve becomes nearly flat, signifying that the yield is close to zero. Further increases in capital will not, by themselves, create much additional output.

If we take the rate of profit to be the yield on investment, Figure 2.3 shows a socialist version of Marx's "falling rate of profit." At first, socialist nations reacted to falling yields by increasing investment in an effort to maintain growth, but eventually they had to give this up because of the negative effect on consumption. Falling investment yields also increased inflationary pressures, because the net tax contribution (taxes minus subsidies) of the enterprise sector depended on its profitability. Decreases in profitability resulting from falling investment yields created or increased budget deficits, which were covered almost entirely by expanding the money supply. As a result, shortages also increased, and households in some of these countries withdrew labor from production in order to spend more time obtaining goods. Together with other disruptions caused by the increases in excess demand, this helped to turn stagnation into absolute decreases in output. Preoccupation by the authorities with maintaining production may also have contributed to the environmental disasters caused by industrial production in every Soviet-type economy.

As early as the mid-1960s, the era of rapid extensive growth appeared to be drawing to a close in several socialist countries.[16] The arrows in Table 6.2 show the growth declines that contributed to decisions to decentralize in the Soviet Union, Hungary, and East Germany at that time. These were reinforced by decisions to raise the relative priorities of light industry and agriculture in order to give a break to the consumer and because investment yields were falling most rapidly in heavy industry. On balance, the need to generate more intensive growth was the main reason for the original reforms and for their renewal in the late 1970s or 1980s—in Hungary, Poland, Bulgaria, and the Soviet Union itself. Reform renewal also followed growth slowdowns that are shown in Table 6.2.

We may draw a limited analogy between the growth of a Soviet-type economy and the growth of a firm in a market economy. When the company is small, its top management will be heavily involved in the details of day-to-day operations. But as the firm becomes larger and more complex, individual managers will specialize. Top management will progressively unburden itself of most of the technical content of everyday business decisions in order to concentrate on designing and implementing the grand strategy of the company's evolution. The

Table 6.2

Per Capita Growth Rates in Eastern Europe (annual averages)

	Western estimate (gross national product)	Official (net material product)
East Germany		
1950–55	7.6%	13.7%
1955–60	5.8	8.0
1960–65	3.0	→3.7
1965–70	3.2	5.2
1970–75	3.8	5.7
1975–80	2.5	4.0
1980–85	1.8	4.6
Hungary		
1950–55	4.4%	4.7%
1955–60	3.5	5.5
1960–65	3.9	→3.7
1965–70	2.7	6.3
1970–75	3.0	5.9
1975–80	1.9	2.5
1980–85	1.3	1.3
Soviet Union		
1950–55	4.3%	9.6%
1955–60	4.0	7.5
1960–65	3.1	→5.0
1965–70	3.9	6.8
1970–75	2.1	4.8
1975–80	1.4	3.5
1980–85	1.1	2.7

Sources: Statistical Yearbooks of countries above (for net material product).

firm will also decentralize internally as it grows larger. Until the 1980s, socialist reform movements also produced mainly technical changes in organization, which allowed greater specialization and division of labor and better use of available resources within the planning hierarchy. The top planners tried to unburden themselves of detail in order to concentrate more on the basic strategy of economic development.

In between, ministries and other intermediate-level planners perceived the greatest threats to their authority and status to be from reforms that would increase the role of market allocation. Consequently, they resisted such reforms and were able to ally with enterprise managers and party secretaries resisting the wider responsibilities, greater risks, and competitive pressures threatened by decentralization. Inside the party, it was hard to develop a constituency with a vested interest in marketization, which would have deprived state and party officials of control over supplies of scarce goods and resources. Thus each reform that tried to raise enterprise autonomy generated a counter-reform of recentralization. As a result, state enterprises received little or no permanent increase in their autonomy. Permanent decentralization was difficult or impossible to bring about. We may even be tempted to apply the Marxian theory of history. To wit, vanishing opportunities for extensive growth make a command economy less efficient relative to the potential of a competitive market system, which provides a better environment for innovation. However, a bureaucratic elite, fearing an erosion of its status and power, resists basic changes in socioeconomic relations, although it does allow some tinkering with the system.

The growth recovery after 1965 in the Soviet Union and in Eastern Europe was due less to reform than to continuing high rates of investment, together with accelerated technology transfer from the West. The latter accompanied détente and the general expansion of East-West relations during the 1970s, but it also ran into problems resulting from a lack of demand orientation on the part of socialist recipients. For example, East European officials made a number of mistakes in deciding which specific technologies to import, and their systems had difficulty absorbing the associated capital and integrating it with the rest of the economy. Neither were they able to develop manufacturing export sectors capable of paying for a continuing flow of imports and technology from the West. Therefore, their hard-currency indebtedness rose dramatically. By the late 1970s, growth had again slowed in the wake of the second energy crisis. With the decline of détente and the reduced willingness to lend to Eastern Europe, the intelligence services of the Soviet Union and other COMECON (Council for Mutual Economic Assistance) nations became preoccupied with industrial espionage.

Moreover, there was a growing tendency to view technology transfer as complementary to rather than as a substitute for internal decentralization. Whereas many socialist officials believed in the 1970s that détente could partly substitute for reform aimed at expanding the role of markets, thinking during the 1980s moved closer to the position that reform and détente should go hand in hand to allow socialist countries to gain the greatest benefit from technology transfer. Technological advances in microelectronics, microbiology, robotization, and other high-technology sectors reinforced this view. These advances created more flexible manufacturing processes, spawned a range of sophisticated products, and broke down traditional barriers in market economies between design, marketing, and production. One of their impacts has been to make possible the automation of multiproduct manufacturing in small batches at low unit cost, and thus to reduce product standardization, while increasing the importance of independent judgment in the workplace. By using computers to retool, a flexible assembly line can turn out small quantities of many different products and models without sacrificing scale economies. As a result, suppliers can better satisfy demand and adjust to changes more readily and at lower cost.

By contrast, in chapter 2 we pointed out that the ability to standardize products and production processes and to routinize work effort was a major ingredient of the Industrial Revolution. Subsequent development of continuous-flow "pipeline" production, culminating in the modern assembly line, pushed standardization, routinization, and simplification of work effort further. It created production systems with large economies of scale, but with built-in rigidities, that are sharply limited in their ability to handle product variety and variability. (For example, Henry Ford once took a year to convert his main factory from production of the Model T to the Model A. With a modern, flexible system, he could have produced both models simultaneously in small quantities while keeping unit costs close to their achievable minima.) In retrospect, Soviet-type economies seem almost designed for these older, more rigid, and standardized production processes, with their larger scale economies. The trend toward flexible systems, as well as the rise of the service sector and of modern high-technology industries, increased the comparative efficiency of market vis-à-vis state-managed economies and helped to turn the latter into dinosaurs of the industrial era.

Nevertheless, progress in increasing enterprise autonomy continued to be slow during the 1980s, as in previous decades, for five basic reasons. First, ministries and other state agencies were reluctant to give up direct control over economic activity and often took advantage of opportunities to recentralize. Second, they were helped in this by a frequent unwillingness of enterprise directors to take initiatives or to assume wider responsibilities for selling goods, procuring supplies, and obtaining financing—especially in competition with other firms. Because of their political ties, many of these directors survived and even prospered. Members of party and state bureaucracies (including enterprise executives) that managed Soviet-type economies belonged to informal networks of mutual self-help and support based ultimately on loyalty. These networks involved continuing exchanges of favors, promotions, and job perquisites on an individualized basis. Such relations were crucial to career success, but they would not easily have survived a shift to anonymous prices and a tax subsidy system that treats firms in a uniform way, since the individuals involved were not chosen because of managerial competence in a competitive environment. Market-oriented reforms threatened such networks, and the ties that bind within them continue to frustrate reform efforts well into the transition period of the 1990s.

Third, there was reluctance within the party—and to a degree within society at large—both to loosen guarantees of job security and full employment and to accept income differences based on differential contributions to enterprise profitability. For many, this was "unsocialist." As well, underemployment within the firm continued to substitute for open unemployment. This has limited the emphasis on profitability or cost effectiveness, again well into the 1990s, because of the threat of increased unemployment. At least within the state sector, a redistribution mentality also tended to compress income differences. In particular, there was a continuing redistribution from profitable to unprofitable firms (the soft enterprise budget constraint), and the state was reluctant to punish managers for poor financial results. To protect the return on its investment, it therefore continued to supervise enterprises rather closely and to stay involved in their management. The state also had to maintain quantitative controls on investment, since the soft budget constraint inflated enterprise investment demand by insulating firms and bank branches from risk of losses on projects undertaken.

Because of irrational, below-equilibrium prices, it was also hard to use profitability or any simple financial index to judge enterprise performance. One firm's profits or another's losses often reflected comparative pricing distortions to a greater extent than comparative efficiency. This is the fourth factor. In addition, rigid, below-equilibrium prices preserved excess demand after reform was under way. This prevented markets from allocating goods or resources. Firms therefore had to depend on their planning superiors for access to inputs, which helped to pave the way for recentralization. Following reform, state agencies increased their output demands on subordinate enterprises—instead of giving them breathing space to adapt to the new rules—which tended to increase shortages and consequent disruptions.

Finally, setting plans from the achieved level discouraged firms from producing beyond what was mandated by their short-term plans. It helped to make enterprise supply curves inelastic. The soft budget constraint and the lack of independent initiative on the part of enterprise directors reinforced this low elasticity of supply. They ensured that, when freed, prices would rise by more (and would subsequently be more volatile in response to shifts in demand) than if firms increased output enthusiastically in response to price increases (or generally moved along elastic output supply curves). This helped to prevent prices from being freed.[17] An East European official once remarked that, after the worldwide revolution to establish socialism, a single capitalist nation would have to remain. "For otherwise, how would we know at what prices to trade?" We may understand this as a comment not only on the irrational nature of prices in Soviet-type economies but also on the difficulty of price reform.

We can illustrate some of the above problems with the aid of Figure 6.2. Suppose a reform reduces the number of input quotas and output targets received by firms as part of an effort to decentralize economic decisions. Prior to the 1990s, the number of targets and quotas was almost never reduced to zero; in this sense, reforms were only partial. Moreover, although revisions to move prices closer to equilibrium levels often accompanied reforms, the new prices remained rigid afterward, and generally below supply-demand equilibria, preserving excess demand. Therefore, following reform, let D_1 and S be the demand for and supply of an industrial input whose production is no longer governed by output targets and whose distribution is no longer governed by input quotas. In a full-

208

Figure 6.2 Price Control and Reform Failure

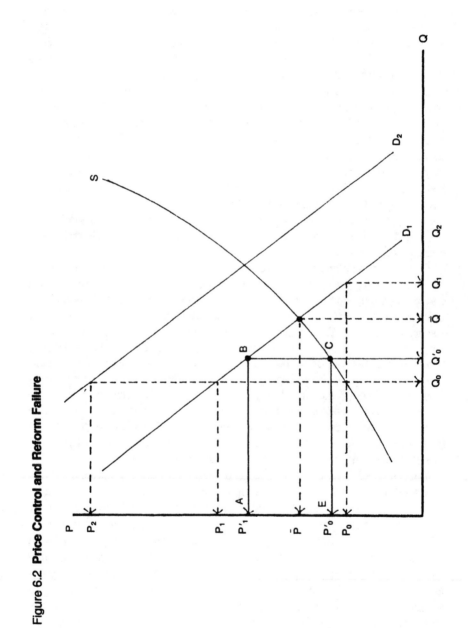

fledged market, the equilibrium price would be $\bar{P}$, which balances demand and supply at $\bar{Q}$. Access to the good would then depend solely on ability and willingness to pay $\bar{P}$ per unit. However, the government of a Soviet-type economy would maintain a lower ceiling at P_0, where quantity supplied is Q_0. Not only would there be a shortage, but the price users would be willing to pay for Q_0 units would be P_1, higher than $\bar{P}$ (and P_0).

In an earlier discussion (chapter 1), we suggested that users will end up paying an average "price" above $\bar{P}$, when all costs of obtaining the good or of going without it because of excess demand are taken into account. Besides P_0, these costs include payments (favors, gifts, bribes, surcharges, etc.) to persuade buyers to supply one potential customer rather than or before another, costs of hiring purchasing agents or expediters (*tolkachi*) to obtain the good, any other costs of searching out scarce supplies, costs of holding up production when supplies arrive late, costs of quality or design defects owing to the sellers' market, and others. Some of these are forms of hidden price increase, so that the effective price received by suppliers rises to P_0', causing quantity supplied to expand to Q_0'. However, not all the above costs paid by buyers are actually transferred to suppliers, and those that are represent relatively inefficient ways of paying for the good. Therefore, the effective price paid by users is above P_0' —indeed above $\bar{P}$—for example, at P_1. The area ABCE represents a waste to society, since it denotes costs borne by users of the good that do not benefit producers.

Under the usual system of allocation by quotas in a Soviet-type economy, the costs created by the scarcity of industrial inputs were mainly borne by low-priority producers as residual claimants to state-controlled supplies. To an enterprise director, "high priority" meant priority in access to inputs. The higher the priority of a firm's output, the better its access to scarce supplies through official channels at low, state-controlled prices and the more it or its downstream customers were hurt by price increases. Low-priority producers were more active in procuring inputs through unofficial channels (the second economy). When formal rationing was removed or relaxed (but official price ceilings remained), they were often able to take advantage of these contacts to improve their access, and they were also better able to compete for inputs whose prices rose unofficially. Low-priority products were usually more profitable to produce because of their historic role, under command planning, of generating savings to finance investment in high-priority (heavy) industry.

By contrast, high-priority producers would find their supply situations deteriorating. In place of their former good access at low prices, they now had to queue and to compete with other users for scarce supplies. This made their own output targets harder to reach, which was also a signal to planners to increase their intervention in the economy. Managers of firms in trouble often appealed for more detailed plans in order to raise their priority in receiving supplies. By requiring more ambitious growth, state agencies helped to generate such appeals.

The effect of this requirement was to increase the demand for nonrationed inputs—for instance, from D_1 to D_2 in Figure 6.2—which increased shortages. Sooner or later, missed targets and bottlenecks in high-priority sectors then threatened to lead to costly disruption or plan failure, triggering recentralization. Following reform, the most favorable action the planners could take to preserve decentralization was to relax their demands for economic growth for a time, so that prices would stay closer to equilibrium levels and everyone would have a chance to adjust to the new system. As indicated, the reactions of state authorities to reform were often just the reverse.

When Communist Party control over Eastern Europe and the former Soviet Union finally ended during 1989–90, the preceding quarter century of reform frustration probably helped to ensure that market socialism would not be seen as a viable option. The question of how (not whether) to privatize thousands of state enterprises quickly became the major issue facing transition economies. Reformers believed that marketization could not occur as long as the state controlled the fate of most major industrial enterprises, and that independence from state control was possible only through privatization. As it turned out, privatization alone did not ensure independence, and persistence of the soft budget constraint prevented efficient financial markets from arising. In turn, this increased dependence on foreign investment to generate growth and technological advance. Before turning to these issues, we shall briefly look at the Soviet Union's final effort at reform, which had the unintended consequence of ending Communist Party rule and dismembering the country.

Perestroika[18]

The end of the Brezhnev era, 1964–82, in the Soviet Union brought a renewed willingness to experiment with economic reform. A new faction of the Communist Party, represented first by Yuri Andropov and later by Mikhail Gorbachev, came to power. These leaders were convinced that significant change was necessary to save the existing economic and political system. By the start of the Tenth Five-Year Plan (1976–80), Soviet growth was stagnating as never before in peacetime, and stagnation continued through the Eleventh Plan (1981–85). This was the context in which Mikhail Gorbachev came to power, in March 1985, following the deaths of Leonid Brezhnev, Yuri Andropov, and Konstantine Chernenko, over the preceding two and a third years.

In presenting ambitious targets for economic growth during the Twelfth Five-Year Plan, 1986–90, and the 1990s, Gorbachev promised a new approach that would switch the economy from extensive to intensive growth. The targets themselves demanded as much, since they could be reached only with major productivity gains. In particular, net material product per capita was to grow by an annual average of 4 percent from 1986 to 2000 versus less than 3.7 percent during the previous fifteen years (Table 6.2). The fall of world energy prices in

1985–86 increased the pressure for improved performance, since natural gas and oil were accounting for 75 to 80 percent of Soviet exports to OECD nations.

The new strategy called for modernization, reduction of waste and inefficiency, and major increases in food output. The main vehicle for achieving these goals was to be a limited but comprehensive reform of economic planning and management, known as *perestroika* or "restructuring," which was passed into law in mid-1987. It sought to go further than previous reforms in the Soviet Union, although in some respects it recalled Liberman's proposals. Gorbachev began by replacing many key government and party officials, which brought his supporters into positions of power and control. Within government, political reform led to contested elections and livelier debate (although not to an end of the Communist Party's leading role), as well as to some decentralization of authority to regional levels, especially the Soviet Union's fifteen constituent union republics. This allowed some republics, including the Baltic states, to proceed more rapidly with reform, but also started the Soviet Union down the road to political dismemberment, which turned each republic into an independent nation in 1992. Gorbachev also aroused hostility by promising to eliminate the special schools, stores, and hospitals for the Communist Party elite. Here quality and availability were well above the norms for other Soviet citizens.

The key economic reform sought to give enterprise managers more rights to determine what to produce and how, as well as to choose among customers and suppliers, to hire and fire workers, and to set prices and wages. Most short-run and many investment decisions were to be transferred to enterprises, along with greater retention rights over profits, losses, and depreciation. Thus greater use rights over capital were to go hand in hand with greater income rights. The state would continue to control much of heavy industry, as well as the basic direction of growth and the division of national income between consumption, defense, and investment. It would also retain responsibility for ensuring plan fulfillment and continue to exercise some control over pricing, as well as enterprise taxation and use of profits.

Firms were also supposed to accept more responsibilities—for marketing products, obtaining supplies and financing, negotiating all types of contracts, maintaining good labor relations, and continually improving products and production methods. Above all, Soviet leaders wanted state firms to shed much of their dependence on government, including their dependence on subsidies. The enterprise budget constraint was to harden, and a new State Enterprise Law provided for bankruptcy and for liquidation of firms that repeatedly made losses, as well as for retraining and reemploying their workers. In all, the reforms threatened some sixteen million jobs as a result of efforts to cut costs and to reduce the role of state planning agencies. To reduce pricing distortions, another major price revision was begun. Enterprises were to divide their retained earnings into three funds: an investment fund, a fund to finance housing and social benefits, and a bonus fund. One purpose was to tie earnings more closely to performance, as measured by profitability, although in fact firms used their new authority over wages to raise them in excess of productivity gains. This increased excess demand and the state budget deficit, since taxes depended on enterprise profits. A centrally decreed increase in earnings on the order of 20 percent also took place from 1987 to 1990, along with a widening of pay differentials that reversed the trend to greater equality over most of the post–World War II era. Moreover, as supplies of consumer goods did not increase, wage gains actually reduced welfare, since goods became harder than ever for ordinary people to obtain.

As noted earlier, efforts to increase enterprise autonomy and to expand the role of markets in a Soviet-type economy encounter widespread resistance. To have a reasonable chance of success, reform must proceed simultaneously along two tracks. First, decentralization must begin within the state-run sector of the economy, and here Gorbachev launched the programs indicated above. On January 1, 1988, firms producing 60 percent of Soviet industrial output gained limited freedom to make production and investment decisions and to choose customers and/or suppliers. In most sectors, enterprises were supposed to receive fewer production targets (which were renamed "state orders"), and state agencies were supposed to prepare fewer materials balances, generally at more aggregated levels. A limited wholesale market was to come into existence to partly replace state management of interenterprise exchange, and planners were to begin concentrating more on the basic strategy of economic development.

However, this reform became bogged down. Party and state agencies maintained most of their former control over firms, just as they had done twenty years earlier in defiance of the Kosygin reforms. Decontrol of prices was also put off for fear of the social and political consequences of resulting price increases. From 1987 to 1991, shortages rose dramatically, although open inflation (amid deteriorating economic conditions) was also high beginning in 1990. The soft budget constraint was at least as soft as in the Brezhnev era, and the bankruptcy/liquidation provisions of the State Enterprise Law were never used.

A reform of the banking system was also begun, and firms were supposed to receive limited rights to issue shares. Eventually loans were to replace most budget grants for investment as part of an effort to allocate funds more rationally. An overhaul of the tax system was begun with the intention of bringing it closer to Western norms. Finally, employees gained the right to elect enterprise directors and other members of the firm's management, generally for five-year terms, although subject to approval by the firm's planning superior. Employees also elected a labor council with powers to oversee management and to make decisions directly on labor-related issues.

Additional changes brought a new approach to foreign trade and Western investment in the Soviet Union, plus an expansion of the agricultural reforms begun by Gorbachev's predecessors. Collective and state farms received greater decision-making autonomy, with the eventual aim of decollectivizing agriculture along the lines indicated later in this chapter. In foreign trade, twenty ministries plus seventy large associations and enterprises (covering more than 4,000 enterprises in all) received the legal right to buy and sell on their own in Western and developing countries at the start of 1987. These entities were required to balance their own accounts in convertible currencies, which is to say that each had to earn at least as much as it spent abroad. The state wanted to tax but not subsidize convertible currency receipts. Beginning in April 1989, virtually every Soviet state and cooperative firm gained the right to engage in foreign trade, subject to this constraint, although the number allowed to do so in practice remained relatively small. The Soviet government also devalued the ruble and announced its intention of achieving eventual convertibility.

To help implement the expanded trading rights (plus the hoped-for expansion of foreign trade), the government made it easier for Western companies to invest in the Soviet Union—notably, in the form of joint equity ventures with Soviet partners and in other forms of cooperation in production and research. Previously, the Soviet Union had not allowed Western firms to own shares of enterprises operating on its soil, and the Western partner was initially limited to 49 percent ownership, although this constraint was subsequently dropped. To make such investment more attractive, as well as to promote exports, the Soviet Union also planned several special economic (or free trade) zones within which all import and export duties would be waived for joint ventures and wholly foreign-owned firms. No customs clearance was to be required for exports from these zones, although permission would be necessary if enterprises within them wanted to sell in the Soviet Union. More than 3,000 joint ventures were established with companies from more than seventy countries, although fewer than 40 percent of these became operational and the total value of Western investment was quite small, owing to insecure property rights for Western investors and political uncertainty. The real value of loans by Western banks to the Soviet Union also increased by several times in comparison with the pre-Gorbachev era.

The second reform track involves the sector of private and cooperative firms operating outside the state hierarchy. This is the second economy, which is largely subject to the market. Successful reform requires it to expand faster than the economy as a whole, and to gain rights to compete with state-owned firms. Because the second economy was poorly represented within the Communist Party, however, the latter step was politically difficult to take. In agriculture, Andropov had begun to implement the "brigade method," according to which farm households or other small work groups could contract with the state to carry out specialized tasks, such as raising poultry or livestock, growing vegetables, tending fruit trees, or providing fodder. These households or work groups received the profit or loss from their own activities instead of having to share the profit residual of a much larger organization (the collective or state farm). In some cases, collective or state land was leased to households whose members farmed the acreage allotted them on their own account.

Regulations announced in August 1988 were designed to end compulsory collectivization of Soviet agriculture by extending this system to most farm families. The land would remain in public ownership, with peasants taking out long-term leases. On paper the system resembled that in China, where agricultural reforms during the early 1980s restored family farming and led to a large increase in food production. Private farmers also gained the legal right to buy tractors, trucks, and other means of production, as well as to use hired labor, as long as they did not pay wages below those on state farms. However, this reform failed. In most places, collectivization continues to exist in 1996, and prospects for a Chinese-style leap forward in food production are remote on most of the territory of the former Soviet Union.

On May 1, 1987, Soviet citizens also received rights to go into business on their own in light manufacturing (mainly consumer goods) and services. It remained illegal for private firms to hire outside labor, which limited such enterprises to household or family undertakings. Private citizens also found it easier to jointly establish cooperatives, however, again mainly in light industry and services, including banking. These firms were subject to the market (and to hard budget constraints), but they were allowed to lease state equipment and facilities, including factory space. As in China, many of them became de facto private firms. In 1991, there were 270,000 cooperatives employing some 5.2 million workers. Only one huge state enterprise was privatized prior to the collapse of the Soviet Union. This was the Kamaz truck factory, which became the property of its 170,000 employees, as well (subsequently) as of its suppliers, customers, and other investors.

The new laws on private and cooperative firms legalized much activity that had been going on illegally or on the margin of legality. The latter occupied at least twenty million people in repair work and other services, most of whom also held regular state jobs. They dwarfed the number of legal permits issued for private businesses. Therefore, it is unclear how much real expansion of the market sector actually took place prior to the collapse of the Soviet Union at the end of 1991. Under Brezhnev, enforcement of laws against private and cooperative production had been relaxed, and a substantial expansion of this sector is believed to have occurred. Gorbachev also launched campaigns against alcoholism, corruption, incompetence, inefficiency, absenteeism from work, and poor work discipline. The first of these expanded the second economy, as local moonshiners compensated for reduced official output of alcoholic beverages, while the other measures restricted black and gray markets by increasing the penalties for illegal operations and making it harder to moonlight. Subsequently, the campaign against alcoholism was toned down, and state production of alcoholic beverages was partially restored. By driving production underground, the campaign had caused a major decrease in tax revenue, which had helped to increase the budget deficit to dangerous heights and to make the economy dysfunctional.

Concluding Comments: The Outcome of Perestroika

In the final analysis, Gorbachev's reforms achieved a greater decentralization of income than of use rights over capital to state enterprises. A strong central planning bureaucracy remained intact, along with price rigidity and excess demand, until the system began to fall apart in 1990 and 1991. Soviet government agencies continued to have responsibility for ensuring plan fulfillment, along with powers to intervene as necessary to carry out this task. They retained responsibility for long-run growth and technological improvement, and they gained specific rights to countervail monopolistic tendencies by enterprises.

In these conditions, the Gorbachev reforms achieved modest gains in industrial output during 1986 through 1989, followed by a decrease in 1990 and an 8 percent decline in 1991, according to official statistics, which were almost certainly overly optimistic. Total factor productivity—or real GNP per unit of combined labor, capital, and resource input—which had been falling between 1976 and 1985, continued its downward trend. Greater income rights for enterprises allowed them to pay higher wages and lower taxes, both of which increased the government budget deficit. The latter rose from 2.7 percent of GNP in 1985 to 8 percent in 1987, 13 percent in 1989, and over 19 percent in 1991. The acceleration of the arms race initiated by the United States in this period also played a role in the state's growing inability to finance its outlays with tax revenue.

Because bond markets scarcely existed, almost the entire deficit had to be covered by money supply expansion, which increased inflationary pressures. Open inflation remained low until 1990, but shortages escalated until the value of excess demand was thirty times as great in 1988 as it had been in 1970. Households reallocated their time away from producing goods toward efforts to obtain goods, as noted earlier, and they also hoarded. Each of these activities helped to make existing shortages worse. As the economy became more and more dysfunctional, the predictable adverse reaction to reform set in, with hard-line centralizers gaining strength within the central government and the Communist Party after mid-1990. This movement climaxed with the August 1991 coup, which briefly deposed Gorbachev before collapsing, owing to the inability and/or unwillingness of coup leaders to back up their decisions with deadly force.

Ironically, an economic system in which money, prices, and finance were supposed to be secondary—and were even viewed with scorn—was done in to no small degree by its inability to impose financial discipline. The money supply rose in 1991 by about as much as during the previous thirty years. Open inflation, which had begun in 1990, accelerated to become hyperinflation in 1991 and grew worse in 1992 after the breakup of the Soviet Union. Since the possibilities for further growth—indeed even for maintaining current output levels—appeared to be exhausted without radical reform, and because of the underlying inefficiencies of the Soviet system, the rift between reformers and centralizers grew deeper from 1990 to 1991.

Unlike previous reform efforts, perestroika was accompanied by *glasnost,* or openness, which encouraged people to air their grievances, to criticize the regime to a limited extent, and even to propose and discuss solutions. Glasnost increased the level of tolerance in the Soviet Union. Past crimes of the regime, including genocide, were revealed, and individuals began to speak out more freely, as well as to organize groups (including political parties) not controlled by the Communist Party. The ability of the latter to interfere in the daily lives of the people was reduced. Non-Russian ethnic minorities began to demand greater autonomy, and there was a revival of Russian nationalism. In consequence, the fifteen union republics—which were both political and ethnic divisions of the Soviet Union—became more independence-minded and gained political strength at the expense of the central or all-union authorities.

In the summer of 1990, when the economic crisis had already begun, Gorbachev accepted a program of radical reform that went far beyond the original goals of perestroika. Known as the Shatalin, or 500 Days', Plan, it called for liberalization of most prices, privatization of most of the economy, reduction of the budget deficit via large spending cuts, and decentralization of most executive authority to the union republics. The Soviet Union itself would become a common market with a common currency, but it would lose its position as the peak of the chain of command through which economic activity was managed.

The Shatalin Plan was never adopted, and it sparked the conservative backlash indicated above. When the August 1991 coup collapsed, central authority collapsed along with it. Within the Russian Republic, power passed to Boris Yeltsin, who had openly defied and faced down coup leaders from his position as this republic's president. Other republic-level authorities gained power as well, and Yeltsin recognized the independence of the Baltic states.[19] The fate of the Soviet Union was sealed. At year's end, its constituent republics became independent nations, although most of these retained the much looser ties of the Commonwealth of Independent States.

When Gorbachev launched perestroika, he intended a series of limited reforms that would reinvigorate the Soviet economy and society. In fact, the chain of events he set in motion destroyed first the Warsaw Pact and then the Soviet Union itself, bearing in mind that these had already been weakened by the time he came to power. His reforms were in the right direction, but they started a process that he did not understand and could not control, exactly the scenario foreseen by Karl Marx for capitalist leaders in the years leading up to the socialist revolution.[20]

Notes

1. This section relies mainly on the following works by Marx: *The Economic and Philosophical Manuscripts of 1844* (New York: International, 1964); "Preface" to *A Contribution to the Critique of Political Economy;* "Alienation and Social Classes"; *The German Ideology, Part 1; The Civil War in France* (with an introduction by Friedrich Engels); and "Critique of the Gotha Program." The last four works may be found in Robert C. Tucker, ed., *The Marx-Engels Reader* (New York: Norton, 1972). Finally, see Edwin West, "The Political Economy of Alienation," *Oxford Economic Papers,* March 1969, and D. Milenkovich, *Plan and Market in Yugoslav Economic Thought* (New Haven: Yale University Press, 1971), pp. 9–21.

2. Marx and Engels, "The German Ideology," in Tucker, *The Marx-Engels Reader,* p. 124.

3. Marx, *The Civil War in France,* including the "Introduction" by Engels, is the main source of the above paragraph.

4. The basic reference is to Oskar Lange's article, "On the Economic Theory of Socialism," pp. 57–143, in B. E. Lippincott, ed., *On the Economic Theory of Socialism* (New York: McGraw-Hill, 1964). See as well Abba P. Lerner, "Statics and Dynamics in Socialist Economics," *Economic Journal,* June 1937, pp. 253–286. For criticism, see A. Bergson, "Market Socialism Re-Visited," *Journal of Political Economy,* October 1967.

5. Lange was chairman of the Central Commission for the Application of Mathematical Methods to Economic Planning and Programming. However, his work on market socialism was banned in Poland until well after his death.

6. See F. A. Von Hayek, ed., *Collectivist Economic Planning* (London: Routledge, 1935).

7. See E. G. Furubotn and Svetozar Pejovich. "Property Rights and the Behavior of the Firm in a Socialist State: The Example of Yugoslavia." *Zeitschrift Für Nationalökonomie,* 1970, nos. 3–4, pp. 431–454.

8. See Ben Ward, "The Firm in Illyria: Market Syndicalism," *American Economic Review,* September 1958; Evsey Domar, "The Soviet Collective Farm as a Producer Cooperative," *American Economic Review,* September 1966; and Jaroslav Vanek, *The General Theory of Labor-Managed Market Economies* (Ithaca: Cornell University Press, 1970).

9. Under perfect competition, the curve would in fact shift backward. See Ward, op. cit., for the short-run case and Domar, "The Soviet Collective Farm as a Producer Cooperative," op. cit., for the long-run case.

10. Indeed, high-seniority workers could do even better than indicated in the text by taking advantage of their monopsony hiring power (since $S_L S_L$ is upward sloping) to set an even smaller low-seniority wage. We could think of a hospital as a physicians' cooperative in which the staff doctors are analogous to high-seniority employees or insiders, while interns and resident physicians are analogous to low-seniority employees or outsiders. See M. Pauly and M. Redisch, "The Not-For-Profit Hospital as a Physicians' Cooperative," *American Economic Review,* March 1973.

11. See L. Tyson, "Liquidity Crises in the Yugoslav Economy," op. cit., and J. Zupanov, "The Producer and Risk," *Eastern European Economics,* Spring 1969. In addition, see the references in note 12 below.

12. Discussions of decision making in Yugoslav firms appear in Joel B. Dirlam and James L. Plummer, *An Introduction to the Yugoslav Economy* (Columbus, Ohio: Merrill, 1973), chaps. 2–3; Jiri Kolaja, *Workers' Councils: The Yugoslav Experience* (London: Tavistock, 1965); Ellen Commisso, *Workers' Control Under Plan and Market* (New Haven: Yale University Press, 1979); Idzhak Adizes, *Industrial Democracy: Yugoslav*

Style (New York: Free Press, 1971); David Granick, *Enterprise Guidance in Eastern Europe* (Princeton, N.J.: Princeton University Press, 1975), chaps. 11–12; and H. Lydall, *Yugoslav Socialism: Theory and Practice* (Oxford: Clarendon Press, 1984). The last gives an excellent general discussion of Yugoslav workers' management in theory and practice. Finally, see L. D'Andrea-Tyson, "Liquidity Crises in the Yugoslav Economy: An Alternative to Bankruptcy?" *Soviet Studies*, April 1977, and J. Obradovich, "Workers' Participation: Who Participates?" *Industrial Relations*, February 1975.

13. Liberman's article, "The Plan, Profits, and Bonuses," is reprinted in Morris Bornstein and D. R. Fusfeld, eds., *The Soviet Economy* (Homewood, Ill.: Irwin, 1966), rev. ed., chap. 22. His "Reply to Critics," occupies chap. 23 of the same book. Premier Kosygin's proposals for more limited reforms in the Soviet Union appear in chap. 20 of the third edition of this volume (Homewood, Ill.: Irwin, 1970), while chap. 19 gives replies to Liberman by other Soviet economists. Finally, a later discussion indicating the fate of the Kosygin reforms is found in Jan Adam, "The Present Soviet Incentive System," *Soviet Studies*, July 1980.

14. Susan J. Linz, "Managerial Autonomy in Soviet Firms." *Soviet Studies*. April 1988.

15. See Gertrude Schroeder, "Soviet Economic Reform at an Impasse." *Problems of Communism*, July–August 1971, p. 41. See as well her "Soviet Economy on a Treadmill of 'Reforms,' " in U.S. Congress, Joint Economic Committee. *Soviet Economy in a Time of Change* (Washington, D.C.: U.S. Government Printing Office, 1979).

16. See Martin Weitzman, "Soviet Postwar Economic Growth and Capital-Labor Substitution," *American Economic Review*, September 1970, for an early analysis of growth slowdown in the Soviet Union owing to diminishing returns. Weitzman writes (p. 685), "Accounting for somewhere around 15 to 25 percent of average output increases, technical change [in the Soviet Union] is not nearly so significant a determinant of economic growth as in some other economies." See as well Z. M. Fallenbuchl, "East-West Economic Relations Since the Beginning of the 1970s," in R. E. Kanet, ed., *Soviet Foreign Policy and East-West Relations* (New York: Pergamon, 1982); and Jan Winiecki, "Are Soviet-type Economies Entering an Era of Long-Term Decline?" *Soviet Studies*, July 1986.

17. Arguably, however, the costs to the regime of freeing prices are mainly those of the resulting redistribution away from households and firms with relatively high access to goods under the low controlled prices to households and firms with relatively low access. The former would include residents of the main urban areas. We shall take up this matter again in chapter 7.

18. See Abram Bergson, "The Soviet Economy Under Gorbachev: The Twelfth Five-Year Plan," Harvard University, Institute of Economic Research, Discussion Paper No. 1275, October 1986; Gertrude Schroeder, "Anatomy of Gorbachev's Economic Reform," *Soviet Economy*, July–September 1987; Gertrude Schroeder, "Post-Soviet Economic Reforms in Perspective," in U.S. Congress, Joint Economic Committee, *The Former Soviet Union in Transition* (Washington, D.C.: U.S. Government Printing Office, 1993); and Anders Aslund, *Gorbachev's Struggle for Economic Reform*, 2d ed. (Ithaca, N.Y.: Cornell University Press, 1991).

19. In fact, Lithuania had already declared independence, and her independence had been recognized by the Russian Republic before the August 1991 coup. However, there was no guarantee that this recognition would be honored until the coup failed. Estonia and Latvia declared independence at the outset of the coup. This was subsequently recognized by Yeltsin.

20. See Marshall Goldman, *Why Economic Reforms in Russia Have Not Worked* (New York: Norton, 1991), and David Pryce-Jones, *The Strange Death of the Soviet Empire* (New York: Holt, 1995).

Questions for Review, Discussion, Examination

1. What would be the key requirement of a Marxian socialist state vis-à-vis its capitalist predecessor? Why would it have this requirement?

2. How would the nature of the socialist system envisaged by Marx depart from a Soviet-type economy in terms of the way Marx expected it to work? In practice, would it be different from a Soviet-type economy? Why or why not? In answering, explain what key ingredient is missing from Marx's system and why this poses a problem. Why might regional decentralization be at least a partial solution to this problem, albeit at some cost? What is the nature of the cost involved?

3. Explain why Lenin's notion of a "vanguard elite" (the Communist Party) is a logical addition to Marx's system. What potential implication does this have for a socialist society?

4. According to the text, "Present-day socialism did not succeed mature capitalism, as Marx had forecast. Instead, most socialist governments came to power in countries where capitalism had not yet reached maturity. This was, in part, the secret of their success in generating rapid economic growth for a time." Explain why this is the case.

5. What broad categories of socialist systems can we distinguish, from the standpoint of plan and market? Indicate why problems may arise in making one type viable and what would have to be done to resolve these problems.

6. Outline Lange's model of market socialism (also known as the Lange-Lerner system). Indicate how prices are set and the responsibilities of enterprise and industry managers. What rules are managers supposed to follow? On a purely theoretical plane, is it an effective answer to von Mises, Hayek, and others who had argued that rational prices could not exist under socialism? Why or why not?

7. Briefly discuss two practical difficulties that would arise in implementing the Lange-Lerner system. Are there advantages in centralizing price setting (or in putting it under the control of a central planning board), or should pricing be decentralized (set by individual buyers and sellers) as a general rule in a socialist market economy? Explain why you feel that one way or the other would be preferable.

8. What are potential efficiency advantages of workers' management? What are potential efficiency disadvantages? (Describe these briefly without going into too much detail.)

9. Why may the tendency of a worker-managed firm to maximize profits per employee create efficiency problems? In answering, explain why such a firm would be more reluctant to expand output and employment than a profit-maximizing firm when economic profit is positive. What does this imply about the importance of having efficient financial markets and low barriers to entry and exit into each industry? Why may the latter be difficult to achieve under socialism?

10. Problems of output and employment restriction resulting from the tendency of worker-managed firms to maximize profits per employee can be overcome via wage discrimination. Show how wage discrimination can lead to output and employment expansion. Are any dangers inherent in resolving problems in this way? If so, what are they?

11. How may workers' management deter entrepreneurship? How may it lead to the soft budget constraint? Why may efforts to increase the incentives for launching new products, starting new firms, and adopting new production methods take a worker-managed socialist economy in the direction of capitalism?

12. Why did Soviet-type economies try to reform—in the sense of expanding enterprise autonomy and/or shifting decisions down the chain of command closer to the scene of production—from the mid-1960s? Explain what this had to do with falling investment yields and why a solution could not be found within the conventional command economy framework. Once stagnation from falling investment yields has set in, will a Soviet-type economy simply experience slow (or zero) growth, or will there be absolute decline? On what factors does this depend?

13. How did détente during the 1970s act as a partial substitute for reform in Eastern Europe and the Soviet Union? Why was it only a partial substitute, and why was there a growing tendency in these countries after the 1970s to think of reform and détente as complementary?

14. Explain why reform of Soviet-type economies was made more necessary by advances in high-technology industries.

15. Prior to 1990, nearly all efforts to reform Soviet-type economies tended to fall short of their goals, and even to reverse themselves, insofar as they attempted to increase enterprise autonomy. Give and discuss five reasons for this.

In particular, planning from the achieved level and rigid prices often thwarted efforts to reform Soviet-type economies. Explain why this was true, and explain as well how actions of state authorities helped to ensure that the reforms would not succeed.

16. Outline the reforms proposed by Yevsei Liberman in the Communist Party newspaper, *Pravda,* on September 9, 1962. How did he propose to make firms more enthusiastic participants in plan formation? How do his proposals suggest a mixture of markets and commands to coordinate economic activity?

17. Outline the Gorbachev reform proposals (*perestroika*). Be sure to deal with proposed changes in the state sector, changes in the market-oriented sector of private and small cooperative firms, changes in social policy, changes in foreign trade and investment, and changes in agriculture. Were Gorbachev's agrarian reforms ever carried out?

18. Although the perestroika reform proposals were intended to reinvigorate the Soviet economy, they ended up helping to make it dysfunctional, which in turn helped to bring about the demise of the Soviet Union itself. Broadly speaking, how did the changes brought about by these proposals have this effect?

Chapter 7

The Problem of Transition from a Soviet-type to a Market Economy

Introduction: The Nature of the Transition Problem

The collapse of Communist Party control in Eastern and Central Europe from 1989 to 1991 began an economic transformation that is gradually turning former Soviet-type economies into market economies. These changes are taking longer to implement and are proving to be more painful, however, than most people expected in 1990. While much progress was achieved between 1989 and 1996, much also remains to be done, and most of these emerging economies experienced negative growth or stagnation, on balance, between 1985 and 1994 (Table 3.2). By contrast, the two Asian transition economies, China and Vietnam, began their transformations earlier and proceeded at first more slowly and deliberately toward a market economy. As a result, their economic growth rates have taken off under transition, to the point where they have become Asia's latest "miracle" economies. Here the Communist Party has retained its monopoly on political power, which may be part of the reason for their success thus far.

In Europe, the start of transition for most countries followed twenty-five years of efforts to decentralize the Soviet-type economy within the framework of socialism from 1965 to 1990. These reform efforts largely failed, although there was a degree of success in the former Yugoslavia, in Hungary, and in Poland, especially after 1979. Initial decentralizations were usually followed by recentralization and reform reversal. This legacy helped to rule out the alternative of market socialism after 1990. Instead, privatization quickly became a major goal of transforming economies, and success in privatizing their vast state sectors has been seen as the key to successful transition. Otherwise it would be impossible to get firms to compete for market share, to minimize costs, to innovate, or more generally to use resources efficiently. Serious problems would arise in particular if the state granted independence to firms (or granted them use rights over capital) while retaining the soft budget constraint (or income rights over capital). In this case, enterprises would have no incentives to use the resources entrusted to them in an efficient way. Moreover, development of efficient financial mar-

Table 7.1

Reform Paradigm

I.	Politicalreform	Replace the Communist Party's political monopoly with competition among political parties for temporary control of government.
II.	Economic reform	
	A. Marketization	Reduce state planning and management of production and interenterprise exchange, and replace this with market coordination of independent firms. Transition cannot be considered successful until most economic activity is market-coordinated and markets are "reasonably" competitive.
	B. Privatization	Reduce government ownership of capital and natural resources in favor of private and cooperative ownership. Harden enterprise budget constraints.

kets—often considered a prerequisite for an efficient and modern market economy—would be out of the question.

Therefore, the goal of socialism has largely been abandoned for now, although in Russia this could depend on future election outcomes. In Russia and in several other Central and East European countries, privatization was well over 50 percent completed by the end of 1995. In China, where the rhetoric stresses market socialism, the reality is that the state's share of gross national product (GNP) has fallen almost continually since the early 1980s and is now under one-third. All but about 1,000 large heavy industrial enterprises are supposed to "go to the sea"—that is, to be privatized. Yet none of these economies has developed efficient financial markets. Within the remaining state sectors, the budget constraint is still soft, and performance is poor. Privatization has not necessarily changed either of these basic facts of economic life, especially when privatization takes the form of handing firms over to their employees or to their managements.

We shall begin our attempt to understand transition with Table 7.1, which identifies two basic dimensions to the transformation process. These are *political reform*, or the introduction of political party competition, and *economic reform*. The latter covers marketization, or the introduction of markets and independent enterprise management to replace state management of the economy, and privatization, or the introduction of private, and possibly cooperative, ownership to replace state ownership of the means of production. Successful transition requires marketization, and in most of these countries the state sector's share of GNP has fallen substantially, although privatization has generally proceeded more slowly than foreseen.

Some observers argue that successful economic reform requires political pluralism, since otherwise there is no guarantee of protection for the rights and freedoms that an efficient market economy requires. Political monopoly means that rule by individuals will ultimately take precedence over rule by law. This increases the risk that property rights will be altered in the future without due process, and the lack of due process protection for property and lives deters investment and economic activity in general. As well, members of the Communist Party are likely to acquire a stake in some enterprises that they subsidize and protect from competition. This is true, for example, in Russia and also in China, which is nevertheless the most successful transition economy (as of the end of 1995) in terms of economic growth.

However, it can also be argued that for now continuing control by the Communist Party provides a more stable political environment and a longer time horizon for public officials. The shorter horizon associated with political democracy (owing to the need for periodic elections that are contested by at least two independent parties) acts as a potential barrier to reform progress, since the transition can promise only long-term gain in exchange for short-term pain. The alternation in power of governing parties or coalitions also causes uncertainty about future property rights, especially since the rule of law is not yet instituted in the fledgling democracies of Eastern and Central Europe.

To make matters worse, different government bodies are often competing for power in Russia and elsewhere in the former Soviet Union, making property rights even less secure. In Russia as well, central and local government bodies have continued to control use and exchange rights to land. In Eastern Europe, efforts to restore state and collective land to former owners have led to the filing of many claims for the same property. Allocation of rights must therefore be decided by the courts, and until claims are settled, it remains unclear who has the right to do what. This deters investment and efficient land use. By contrast, decollectivization of land in China, under Communist Party control, proceeded quickly and resulted in well-defined use and income rights.

On balance, it is unclear whether democracy helps or hinders the process of economic transition, which requires changes in property rights, institutions, and social attitudes that are revolutionary in scope. In such an epochal makeover, two basic dangers arise. The first is that the old system will persevere, perhaps in altered form. In this case, the economy is likely to be even less efficient than before, since the firm hand of old that the central government was able to wield over economic activity will now be weaker. In Russia, for example, many former state enterprises appear to be almost adrift, producing well below capacity and still protected by a continuing soft budget constraint. Underemployment in these firms is greater than during the Soviet era, and they are making little progress in adapting to a market economy, even though they are now legally private companies. Here the old system persists under the facade of the new.

The second danger is that reformers may succeed in destroying the old property rights associated with a Soviet-type economy (notably the right of the state to manage production and interenterprise exchange) but fail to replace these with new rights. Property rights are then ill-defined, which deters investment and production. Perhaps worse, ill-defined rights create a vacuum into which exploitive forces are likely to enter, including organized crime, with its own style of property rights creation and enforcement. The shortest distance from a Soviet-type to a market economy leads to monopoly rather than to competition, with high prices and profits and restricted outputs. There is always a risk that transition will be hijacked by elements seeking monopoly profit instead of economic growth. These include members of the Communist Party elite (*nomenklatura*), who are often well placed to establish and benefit from monopoly power, as well as to loot the state enterprises under their control.

Both dangers have materialized in transition economies. Property rights have been poorly defined and contested, and monopoly power has been hard to erode. Russia, in particular, has been hit by a crime wave. In one part of the Russian economy, organized gangs battle to extend their control and carry out intimidation and enforcement on a massive scale. Government authorities often act arbitrarily and are themselves struggling to redefine and expand their jurisdictions, as well as to increase their revenues. In another part of the economy, many large and midsized state and former state firms carry on much as before, except at a lower level of efficiency. For them, the budget constraint remains soft, as indicated above, a major reason why venture capital is scarce in the rest of the economy and efficient financial markets have failed to emerge.

A key factor in making transition long and hard is the need for highly specialized skills to make the institutions of a modern market economy work efficiently. In any economic system, institutions and skills are interdependent.[1] For example, suppose we reform the banking system by breaking up the monobank of a Soviet-type economy into a Western-style central bank, on one hand, with responsibility for monetary policy, and commercial banks, on the other, which deal directly with households and firms. On paper, the new arrangement may resemble that in the West, but it will not work in the same way, at least at first. It may well continue to function much as did the prereform monobank. A Soviet-type economy has no monetary policy, in the sense of efforts to dampen the business cycle or to maintain currency values or balance-of-payments equilibrium, and its monobank has no experience in checking creditworthiness or in dealing with business firms on an arms-length basis. It has little experience of any sort in dealing with households. The parliament of a transition economy may pass a Western-style contract law, but the supervisory and legal skills needed to make it work properly, as well as the legal precedents, are missing.

The absence of market economy skills makes it easier for public officials to cooperate with bank and enterprise managers to preserve the Soviet-type economy, which everyone understands and is familiar with. One author writes:

The market mechanism and freedom of actions of individuals [in Western market economies] not only insure the right amounts of goods and services (with well-known exceptions) . . . [t]hey also [help to] ensure the right amounts of skills and the right kinds of institutions. . . . Over several decades, advanced western economies have achieved a sort of social "ecological balance" among their institutions and the available skills. The demand for certain skills (accountants, tax lawyers, economists, managers, engineers) and certain institutions (commercial banks, savings and loans institutions, futures markets, real estate markets, regulatory agencies, investment banks) has brought [these] into existence, so that some kind of institutional and professional equilibrium has been established.[2]

By contrast, a transition economy has to build a business middle class, starting nearly from scratch, which can easily take a generation. Managerial skills are in especially short supply at the outset, but the same is true to varying degrees for accountants, financial experts, lawyers, and even government regulators, since the regulatory role of the state in a market economy is quite different from that in a Soviet-type economy.

On balance, it is hard to understand some forecasts made in 1990 and 1991 that predicted a successful transition within five years. In fact, these years witnessed high inflation, growing inequality, stagnant or falling output, and disappointing progress toward the end goal of an efficient market economy in Eastern and Central Europe. Death rates have risen, and many people have become destitute, while others have gotten rich beyond previous imagination. Transition has been especially hard on the elderly, and many others have watched their living standards fall, while the Communist Party elite and organized crime elements have gained. Of all age groups, the young stand to benefit most from transition, since they will have the best opportunities to acquire professional, technical, and linguistic skills at a time when these are in short supply. They are also most likely to live long enough to enjoy the eventual fruits of marketization. In this context, although the basic picture is not yet rosy, there were signs of a turnaround in a number of European transition economies by the end of 1995, and a few were even showing healthy growth. This came after decreases in real GNP on the order of 20 to 40 percent, the largest of which occurred in Romania, Russia, Ukraine, and several other former Soviet republics.

To help us understand the challenges of transition better, Table 7.2 gives a sequence of reforms, together with explanations, that would lead gradually from a Soviet-type to a market economy. This is a sequence that might be recommended in the absence of political constraints, as well as foreign pressures (notably to open domestic markets). Political constraints are bound to be important because of the revolutionary nature of the changes required, and also (for countries that become political party democracies) because transition invariably lasts longer than the period between elections. Therefore, we shall also consider what must be done to ease these constraints on the transition process. (Since every nation is unique and will therefore choose a transformation path that is somewhat unique, we must bear in mind that no sequence will fit all cases.)

In fact, the sequence given in Table 7.2 better describes the course of reform in China since 1979 than it does the course of events in European transition economies, with the exception of Hungary. There a long tradition of gradual reform, dating from 1968, had achieved significant changes by the fall of the Berlin Wall in November 1989. Hungary has nevertheless suffered stagnation rather than growth, although a turnaround may now have occurred. Moreover, two reasons for stagnation or decline in Hungary and elsewhere in Central and Eastern Europe that should not be blamed on transition are the worldwide recession of the early 1990s and the collapse of the COMECON market for East European products between 1989 and 1991. COMECON was the trading bloc linking the former Soviet Union and its political allies whose demise weakened transition economies and caused decreases in production and exports at the worst possible time. This collapse did not affect China, which had already reoriented her trade toward nonsocialist Asia and the West during the 1960s and 1970s.

Sequencing of Reforms in Gradual Transition

Because of the comprehensive nature of the changes required to go from a Soviet-type to a market economy—which affect every aspect of social and economic life—some sequencing of these reforms is unavoidable. They cannot be made all at once. In Table 7.2, the major changes are divided into three categories. First, come those reforms that should be started without delay, because they take a long time to complete and/or are key prerequisites for other changes. Second, come changes that are the heart of reform in the sense that there can be no efficient market economy, and hence no real transition, without them. Finally, some reforms will inevitably be delayed and others should be, since the number of urgent changes is already sufficient to overwhelm the societies that undertake them.

At the outset of transition, the information needed in order to bring about some of the most important reforms is missing. Most serious is the absence of rational prices. Not only is the value of products to users unknown, equally unknown is the value of the firms that make these goods and services, since there are no capital markets and enterprise value depends on the prices that firms charge and pay for their inputs. Valuation difficulties are least serious in the case of small firms in light industry and services, which historically have operated at least partly on the second economy, and greatest for larger enterprises, especially in heavy industry, where prices have been most distorted. As a result, privatization of most large firms will have to await the freeing of prices to respond to supply and demand. In the meantime, the hardening of budget constraints for state enterprises should begin, and in general these firms should be treated more

Table 7.2

Sequencing of Reforms in Gradual Transition

I. Changes to be started as soon as possible

A. *Development of market economy skills.* This will be one of the hardest and longest tasks of all, requiring the development of business, and especially management skills, but also many others, including regulatory skills. In addition, a start must be made in reorienting government administration away from management of the economy toward maintaining health, safety, and environmental standards and in acquiring the legal skills required by an efficient market economy.

B. *Creation of private property rights.* The economy urgently needs laws governing contracts and other new legislation, including a bankruptcy law to facilitate efficient markets and hard budget constraints. It should become easy for citizens to start small private and cooperative enterprises. The success of transition depends in no small measure on the growth and vitality of this sector. New legislation should also ease the transition from a society governed by individuals to one subject to the rule of law.

C. *Change of economic priorities.* Investment should be reoriented away from heavy industry, with its phenomenal waste, toward infrastructure, light industry, services, and agriculture. The first steps toward hardening budget constraints of state firms should also be taken as soon as possible. Because transport (especially road) and communications investment were neglected in Soviet-type economies, the need for upgrading here is urgent. As well, there is a need for a better network of retail and wholesale enterprises and a better system of payments and settlements.

D. *Initial freeing of prices and enterprise restructuring.* Ideally prices would be freed gradually, since most will rise owing to the shortage nature of the Soviet-type economy. This will cause a price "shock." We can begin by freeing prices of luxury goods and of other "nonessential" products. (Inevitably a value judgment will have to be made as to what to include here.) We can also free prices of goods for which price increases will lead to a vigorous supply response. To guard against monopoly pricing, we must start creating conditions favorable to competition, where necessary, by splitting up large state enterprises and trusts and making it easier to start new private and cooperative firms.

E. *Welfare reform and hardening of enterprise budget constraints.* Welfare must become the responsibility of government rather than of state firms, and the task of reducing underemployment within the state sector must begin. This implies a progressive hardening of enterprise budget constraints, albeit without moving so quickly as to cause massive unemployment. Subsidies to firms must be reduced and transfer payments to households increased.

F. *Tax reform.* Taxation has to be shifted away from profits (or capital) toward labor and added value. The taxation of investment returns discourages investment, when taxation should be doing just the opposite—that is, encouraging saving and investment. Also, transition economies will have to

(continued)

Table 7.2 *(continued)*

begin harmonizing their taxation with West European economies and will have to upgrade their tax collection machinery in order to avoid massive evasion. (Under the Soviet-type economy, taxes were collected mainly from large state enterprises.)

II. Changes that constitute the heart of reform

A. *Price liberalization.* The preceding measures are preconditions to price liberalization. There can be no market economy unless prices are ultimately freed to coordinate economic activity in place of the state. But price liberalization usually implies sharp price increases that inflict pain on some households and firms. This suggests a gradual liberalization of prices as a welfare system is put in place to cushion the blow to those who are hurt the most and as improved management and competitive conditions emerge to increase the elasticity of supply in response to price changes.

B. *Enterprise restructuring and infrastructure upgrading.* There is little point in shifting from a Soviet-type economy to a market economy dominated by monopolistic elements. However, there is always a danger of this, since the latter is the kind of market economy that is closest to a Soviet-type economy. Therefore, it is crucial to finish the process of splitting large firms and trusts begun under item I.D, especially since these are often the least efficient enterprises of a Soviet-type economy and rarely realize potential scale economies. Some reliance can also be placed on competition from the nonstate sector and from imports. As noted under item I.C, infrastructure was neglected by the Soviet-type economies. Moreover, improvements in transport and communications will enable firms to enlarge their markets and access to inputs and will therefore increase competition. Since heavy industry will have to reduce its labor force and capital, some of the resources freed can be transferred to building infrastructure.

C. *Bank and financial sector reform.* The efficiency and prosperity of a modern market economy depend in no small measure on the ability of its financial sector to channel savings into the most productive investment opportunities available. There are no financial markets in a Soviet-type economy, requiring these institutions to be built from scratch. The first step is to separate the state monobank into a central bank responsible for monetary policy and into commercial banks that deal with the public. Eventually most of the latter should be privatized. Transition economies also need stock and bond markets, together with a favorable environment for their expansion. Securities markets are essential not only to help get investment funds to projects and enterprises with good prospective returns but also to enable government to finance deficits without expanding the money supply, which causes inflation.

D. *(Further) privatization of small firms and some large ones.* Even in the West, where government enterprises account for 10 percent of GDP or less and capital markets are well developed, privatization of such firms becomes a long, drawn-out affair. For example, the Thatcher government's privatization in the United Kingdom reduced the share of GDP produced in state firms from 11.5 to 7.5 percent over eight years. In European former Soviet-type economies, state firms, collective farms, and other large collective enterprises that were treated like state firms typically accounted for 80 percent of GDP or

(continued)

Table 7.2 *(continued)*

more. Therefore, privatization of state enterprises is bound to be a long, drawn-out affair, if by "privatization" we mean not only a nominal change of ownership, but removal of the soft budget constraint and other ties to the state that are not typical of a market economy (although there is much variation in the practice of different market economies and consequent room for interpretation of this requirement). Small and midsized firms should be privatized first, because it is easier to find domestic buyers (the resources needed for purchase are less), and valuation of large enterprises must await rational prices for their products and for their inputs.

E. *First steps in liberalizing foreign trade and payments.* In order to give domestic producers more rational price signals and to increase competition from imported products, transition economies should begin dismantling the elaborate system of controls over foreign trade typical of a Soviet-type economy. As a rule, trade was one of its most closely controlled sectors. The ultimate goal may well be free trade plus a uniform, flexible exchange rate and a convertible currency, but there are two reasons not to proceed too rapidly toward this goal. First, transition economies will probably want to negotiate a mutual lowering of trade barriers with other nations and trading blocs. To do this requires them to reduce their own barriers only as a quid pro quo. Second, as domestic producers adjust to market conditions, we can reasonably expect them to be able to bring down their costs and improve their products. Firms that could compete successfully with foreign producers after an adjustment period would be forced into bankruptcy if exposed to such competition too soon. To put it another way, there are likely to be significant experience economies in adjusting to a market environment.

III. Changes to be delayed

A. *(Further) privatization of large firms.* This must be constantly pushed forward in order to succeed, but completion of this program is bound to take many years, for at least three reasons. First, there is a danger of selling too many of the potentially most efficient enterprises to foreigners, which could threaten national control over domestic policy making later on. Second, if hard budget constraints are applied too quickly to too many of these firms, massive unemployment will result, which is undesirable on efficiency grounds alone. Third, as indicated earlier, the value of these enterprises is nearly impossible to determine until rational price signals are available for their products and their inputs. Once we have a good idea of what they are worth, we may wish to make easy credit available to domestic buyers and/or to give each citizen a voucher that can be used to buy shares of state firms or mutual funds that become part owners of these enterprises. This voucher would represent his or her ownership share of the state sector by virtue of having been a part of the "whole people" under the Soviet-type economy. This is also a way of encouraging domestic ownership. Foreign investment is needed, although subject to the constraint that foreign control not be "excessive." In some cases, state enterprises should be closed and their assets sold. Unfortunately, this will often be true of heavy industrial firms employing many workers and with a history of paying relatively high wages.

(continued)

Table 7.2 *(continued)*

B. *Further foreign trade liberalization.* Several of the smaller European transition countries are looking forward to joining the European Economic Community (EEC), and all may eventually be forced to join larger free trade areas. While it is important to expose domestic producers to international competition, as well as to opportunities to gain export markets, it is also necessary to do this in a gradual way, as noted above, in order to give domestic firms a chance to improve their operations to the point where they can compete.

C. *Further reform and liberalization of the financial sector.* This is another reform that is bound to take a long time. In some cases, transition economies may opt for finance capitalism (or close associations between banks and firms, including ownership ties), since banks can become centers of entrepreneurial and technical expertise that is spread over many firms. Latecomers to economic development during the nineteenth century (including Germany, France, Sweden, and Japan) relied on this type of financial intermediation.

---

and more like public enterprises in the West. Here transition governments would ideally walk a tightrope, taking care to constantly push ahead, but not so quickly that unemployment becomes too high.

While enterprise values are unknown at the outset of reform, transition governments can determine what kinds of skills an efficient market economy will require and what kinds of laws are necessary to make markets work effectively when the requisite skills are in place. Because acquisition of the necessary business and regulatory skills, plus the knowledge in applying them that only experience can bring, could take a generation, a start on this journey must be made as soon as possible. The longer it takes to develop these skills, the easier it is for the reform to be subverted by one or both of the two basic dangers outlined in the previous section. However, even the best managers will not produce results in an environment in which state authorities can interfere and change the rules governing enterprises in an arbitrary way. Such actions will discourage investment and entrepreneurship, as well as preserve the dependence of firms on the state.

The need for legal reforms is therefore urgent in order to legalize private property in the means of production and to support contracts between independent parties, as well as to give state authorities well-defined responsibilities and jurisdictional boundaries. Such laws are the legal foundation of Western market economies. In addition, since heavy industry was overemphasized in the Soviet-type economy and investment in other sectors was far too low, it is clear that investment priorities must change in favor of infrastructure, light industry, services, and agriculture, and against heavy industry. This will not only help to increase efficiency by tailoring production more closely to demand but will also create more jobs for a given investment outlay, since light industry, agriculture, and services are much more labor intensive than heavy industry. Finally, tax and welfare reform should broaden the tax base and shift responsibility for welfare from the enterprises to government. Otherwise, it will be impossible to harden enterprise budget constraints and make firms cost conscious.

Gradual Transition versus "Big Bang"

As Table 7.2 contains much of the explanation of the importance and sequencing of the reforms given there, we shall now turn to the main alternative sequencing that has been followed in practice. This is the "Big Bang" approach, notably used in Poland and Russia, but also in Czechoslovakia, Bulgaria, and Romania. Modeled on the post–World War II currency reforms in Italy and West Germany, it features liberalization of most prices in one shot, without first preparing the way via the measures under item I in Table 7.2. When prices are freed, barriers to imports are also supposed to be lowered and major progress achieved toward making the domestic currency convertible in terms of Western currencies. (Under the Soviet-type economy, domestic currency was greatly overvalued.) Finally, price liberalization is supposed to be accompanied by "macrostabilization," meaning that the government reduces its budget deficit and acquires the ability to finance the remaining deficit in a noninflationary way. This requires a securities market on which it can sell bonds as an alternative to increasing the money supply. Macrostabilization, therefore, covers measures under items I.E, I.F, and II.C in Table 7.2.

In practice, however, macrostabilization has proved elusive. Not only did Poland and Russia get the expected one-time jump in prices, but they also experienced far higher inflation rates between 1985 and 1994 than did Hungary or China, where prices were freed gradually and more was done in advance to prepare for a market economy. In neither Russia nor Poland is there strong evidence that sudden price liberalization, without preparing the way via legal, institutional, and skill-oriented reforms, speeded up the transition as a whole.

Political constraints—and, in the case of Poland, a desire to join the European Common Market—are often cited as justification for the Big Bang.[3] In chapter 6 we saw that the nations of Central and Eastern Europe had a history of reform setbacks from 1965 to 1990. Therefore, something had to be done near the start of transition to signal that government policy had really changed and that firms and households would henceforward be subject to new rules, implying new opportunities and constraints. The years of "reform-pretend" were finally over. However, such a signal can be given in more than one way. In this respect, China's counterpart of the Big Bang was decollectivization from 1979 to 1984, in which the communes were dismantled in favor of a return to family farms, although the state retained legal ownership of the land. This reform affected 700 to 800 million people. Together with increases in prices paid to farmers, it led to a nearly 34 percent jump in grain output between 1979 and 1984, in a country that had known widespread starvation as recently as 1961–62. This lifted political constraints on China's leaders by creating a constituency in favor of reform, which is basically how the political constraint on reform must be overcome.

In Poland, by contrast, farms were already in private hands, while in Russia, decollectivization became legal but has yet to occur in most places. This is because central and local government bodies have retained de facto control over the use and sale of land. In particular, they have supported efforts by collective farm managements to prevent peasants who belong to these farms from withdrawing their land. Such withdrawals would threaten to break up these large, but notoriously inefficient, enterprises. One consequence is that the crisis in food production is now worse than ever. The 1995 fall grain harvest was the worst in thirty years. It was to overcome the resistance of government authorities and farm managements to decollectivization, as well as to gain political favor, that Boris Yeltsin issued a decree in March 1996 providing land ownership certificates to peasants and others who use rural land. Each individual is supposed to receive a deed to land that he or she uses. The idea was to make full private ownership of land a reality instead of a legal fiction, although it is too soon to know as of this writing whether the effort will succeed.

At the start of transition in any country, many people are at risk of losing income and status because of the intended changes, at least in the short to medium term. These include the state bureaucracy and management personnel of state enterprises, but also ordinary workers in these firms (many of which are inefficient) and weaker groups in society, including pensioners. Therefore, there is certain to be a potential constituency against reform, whose livelihoods are threatened. This makes it crucial to create a constituency with a vested interest in successful reform and to do so by creating additional wealth. Simple redistribution can only intensify social conflict, whereas wealth creation holds out the prospect of spreading the gains to those who miss out initially. The price shock of the Big Bang did not lead to wealth creation, at least in the short run, and it is unclear whether wealth-creating measures were available to these governments that could have advanced reform and bought time for a more gradual implementation along the lines suggested by Table 7.2.

What exactly is wrong with the Big Bang? Sudden liberalization of prices will cause them to rise, given the pervasive shortages of the Soviet-type economy, but such increases will also eliminate the shortages. The costs of waiting and queuing will go down, as will the costs of doing without products that one can afford to buy. For many households, goods that used to be unavailable are now available, but they are unaffordable. For others, products that used to require patience and legwork or long periods of waiting to obtain can now be found more readily, although at higher prices. Buyers formerly constrained by availability are now more constrained by their budgets, as are buyers in Western countries. This does not necessarily leave them worse off, however, which is why we need to take a closer look at the effects of price liberalization.

The Effect of Freeing Prices in a Transition Economy

We recall that supply curves in a Soviet-type economy are inelastic (and sometimes backward bending) for at least four basic reasons. First, planning from the achieved level makes firms unwilling to increase supply above targeted levels—unless the above-plan output escapes the official records of planning superiors. Second, the soft budget constraint removes the firm's financial interest in above-plan production. Third, even if the first two constraints are weakened, enterprise management is generally chosen for its loyalty, for ideological reasons, and for its willingness to depend on planning superiors. It is not chosen for independence or initiative. Fourth, potential supply outside the state plan, which would come from the second economy, is constrained by controls on extra-plan investment and production. When transition gets under way, the easiest of the above to bring to an end is the first—by eliminating state management of the economy. But this does not necessarily make supply curves elastic, which is to say that it does not necessarily make producers price sensitive. From one point of view, the changes under item I in Table 7.2, along with those under items II.B through II.E, are designed to increase supply elasticities, as well as cost-effective production of a wider range and variety of products, and innovation. Without these changes, supply will continue to be inelastic, and there will be a sluggish response on the part of producers to financial opportunities and constraints. If the state bureaucracy remains in place, it may have a further deadening effect on initiative.

In these conditions, suppose there is a general freeing of prices, and let Figure 7.1 describe what happens for a "typical" good or service. Although price changes for many products at the same time are likely to cause most demand curves to shift—some will rise and others fall—we hold the demand curve in Figure 7.1 fixed in order to simplify the analysis.[4] The supply curves, SS and $S'S'$, give alternative output expansion paths under two different assumptions. At first the state price of this product is frozen at P_0, or 10 rubles, and subsequently is freed. With inelastic supply SS, the price then jumps to 23 rubles and quantity increases to 112,000, whereas with elastic supply $S'S'$, the price rises only to 14 rubles and quantity expands to 150,000. For customers, elastic supply responses are better, since the resulting price increase is smaller and quantity increase is greater. Moreover, the widespread underutilization of inputs in a Soviet-type economy implies a potential for output expansion in response to demand stimuli.

Even with inelastic supply, however, the price will not rise above the former demand price (30 rubles) unless output actually falls when controls are lifted.[5] For products of such low appeal that their demand prices are below their administered prices under the Soviet-type economy, output decreases are desirable. The same is true of goods and services whose liberalized costs rise above their demand prices, except in some cases in which increasing returns to scale prevail

Figure 7.1 **Price Increase and Elasticity of Supply Response**

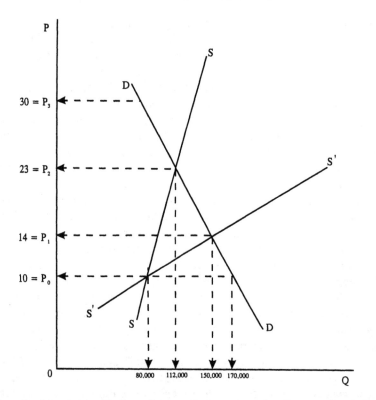

(as described in chapter 3). For other products, output should expand—or, at the very least, not contract. If all outputs fail to change—in which case the supply curve in Figure 7.1 would be vertical—actual prices will simply rise to the levels of former demand prices for the same products.

In chapter 1, we saw that buyers of a good or service in short supply will usually pay more than the ceiling price if we take into account all their costs of obtaining or of doing without the product. The former include costs of queuing, searching, hoarding, and/or of paying higher black market prices. The full price paid is likely to be closer to P_3 than to P_1.[6] Indeed, suppose that a freeing of all prices causes no change in any output, while actual prices rise to former demand price levels. Logically there should be no change in aggregate real output or in real GNP. In the aggregate, citizens are no worse off and no better off than before, although the distribution of products among buyers is likely to change. Otherwise, Big Bang simply makes the implicit or hidden (or second economy) portions of prices explicit. In the process, it brings to an end the "monetary overhang" of surplus savings in a Soviet-type economy that results from the relatively low availability of products.

It also creates prices that reflect true values of goods to users and therefore sends the "right" signals to actual and potential suppliers. The information vacuum of a Soviet-type economy comes to a sudden end. We may then ask why anyone would prefer the gradual liberalization of prices suggested by Table 7.2, especially since a drawn-out program often involves an intermediate step in which many goods have two or more prices. In China, products had low, controlled prices for deliveries under the state plan but higher prices for above-quota production. Such prices were gradually freed (with a few exceptions) as the sphere of economic activity covered by mandatory planning retreated. In order for the system to work, producers had to believe that today's above-target output would not become part of future targets. Moreover, there was an incentive to buy at the low price (by acquiring supply quotas under the plan, but with no intention of using these products as inputs into further production) and then sell the same goods at their higher market prices. The Big Bang eliminates this incentive and gives the right price signals immediately, even if a large jump in prices is necessary. In Russia, consumer prices rose to about three times their levels at the end of December 1991, on average, in January 1992.[7]

Thus the problems with Big Bang are subtler than they may at first appear to be, but they are nevertheless potentially serious. In the West, it is easy to take for granted the legal and institutional foundations of markets, because these have existed for many years and are gradually adjusted over time as conditions change. When opportunities exist to make money by expanding supply, it is generally assumed that this will happen and that governments will promote at least limited competition to restrict the profits gained via exercise of monopoly power. Work habits and attitudes have evolved that are compatible with an efficient market economy. There is tolerance of inequality based on skill and entrepreneurship, less tolerance of inequality based on theft or monopoly power. Partly because of such attitudes, and also because of effective contract laws, Western and Asian economies have found ways of channeling competition for scarce resources into avenues that lead to wealth creation. Imperfect as these societies often appear to be, this is a major achievement. It accounts for much of the prosperity that attracted the European transition economies to markets in the first place.

In former Soviet-type economies, we can take for granted neither the legal or institutional underpinnings of markets, nor the proper work habits or social attitudes for an efficient market system. Work habits tend to be poor because of years of overstaffing of enterprises. For forty years in China and in Eastern Europe and for seventy years in the former Soviet Union, people were constantly told that all capitalists were exploiters and that competition was not an effective way to hold down prices. Capitalism was viewed exclusively as monopoly capitalism, with no distinction between those who got wealthy by innovating and those who made their riches by exploiting protected monopoly power. (The existence of the former was simply denied.) Over time, theft of state property in Soviet-type economies also became common and tolerated.

In such conditions, competition for scarce resources can easily become destructive, as it has time and again throughout history. This is likely when the property rights of an old system are destroyed but those of a new system, together with their supporting institutions, are not yet in place. The Big Bang creates such a property rights vacuum. To avoid the waste associated with communal rights, suppliers and government authorities will try to establish new rights, together with enforcement. Specifically, they will try to gain control over supplies of goods and services and to enforce their control with such means as are available to them. Given the shortage of business skills and of legal and institutional support for workably competitive markets, the likely outcome is monopoly control over supply, although without the output targets that provided some check on the exercise of monopoly power in the Soviet-type economy. Worse, criminal elements may become the power behind the monopoly, bringing their own extra-legal style of property rights creation and enforcement.

If monopoly elements gain control of supply, output may well be restricted below levels available under the Soviet-type economy in order to maximize monopoly profit. The actual price will then rise above 30 rubles in Figure 7.1— which is to say, above the former demand price—even if unit cost is less than this price. In Poland, there is evidence of monopolistic influences on pricing, while in Russia few transactions in urban areas occur without payoffs to criminal elements.[8] In such conditions, the worst-case scenario of capitalism depicted by Communist propagandists may become reality, which helps to cause a political backlash against reform and to prevent social attitudes favorable to an efficient market economy from emerging.

Of course, different criminal gangs compete with one another, but rarely by trying to develop better or cheaper products than those of rivals. Instead of competing in the marketplace, they compete for monopoly control over market supply. The former is wealth-creating competition, while the latter is destructive of life and property. It is monopoly profits that finance the lifestyles of the rich and infamous. Monopoly behavior reduces output and raises prices, profits, and inequality. Control over monopoly profits by organized crime probably reduces the propensity to invest as well, since the risky lifestyle of a criminal in today's Russia tends to favor short time horizons and lavish consumption (or repatriation of profit to Swiss bank accounts) over investment.

It would be wrong to attribute the rise of organized crime in Russia or its control over product supply entirely to the Big Bang (or to the liberalization of most prices before the institutional and legal foundations of markets were in place). But it did help to create conditions under which criminal organizations could increase their power and economic role. Other elements have also conspired to prevent the elastic expansion of supply on which the success of reform depends. These include arbitrary taxation, frequently at confiscatory levels—although with generous tax breaks for companies with the right political connections—plus myriad rules and restrictions that have in particular preserved and even amplified the inefficiencies of collective agriculture. The latter is critical, because lower food prices would do much to alleviate poverty in Russia, where pensioners often cannot afford to eat and must scavenge just to survive.

The alternative of gradual liberalization involves dismantling the Soviet-type economy, not all at once, but bit by bit and sector by sector. As the planned economy retreats, the old property rights and institutions are progressively replaced by new ones favorable to competitive markets. Only after this is done and at least a start is made in developing the necessary market economy skills would prices be fully liberalized. Thus the retreat of the old set of property rights is followed by the advance of the new, with minimal opportunities for poorly defined or enforced property rights to emerge. Along the way, it will be possible to experiment with different legal and institutional reforms in just a part of the economy before extending these to the whole country. An all-at-once price liberalization has its greatest chance of success when the property rights and institutional support necessary for a market economy are already in place, along with the required business skills, and economic activity is restrained primarily by price controls and other government restrictions. This was the case in West Germany in 1948, but was hardly so in Russia in 1992. Real consumption per capita rose by over 6 percent per year between 1948 and 1958 in the Federal Republic of Germany, but it has thus far fallen in Russia, although a turnaround may have finally been achieved in late 1995.

Transition is often accompanied by other changes that impact economic performance. In most cases, a reorientation of priorities has occurred, along the lines suggested in Table 7.2, which has reduced the demand for heavy industrial output, especially where this is related to defense and/or exploration of space. The worldwide recession of the early 1990s plus the collapse of the Council for Mutual Economic Assistance (COMECON) further deflated the demand for manufacturing output in Eastern and Central Europe, as noted earlier. COMECON was a system of managed trade between the former Soviet Union and its allies that was originally designed as an answer to the European Common Market. Most of the trade flows within COMECON involved exchanging Soviet energy (mainly oil and natural gas) for manufactured products of the Soviet Union's European allies. The latter became dependent on the Soviet Union's supplies, and also on the Soviet Union as a market for products of generally modest quality that would have been difficult or impossible to sell anywhere else in the world. By the 1980s, the net result was a subsidy from the Soviet Union to her European allies in return for which she ensured the economic dependency of the latter. The "collapse" of COMECON occurred when the Soviet Union cut her deliveries to Eastern Europe, partly because of output reductions and partly because she needed the higher, convertible currency earnings obtainable for supplying energy to the West.

The result was devastating to East European countries, which suddenly had to find new export markets in the midst of a recession for products that were historically not competitive and which (in the case of food exports) also faced trade barriers in the West. It is hard to know what part of the poor performance of these economies from 1985 to 1994 was due to this factor and what part was due to transition. By contrast, China did not face this demand deflation, as she had already reoriented her trade toward Asia and the West following the Sino-Soviet rift in 1960. Where transition led to monopoly pricing (or, more generally, to inelastic or backward-bending supply responses in sectors with potential to expand), it reinforced the effect of demand deflation owing to reorientation of priorities and the demise of COMECON. In order to avoid either open unemployment or even greater underemployment of productive inputs (notably labor) than under the Soviet-type economy, a substantial reallocation of resources from declining to advancing sectors had to occur. A sluggish or negative supply response in sectors with growth potential would help to trap resources in declining sectors or in open unemployment. Unfortunately, this is what happened.

Output therefore declined in the initial years of transition, as production decreases in sectors with falling demand exceeded production increases in sectors with rising demand. In many cases, the latter were restrained by poor access to financing and other resources, and monopolistic restrictions on output also appear to have played a role. In addition, countries of Eastern and Central Europe were hurt by the collapse of COMECON demand. Within the state sector, output decreases were intensified by supply and organizational disruptions. Suppliers of raw materials and of other crucial inputs for state manufacturing firms now found it lucrative to divert output to private or foreign-invested enterprises. Some of the ablest individuals left the state sector, which became a less attractive employer in terms of earnings and career prospects. In the final analysis, both state and nonstate sectors have had supply problems. Even with subsidies, the state sector could no longer afford crucial inputs allocated through the market. The nonstate sector had relatively low access to inputs that were still rationed and suffered from a shortage of market-economy skills, as well as of infrastructure and legal and institutional support.

Following price liberalization, redistribution also occurred as shortages disappeared and prices rose to reflect user values. Those households and firms with relatively good access to supplies under the Soviet-type economy were often penalized, while those users with poorest access before were helped, since access to many goods and services came to depend solely on payment of market prices. Many heavy industrial firms were in the former category, while among households, those living in urban areas had better access to goods than those in the countryside, and those living in the largest cities had better access still. The party elite (*nomenklatura*) enjoyed the greatest availability, since they were able to shop at special stores.

Following the liberalization of prices, governments often tried to shield some firms and households from the effects of this redistribution. To a degree this depended on whether the Communist Party or a successor remained in power, but no government can afford widespread unemployment, especially if concentrated in specific regions or localities, and particularly if a "reasonable" social safety net is not yet in place.[9] Governments provided such a shield by subsidizing firms in one form or other, and thus by prolonging the soft budget constraint. Indeed, budget constraints for state and some former state firms often became softer following transition, since other historical devices for protecting these enterprises, notably rigged pricing and guaranteed markets, disappeared or grew less effective. In addition, many members of the *nomenklatura* were able to use their insider positions and knowledge, as well as their personal ties, to preserve or increase their affluence—frequently by looting the assets of firms under their control.

However, while some entities have been protected from the effects of redistribution, others have not, and as in the West, the latter are often the most vulnerable elements of society. As part of Russia's Big Bang, for example, subsidies used to hold down prices of some foodstuffs were reduced or eliminated. These subsidies shifted supply curves outward, and therefore reduced the shortages associated with any given low price (or reduced the price associated with any given shortage). They were especially helpful to pensioners and to others on relatively low incomes, because they made it possible to at least eat enough to survive. Subsidized rents also made housing affordable, although it was cramped and of low quality. Now pensioners are often barely able to survive, and transition economies have large numbers of destitute and homeless people, a problem that they share with Western countries.

As indicated in chapter 6, the Soviet Union was experiencing massive budget deficits prior to its dissolution, which was closely followed by the Big Bang. Price subsidies were reduced as part of an effort to bring down the deficit. As in Poland, this "shock therapy" was a stated precondition for international assistance, especially from the International Monetary Fund (IMF). But while poorer elements in society were indeed jolted, subsidies to large state and former state firms continued. The persistent soft budget constraint in one form or another affects nearly all transition economies and has had the effect of converting what might have been one-time price increases following liberalization into ongoing inflation.

The Soft Budget Constraint and the Nature of Financial Markets in Transition Economies[10]

The soft enterprise budget constraint in transition economies takes the form of outright subsidies and tax forgiveness, but to an even greater extent of soft loans from banks and other firms, including suppliers. These loans are often repaid late, only partially, or sometimes not at all (i.e., are forgiven). To the extent that they are not repaid and become a part of government expenditure in any fiscal year, they must be financed by the government. In an environment with rudimentary capital markets and a low capacity for government to borrow by selling interest-bearing debt (bonds or treasury bills)—or for that matter to collect taxes—they end up being financed mainly via expansion of the money supply. Similarly, the governments of these countries finance subsidies and tax forgiveness largely by money supply expansion. Explicit or implicit subsidies account for most or all of their government budget deficits (in the sense of the government's borrowing requirement).

The persistent soft budget constraint causes the *macroeconomic* problem of rapid expansion of the money supply, resulting in inflation. The expenditure financed by money supply creation becomes part of incomes, and therefore raises demand through the income effect. Continuing money supply increases mean continuing increases in the money value of aggregate demand, and therefore continuing inflation when these increases are foreseen, as appears likely in a transition economy. The soft budget constraint also causes the potentially more serious *microeconomic* problem of poor allocation and use of investment funds—and therefore of other resources as well—within the state sector and over the economy as a whole. The soft budget constraint applies mainly to large and medium-sized state firms and to some former state firms that were privatized by selling or giving a majority of shares to their managements and/or employees, with control generally winding up in the hands of management. In Russia, the latter category includes several thousand firms. The rest of the economy, including private and cooperative enterprises, joint ventures, and other firms with strong foreign participation, benefits less or not at all from soft budgets.

Thus budgets are often softest for the least efficient firms, where the lion's share of domestic investment and working capital is tied up. The more efficient sector of nonstate firms with greatest growth potential remains short of credit and undercapitalized, except where sufficient foreign funds are available. The concentration of financial capital in relatively large but inefficient state and former state enterprises also helps to hold labor and other productive inputs in this sector. The shortage of capital holds back expansion of the nonstate sector, complementing and reinforcing the effect of monopolistic practices here. (The shortage of financing acts like a barrier to entry and to expansion, while the soft budget constraint is a barrier to exit, downsizing, and restructuring of inefficient firms.) Ironically, the nonstate sector is more labor intensive and more responsive to product demand, so that a given investment there creates more productive jobs than are preserved with the same outlay to state enterprises. However, the jobs in question would usually not go to the same workers—at least without retraining—nor would they be created in the same industries or locations in many instances, and they may take several months or even years to materialize.

In short, financial markets in transition economies work poorly and remain underdeveloped. Stock and bond markets lack capital and remain small, while bank loans go mainly to large state or former state enterprises, which still treat financial constraints as secondary. These loans are not made on the basis of creditworthiness, and indeed they go mainly to the least creditworthy part of the economy. Here enterprises sometimes produce well below capacity because there is now reduced demand for their products and/or because supply disruptions have increased, and they resist efforts to make them reform. As a rule, these are also "buddy" loans, honoring political ties and connections between the banks and enterprise managements left over from the Soviet-type economy (when the bank may have been a branch of the former monobank and still functions much as it did then). In these conditions, the bank also benefits from the soft budget constraint, and creative ways of subsidizing banks have emerged. These include allowing them to lend to the government (buy government bonds) at high real interest rates and to purchase equity in resource industries at low prices.

Thus credit markets are segmented. Some relatively inefficient firms have good access to loanable funds and can afford to be lax in repayment because banks perceive repayment to be effectively guaranteed by the state. Such loans are nearly free of risk to lenders, and the possibility of making them frees banks from having to learn how to assess creditworthiness and manage risk efficiently. By contrast, domestically owned private firms have low access to credit and face hard budget constraints. Banks consider that loans to this sector usually involve unacceptable risk, partly because of their low capabilities in managing risk and in assessing loan applications. Interest rates do not ration loans and are generally far too low to do this. They continue to provide no information about potential returns on investment. In many cases, they have been below the rate of inflation, so that the loans have been to some extent grants, even if paid back on time. In this way, a perverse system of credit rationing based on political and economic connections is in effect. These connections are left over from the former Soviet-type economy and help to explain why many enterprises privatized by selling or giving a majority of shares to their employees end up being controlled by their managements (which are usually minority shareholders). The web of relations that guarantees customers, supplies, and easy credit to a firm is based on personal ties, and the guarantees in question might not carry over if its managers were forced out.

In the above conditions, suppose that government wants to reduce inflation and therefore to tighten monetary policy. Such a policy cannot be implemented through higher interest rates, since these higher rates will be paid mainly by government itself under the soft budget constraint. Instead the budget constraint has to harden, implying that the flow of net subsidies and/or soft loans to firms must be reduced. However, such measures are bound to affect the viability of some enterprises and the ability of others to continue paying wages and salaries at previous real levels. In order to survive while cutting back employee earnings as little as possible, the firms in question begin to delay payment of their bills. For their suppliers, accounts receivable begin to rise as a percentage of sales, forcing them to delay payment of their own obligations.

The result of a tightening of monetary policy is therefore a mushrooming of interenterprise debt. It becomes common to delay payment of bills, and accounts receivable pile up. Suppliers are then lending to their customers, replacing to some degree the soft loans from banks that have become less plentiful. A given firm will often be delinquent in paying its suppliers and also unable or unwilling to collect from its customers. Such phenomena are relatively rare in Western market economies, because failure to pay would more quickly result in a cutoff of credit and supplies. The debtor would be pursued by creditors and the law, and might eventually have to declare bankruptcy (or be restructured in such a way that management lost control of the debtor firm).

Within the state sectors of transition economies, however, debtor firms receive kinder, gentler treatment from the government, which is still reluctant to force such enterprises into bankruptcy. One might expect suppliers to cut off their late-paying customers, but often this fails to be done as well. We have seen that many firms retain management personnel from the Soviet-type economy, and personal ties within this group of old comrades are often strong. In such a milieu, it would be considered dishonorable to force a customer into bankruptcy, a holdover from anticapitalist attitudes that were nourished under socialism. Should he cut off credit and supplies, moreover, a supplier might feel that he will receive harsh treatment from government authorities that are wary of unemployment and social unrest. Finally, many suppliers may expect their own survival to be threatened should one or more major customers go bankrupt. These customers may be hard for suppliers to replace, especially if we keep in mind the nature of enterprise managements in a Soviet-type economy. Often a supplier will bail out a customer, or even a customer of a customer, at least partly to save his own skin.[11] By the same token, customers try to prevent the loss of key suppliers, although not always with success.

When interenterprise debt becomes large as a percentage of sales—as is the case in both China and Russia as of early 1996—the government is faced with a potential crisis. If it sticks to its tight money policy, the state sector may in time become nearly dysfunctional in the sense of lacking the working capital required to go on operating and paying wages and salaries. Strikes or other forms of labor disruption also become a real possibility. Since many firms are finding their accounts receivable hard to collect, some of those threatened are enterprises that would be efficient and viable in more normal times; the widespread interenterprise debt conceals differences between efficient and inefficient firms. To an extent, the problem can be dealt with through the mutual cancellation of debt, but this is not always practical and usually leaves too many firms—and the banks or bank branches that lend to them—in danger of collapse.

In the end, the government has to give in and relax its monetary policy by resuming the flow of soft loans or increasing the flow of subsidies. An example of such a relaxation occurred in Russia in February 1996, following a coal miners' strike and threats of work stoppages in other sectors. The resumption of soft money allows debtors to speed up payment of arrears to customers and employees, which reduces the ratio of accounts receivable to sales. But it also defeats the government's effort to tighten monetary policy, except within fairly narrow limits. Tightening of money and credit leads to a mushrooming of inter-enterprise debt, which is eventually monetized. As a result, the inflation and misallocation of resources previously described come to be locked into a transition economy. Inflationary money supply expansion is a legacy of the previous Soviet-type economy in that the soft budget constraint for state and former state firms is continued into transition. But it is also a legacy of the Soviet-type economy in a more basic sense. The decision to accept inflation is taken to avoid something that is considered worse—namely, a more rapid loss of jobs in these enterprises plus a demotion of their managements to unemployment or to less prestigious and lucrative employment.

Therefore, the real legacy of the Soviet-type economy is its myriad of poor investment choices—resulting in inefficient and noncompetitive enterprises—plus its creation of a managerial class highly dependent on state support for survival and ill-equipped to manage in a market economy. The low quality of management—chosen for loyalty, political correctness, and rather narrow technical skills—may be the legacy of the Soviet-type economy that takes longest to overcome. In the meantime, financial discipline within part of the economy is impossible to enforce without unacceptable loss of jobs, income, and status. The reorientation of priorities and the collapse of COMECON, have made the problem worse, especially where heavy industry is concerned. Within these enterprises, there is still a low incentive to control costs, to tailor products to user wants and needs, to improve technology, to innovate—in short, to do all the things that firms should do in an efficient market economy—because of the soft budget constraint.

Over time, it is possible to reduce the share of GDP supplied by firms subject to the soft budget constraint and to gradually harden this constraint within the sector that benefits from it. State and former state enterprises thereby receive badly needed time to adjust, but they are also under pressure to make the transition. To this can be added the carrot of opportunities to learn the business skills needed to survive in a market economy. To reduce the opposition to transition, the enterprise managers and government officials best placed to thwart reform progress will have to be given good opportunities to acquire these business skills, even though the resulting perpetuation of their elite status will be distasteful to many.

If transition succeeds, many bureaucratic positions will also disappear. In the former Soviet Union, for example, thousands of officials did little except set prices. Most of these jobs are now gone. The task of pricing has been shifted largely to the enterprises, where different principles and methods are used. But, by the same token, a number of legitimate functions of government in a market economy, notably taxation and regulation, are now done poorly or not at all in transition economies. Tax collection has been a major problem. In the Soviet-type economy, nearly all taxes were collected from large and medium-sized state firms. This eased the task of raising revenues but left the successor transition governments ill-equipped to do this, since a larger and larger share of GNP is generated outside the state sector, which itself is ill-equipped to meet tax obligations but has also become adept at avoiding them.

In order to broaden the tax base and raise adequate revenues, most taxes should now be collected from households and nonstate firms. Failure to do this efficiently has motivated the setting of tax rates that are probably too high to maximize tax revenue because they lead to massive tax avoidance in most transition economies. As a result, the underground economies of these countries are now larger than ever. Ideally tax rates would be lower, and there would be less evasion. But aside from the need to design and to implement more efficient methods of collecting taxes, transition governments must also deal with built-in adverse expectations. Based on past experience, their citizens believe that, if they make money and report it to the state, the latter will find a way to take a large part of it. Announcements of lower tax rates lack credibility, to no small extent because the rule of law is not yet established and budget deficits are so high.

Therefore, a simple lowering of tax rates to levels at which evasion would not pay would not raise more revenue until expectations changed, which would be likely to take a while. As a result the revenue shortfall continues, prolonging budget deficits and the need for inflationary financing. Inflation is a tax on holders of money balances, and these holders have learned ways of evading this tax—by exchanging their rubles or zloty or whatever for U.S. dollars or German deutsche marks or by investing them in goods or property whose value appreciates with inflation. At the start of this chapter, we said that a major argument in favor of allowing private ownership of the means of production versus maintaining strict market socialism was the need to build a network of financial intermediaries that would efficiently channel savings into productive investment. Arguably, efficient market economies have all developed such intermediaries, but transition economies are a long way from doing so. This is partly because too much capital is tied up in money-losing state or former state firms, owing to persistence of the soft budget constraint. In addition, the near absence of bankruptcy for large firms in some transforming economies, including Russia, helps to forestall the development of legal loanable funds markets. A firm often cannot put up security or collateral for a loan, since in the event of default there may be no way for a bank or other lender to seize these assets and use them to its own advantage. (This is not necessarily a problem for extralegal loanable funds suppliers, such as the Russian mafia.)

The solution, however, is not to turn back the clock by introducing enough restrictions on financial markets to make the economy socialist in the property rights sense. The problem is that these markets are already too close to what we would expect under socialism. Instead, the goal should be to press ahead with reform, gradually reducing the sector covered by the soft budget constraint and hardening budgets for firms that remain in this sector. Here there is a role for the West and for international institutions to play, not only in helping to build the human capital that an efficient market economy requires but also in providing financing to help the nonstate sector to expand. Although this sector has little access to domestic financing, its success or failure will determine the overall success or failure of transition.

Conclusion: The Current Status of Transition

As of early 1996, about a third of the world's population was living in transition economies that have been transforming themselves from Soviet-type into market economies. This is one of history's great social and economic experiments, one that has thus far been carried out peacefully, but scarcely without hardship. The privatization aspects alone dwarf anything attempted previously. In Russia, more than 15,000 large firms and 100,000 enterprises in all were privatized by the end of 1995. Over 60 percent of the industrial labor force works in these large, privatized firms. This has probably been the largest, fastest denationalization in history.[12]

On closer examination, however, such changes often turn out to be more superficial than is at first apparent, at least in the short run. Like Czechoslovakia and Slovenia, Russia relied partly on voucher privatization. Some 148 million vouchers, each with a face value of 10,000 rubles, were distributed to all Russian citizens. These vouchers could be used like cash in buying shares of former state enterprises but could not be spent (at least legally) on other types of products. They could be bought and sold, however, and a market for them quickly sprang up, with banks among the major buyers. Many individuals also bought shares of mutual or investment funds, allowing these institutions to accumulate large numbers of shares in individual firms.

Nevertheless, the Russian privatization has also allowed employees of large enterprises to buy up to 51 percent of the shares in their firms at a nominal price and to pay for half of these with their vouchers. Each individual was limited to 5 percent of the equity in any one firm initially, but many employees then sold their shares to management, and the latter has usually been able to retain control of the enterprise, even if it has owned a minority of shares.[13] In nearly all cases, this is the same management that was in charge at the end of the Soviet era. Most of these enterprises have done little to restructure or to change their methods of operation. A real change in behavior may not occur until there is a transfer of control to outside investors, which has so far happened in only a relatively small number of cases. Many large state and former state enterprises are now combined into associations, reproducing to a degree the old ministerial groupings of the Soviet-type economy. Russia also lacks the multitude of small and medium-sized firms that account for most of the innovation and much of the competitive pressure on large firms in the West. Many of the smaller and midsized firms that have been privatized were effectively sold to their former directors at attractive prices. These enterprises are also operating much as in the old system.

In agriculture, large collective farms are still in place in Russia, supported by central and local government authorities. By law, any member wishing to leave a collective farm to go into private farming can withdraw his or her share of land for this purpose. However, less than 10 percent of the land is owned by individual peasants, who are hampered by government restrictions, as well as by resistance of local officials and collective farm managements, as indicated earlier in this chapter. They have also found it nearly impossible to obtain the equipment and working capital necessary to set up individual farms. At the same time, a serious decrease in food production has taken place since 1991. By contrast, in China the land is still owned legally by the state, but decollectivization has long since taken place, and there is an active market in land use rights. Total agricultural output approximately doubled between 1978, the last prereform year, and 1995.

More generally, transition has led to coexistence of two economic systems within nearly every transforming economy. The reformed system consists of the portion of the nonstate sector that no longer benefits from the soft budget constraint. Broadly speaking, there are three kinds of firms here: large former state firms with little or no foreign investment, small firms that are owned domestically, and foreign-invested firms. The unreformed system comprises mainly state and former state enterprises, as well as collective farms, that continue to benefit from the soft budget constraint. Here the main change from the Soviet-type economy is that the state no longer manages production and interenterprise exchange to the same extent as before. Increasingly, the unreformed sector has consisted of firms that were privatized by handing over their assets to their managements and other employees. Often this has resulted in little or no actual behavioral change, except that management is sometimes able to strip the firm of its assets.

Therefore, while the Big Bang countries, Russia and Poland, are well ahead of China and Hungary in percentages of large state firms privatized, this is because the latter two have made less use of privatization via the turning of enterprises over to their employees (although China is now carrying out such a process). In changing enterprise behavior, China and Hungary are ahead of Russia and of most transition economies, even though the former pair deliberately chose gradual approaches to reform. Moreover, Russia still has a state bureaucracy at least as large as that of the former Soviet Union, with twice Russia's population, although the market economy functions of regulation and taxation are performed poorly when they are performed at all.

Within the unreformed sector, firms resist making the changes that transition requires, and they are often helped in this by government agencies. Thus they try to preserve prereform management structures within the enterprise, as well as the historical networks of relations among suppliers, customers, bank branches, and public officials. One enterprise in this sector will often lend money to a customer—or even to a company further downstream—in an effort to ensure its own survival. One reward for such holding actions would be a political backlash against reform, leading to a slowing down or even a reversal of the transition process. Given the widespread pain caused by the transformation in Europe, such backlashes are not only possible, but to an extent have already occurred.

In some countries—China, Vietnam, Poland, Hungary, the Czech Republic, Slovenia, and the Baltic states—the reform now appears to be irreversible, except possibly as a result of foreign intervention. In others—Russia, Ukraine, Belarus, Bulgaria, and Romania, among others—irreversibility is not yet assured. Although a return to the former Soviet-type economy is unlikely, we could continue to see larger state-supported and unreformed sectors than in the first group, in the sense that such firms account for a larger share of GNP. Given the priority claim of this sector on resources and its need for protection, we would also expect a less robust growth of the nonstate sector that is subject to hard budget constraints. Such economies are likely to remain further than the first group from the market economies of Western Europe and North America for a number of years.

Nearly all transitions have led to inflation rates well above levels now deemed acceptable in the West, and most appear to have increased inequality, as well as made this more open.[14] In China, reform mainly benefited the rural areas in its early stages, owing to decollectivization and increased prices of farm produce, but subsequent reform measures have partly restored the former advantage of the cities.[15] While GNP growth in China and Vietnam has been healthy and even close to "miracle" levels, growing inequality in Europe has been sharpened by falling real GNP per capita. Official statistics have overstated these decreases. Under the Soviet-type economy, firms often had an incentive to over-report production in order to collect rewards for meeting production-related targets. In the new system, high tax rates give an incentive to under-report production in order to escape taxes. Nevertheless, it is clear that income and output fell sharply, especially from 1990 to 1993, although consumer goods production declined much less than output of heavy industry, which contributed little to overall living standards. A favorable sign is that several of these economies had apparently reached bottom and rebounded by early 1996. Poland and the former East Germany showed the highest growth rates over 1994–95, although the latter benefits enormously from West German assistance.

Let sector A be the unreformed sector of state and former state firms, as well as collective farms, that continues to benefit from the soft budget constraint. Let sector B be the largely marketized sector of a transition economy. Then progress in transition can be measured by the share of gross domestic or gross national product generated in sector B, as well as by the growth of real per capita GNP in the economy as a whole and other overall measures, such as inflation, unemployment, and inequality. An important milestone is reached when over half of GNP is generated in sector B. Such a threshold has now been crossed by several European transition economies, including Poland, Hungary, the Czech Republic,

Estonia, and Slovenia. China is again well ahead of these countries, with less than one-third of her GNP accounted for by sector A. To date, reform progress in China has been built on her initial decollectivization, followed by an explosive expansion of the mainly small and labor-intensive rural enterprise sector. This supplies over 30 percent of her exports and accounts for much foreign investment, as well as a greater employment than state industry. In addition, China has been more successful than most European transition economies in attracting foreign investment.[16]

Aside from the shortage of market economy skills, at least three factors have been holding back the expansion of sector B to varying degrees in all transition economies. First, financial markets are underdeveloped and loanable funds markets are segmented, with most bank loans going to sector A. Sector B is under-capitalized and short of financing for investment and working capital. Because subsidies that mainly benefit sector A (partly in the form of soft loans) are paid for in large measure with increases in the money supply, nearly all transition economies have high rates of inflation. Inflation has persisted well beyond the initial price jumps that occurred when prices were first freed. Pressures to expand money and credit, as an alternative to greater decreases in output and employment in sector A, have prevented these economies from tightening monetary policy in any way that is effective. Efforts to tighten cause an expansion of interenterprise debt, much of which is monetized sooner or later.

The second factor is the appearance or persistence of monopoly power, which is used to restrict supply and keep prices high. In Russia, and to a degree in other transition economies, organized crime is involved in creating and maintaining monopoly cartels, but even in China local Communist Party and government officials often promote geographical segmentation of markets and thus local or regional concentrations of market power. A monopolistic economy is closer to the old Soviet-type system than is an economy built on workably competitive markets. In Russia, the Big Bang approach probably worsened the problem, because prices were freed before the legal and institutional foundations or the skill requirements of a market economy were available. Organized crime then supplied much of the missing property rights creation and enforcement.

The third factor is the external environment, together with the reorientation of priorities that accompanied reform. Eastern and Central European economies were hurt both by the worldwide recession of the early 1990s and by the collapse of COMECON and the resulting loss of the former Soviet Union as an export market. This raised the prices that they had to pay for energy. Moreover, exports to the Soviet Union consisted in no small measure of manufactured goods of modest quality for which substitute markets could either not be found on short notice or which could be sold (often in developing countries) only at a loss. Here Western powers were less than helpful, since their restrictive trade practices prevented transition economies from increasing exports of food, textiles, coal, and steel. In particular, the European Economic Community (EEC) continued to protect its powerful vested interests in these areas.[17]

The desire to join the EEC as soon as possible was a major reason for adopting the Big Bang in Poland, which wanted to complete its transition quickly. At least for Poland, Hungary, and the Czech Republic, eventual EEC membership now seems assured, but it is doubtful that the Big Bang speeded up the transition in Poland or the Czech Republic. By helping to cause a political and social backlash in Poland, it may have done the reverse. Moreover, among European transition economies, it is Hungary that has benefited the most from foreign investment. By the end of 1995, she had captured as much direct investment as all the other smaller Central and Eastern European countries combined, and more than Russia, which has fourteen times her population.

By now lights are dimly visible at the ends of several transition tunnels. With luck, many of these economies will eventually achieve day-to-day efficiency levels characteristic of Western Europe. A positive sign all along has been the willingness of would-be entrepreneurs to step forward and assume the risks of doing business in their fledgling market economies. Forty years or more of Communist propaganda did not destroy the spirit of entrepreneurship, and these individuals persevere despite restrictions and red tape, threats and outright murder, demands for bribes and protection payments, and so on. Recently an expatriate visitor returning to his native Ukraine after many years of absence marveled at the persistence of such people in the face of all manner of discouragement. "The road to a free economy is long and hard," he said, "and I don't know if we shall ever arrive. But we have at least to try."

Notes

1. This point has been made by Vito Tanzi, among others. See Vito Tanzi, "Financial Markets and Public Finance in the Transformation Process," International Monetary Fund Working Paper no. WP/92/29, April 1992.

2. Ibid., p. 1.

3. See Shafiqul Islam and Michael Mandelbaum, eds., *Making Markets* (New York: Council on Foreign Relations Press, 1993), especially the papers by Islam, Mandelbaum, and Jeffrey Sachs. See as well David Lipton and Jeffrey Sachs, "Creating a Market Economy in Eastern Europe: The Case of Poland," *Brookings Papers on Economic Activity,* no. 1, 1990. The "Big Bang" was imposed on several East European countries (Poland in particular) by their desire for early entrance into the European Economic Community. As a result, they wanted to shorten their transitions as much as possible, although one could argue, as in the text that follows, that the Big Bang probably did not have this effect. (In any event, Poland will most likely join along with the Czech Republic and Hungary, which followed a more gradual approach to transition.) Two discussions of the sequencing of reforms are Hans Genberg, "On the Sequencing of Reforms in Eastern Europe," International Monetary Fund Working Paper no. WP/91/13, and Stanley Fisher and Alan Gelb, "The Process of Socialist Economic Transformation," *Journal of Economic Perspectives,* Fall 1991.

4. This will allow us to isolate the basic impact of different elasticities of supply response. We note that SS and $S'S'$ in Figure 7.1 are not, strictly speaking, supply curves in the usual sense, because the rules and incentives facing producers are likely to change

when prices are freed. We also note that demand curves relate quantities demanded to prices buyers are willing to pay. These are called "demand prices" in the text. They are generally higher than actual prices in a shortage economy. When prices are freed, demand prices and actual prices converge.

5. A completely inelastic or vertical supply response would lead to no change in the demand price. We must also bear in mind that, in the very short run, a vertical response is more likely than over a longer time horizon—which allows movement of resources into production of goods in greatest demand. The supply response also depends on how accurately and how far in advance the effects of price liberalization are anticipated.

6. See the discussion surrounding Figure 1.2.

7. See Abram Bergson, "The Big Bang in Russia: An Overview," Harvard Institute of Economic Research Discussion Paper 1730, July 1995, p. 5. By contrast, Cochrane and Ickes indicate a 245 percent increase in consumer prices during this month. See John Cochrane and Barry Ickes, "Macroeconomics in Russia," Pennsylvania State University, Department of Economics, Working Paper no. 7-94-2, July 29, 1994. Some price controls remain, primarily on energy, transport, and apartment rentals.

8. The influence of organized crime in Russia is widely reported in the press. Regarding Poland, see Adi Schnytzer and Avi Weiss, "The Failure of Supply Response in Transition: A Market-Based Explanation," *Economic Systems,* October 1992, pp. 189–203.

9. Social safety nets in most transition economies are grossly inadequate, whether we are talking about unemployment compensation, pensions, or health benefits. They have been greatly eroded by inflation.

10. The following discussion relies in part on a series of excellent working papers from the Penn State Economics department. These include Cochrane and Ickes, op. cit., as well as Barry Ickes and Randi Ryterman, "Roadblock to Economic Reform: Inter-enterprise Debt and the Transition to Markets," Working Paper no. 2-93-1, February 22, 1993, and Barry Ickes, "Stabilization and Privatization in Russia: An Attempt at Perspective," Working Paper no. 8-94-2, August 1994. See as well Peter Bofinger, "The Experience With Monetary Policy in an Environment With Strong Microeconomic Distortions," *Economic Systems,* October 1992, pp. 247–268, and Michael Bruno, "Stabilization and Reforms in Eastern Europe," International Monetary Fund, Working Paper WP/92/30, May 1992.

11. See Bofinger, op. cit., and Ickes and Ryterman, op. cit., as well as Barry Ickes and Randi Ryterman, "From Enterprise to Firm: Notes for a Theory of the Enterprise in Transition," Pennsylvania State University, Department of Economics, Working Paper no. 10-93-7, July 27, 1993. To see that history is repeating itself, read Laura D'Andrea-Tyson, "Liquidity Crises in the Yugoslav Economy: An Alternative to Bankruptcy?" *Soviet Studies,* April 1977. Tyson describes the growth of interenterprise credit in the face of efforts to tighten monetary policy in the Yugoslavia of the 1970s.

12. Ickes, op. cit., suggests that this is the case.

13. Regarding voucher privatization in Russia, see Bergson, op. cit., pp. 9–10, and Ickes, op. cit., pp. 14–18.

14. Regarding inflation, see Table 3.2. Inequality is more difficult to measure, especially in a Soviet-type economy, where it takes the form of differential access to goods and services. Therefore, the widespread complaints about growing inequality in transition economies are probably based in part on inequality becoming more overt. But a much larger fraction of the population of nearly every European transition economy is below the poverty line than previously, and the revival of Communist and former Communist parties in this area appears to benefit from this, even though many former members of the *nomenklatura* elite have prospered from transition as a result of their connections. In former East Germany, this elite became on average much better off during the transition to capitalism than before, and this advantage cannot be explained by ability or human

capital. See Edward Bird, Joachim Frick, and Gert Wagner, "The Income of Socialist Elites During the Transition to Capitalism: Credible Evidence from Longitudinal East German Data," University of Rochester, W. Allen Wallis Institute of Political Economy, Working Paper no. 6, September 1995.

15. See J. C. H. Chai and K. B. Chai, "Economic Reforms and Inequality in China," University of Queensland, Department of Economics, Discussion Paper no. 141, February 1994.

16. See J. H. Chai, "Transition to Market Economy: The Chinese Experience," University of Queensland, Department of Economics, Discussion Paper no. 133, October 1993. Chai points out that China benefited from a more stable political environment in attracting foreign investment within the context of her Open Door policy, which was designed in part to transfer advanced technology and modern management methods to China. Other reasons for China's success to date, according to Chai, are her more gradual approach to reform, the fact that she had already reoriented her trade away from the Soviet bloc, her successful decollectivization of agriculture and subsequent explosive growth of rural enterprises, and the soft budget constraint for sector A (large and midsized state firms), which prevented that sector from contracting and even allowed it to expand (although less rapidly than sector B). To some extent, however, the soft budget constraint has reduced the fall of output—and even more so of employment—in sector A in nearly all transition economies. Chai cautions that it would be premature to assert superiority of China's transition model, owing to the slow progress of reform within her state sector (as of 1993). As indicated in the text, however, this is a problem that is to some degree common among all transition economies.

17. See Renzo Daviddi, "From the CMEA to the 'Europe Agreements': Trade and Aid in the Relations Between the European Community and Eastern Europe," *Economic Systems,* October 1992, pp. 269–294.

Questions for Review, Discussion, Examination

1. What two basic types of reform can we identify in transition countries? Briefly describe each. Are all transition countries undergoing both types of reform? Explain briefly. Give one argument for and one argument against political reform as part of the transition process.

2. What two basic types of *economic* reform can we identify in transition economies? Briefly explain the difference between them. Which type of reform is absolutely necessary if reform is to succeed? Why are most former Soviet-type economies undertaking both types of reform?

3. What two basic dangers arise that could prevent successful economic transition? Briefly describe each. Explain why the "Big Bang" approach may heighten at least one of these dangers. (In answering, be sure to explain what the Big Bang is.)

4. As part of her gradual approach to reform, China started a Western-style MBA program plus an "open door" approach to foreign investment—in part with a view to acquiring advanced technology and modern management methods— well before most prices were liberalized. China also freed prices and abandoned formal rationing of most products gradually.

(a) How does this depart from the Big Bang approach to transition?

Give at least two arguments in favor of the Chinese approach. If you wish, give arguments in favor of the Big Bang or another alternative to the Chinese approach.

(b) One of the first steps taken by China in her reform was to decollectivize agriculture and raise prices paid to farmers. The latter led to increased subsidies to hold down prices for urban consumers, and therefore to budget deficits (which were also fed by subsidies to state firms). Nevertheless, decollectivization was crucial to reform success. Briefly explain why.

5. Economic systems in Central and Eastern Europe and the former Soviet Union are now in the process of transformation to market economies with increased private ownership of the means of production. Unfortunately, there is always a danger of backlash against reform, and also the danger that the reform will stall or even reverse.

(a) These reforms embody several interrelated changes. In order that the reforms may succeed, which changes should come first, and why? Which changes should be delayed to last, and why?

(b) Which changes constitute the heart of the reform process in the sense of being absolutely crucial to its success? Explain why success in making these changes is necessary to the overall success of the reforms.

6. Give four reasons for inelastic supply in Soviet-type economies. Which of these carry over into transition economies? What factor or factors can prolong inelastic supply? Explain briefly. Would buyers prefer an elastic or inelastic response when prices are freed? Explain briefly.

7. In the former Soviet Union, real industrial wages (a wage index divided by a consumer price index) officially rose by 79 percent between 1985 and the end of 1991. Yet the total supply of consumer goods did not increase at all. Then in January 1992, the month of Big Bang, real wages fell by over 50 percent, again according to official statistics. Explain why both the increase between 1985 and 1991 and the decrease in January 1992, as officially measured, greatly exaggerated the true changes in real wages.

8. Economies in transition usually have relatively high rates of inflation.

(a) Explain what causes this inflation and why the problem is difficult to bring under control. In what way are these inflationary pressures a legacy of the former Soviet-type economy? Discuss briefly.

(b) Sometimes economists describe inflation as a *macroeconomic* problem. Nevertheless, we might argue that inflation in former Soviet-type economies is also a symptom of a *microeconomic* problem, namely, poor allocation and use of resources. Explain this, and briefly discuss the nature of credit (or loanable funds) markets in transition economies. Are these markets efficient? Why or why not? What are the implications for future growth and prosperity?

(c) Inflation often redistributes income, making some people better off and others worse off. Identify some groups that have been made worse off in former Soviet-type economies and some that have been made better off by price changes that have accompanied the transition. Explain briefly.

9. Economies in transition have had diverse experiences regarding economic growth. In Central and Eastern Europe, however, the general rule has been slow growth at best and, more often, stagnation or decline.

(a) What aspects of the Soviet-type economy work to make growth and full employment difficult to achieve once the transition process gets under way? What problems do transition economies inherit that inhibit the growth of their financial markets and help to ensure public sector deficits, even as their social safety nets are becoming less and less adequate?

(b) What is the cost of poorly functioning capital markets in transition economies? In what ways can this lead to a backlash against reform? Explain how this makes the role of foreign capital and of international assistance more important.

(c) What events at the outset of transition (but not directly related to it) have played a major role in causing output declines?

10. Why is it difficult for a transition economy to have an independent monetary policy? What constrains monetary policy in transition economies, and what has this to do with interenterprise debt? How is this constraint a legacy of the Soviet-type economy?

11. Several economies in transition have been plagued by increases in the power and influence of organized crime. Russia, in particular, is in the midst of a crime epidemic.

(a) Some observers argue that the nature of the transition process in several countries, in combination with the nature of the former Soviet-type economy, has created an ideal environment for organized crime. Which aspects of the old system and of the transition process could be suspected of having this effect? Explain.

(b) In what basic ways does organized crime work to defeat the goals of transition and to preserve inefficiency, as well as inequality? Discuss briefly.

12. Several transition economies have used vouchers in their privatization programs. A voucher is like cash, except that it can be spent only for designated items—here shares in former state enterprises or in mutual funds that buy shares in such firms. The basic idea is that vouchers are issued free of charge to all adult citizens, who may then use them to buy into certain enterprises or mutual funds or sell them to others who will do this.

(a) What aspect of the former Soviet-type economy could be interpreted as entitling every citizen to such a voucher?

(b) Vouchers were bought and sold for prices that were below their face values. Explain why the exchange value of a voucher on such a market would be lower than its face value in buying shares. (*Hint:* What is the demand for vouchers at face value?)

(c) Most Russians sold their vouchers for their lower exchange value. Give at least one potential advantage and one potential disadvantage of this as opposed to each citizen's using his or her voucher to buy equity. (*Hint:* A major disadvantage of Russian privatization was the tendency for the former management to retain control of the enterprise. How could a market for vouchers help to defeat this tendency in some cases? What distributional problems may such a market create?)

(d) Give at least one advantage and one disadvantage of a privatization program that includes vouchers versus one that is strictly for money. (*Hint:* What will be the short-term inflationary impact of a voucher program, as opposed to one that sells state firms for money only?)

13. As of the end of 1995, Moscow was in the midst of a construction boom fueled by some of the world's highest rents for new office space. A feature of this boom has been that building starts when financing becomes available, then often has to stop when the money runs out, then resumes when more financing is found. According to the *Wall Street Journal,* two Russian entrepreneurs, partners in an office building, ran out of funds and spent nineteen days playing roulette in a Moscow casino. Finally, they had won enough to complete their project, which has since been profitable.

(a) Assuming that profit prospects were good when construction began, explain what feature of financial markets in Russia (and in transition economies more generally) accounts for the difficulties in obtaining funds and thus for the unusual source of financing, as well as for the stop-go nature of commercial construction in Moscow. Is office construction likely to be part of sector A or sector B? Why?

(b) Explosive growth in the service sector has been driving Moscow's construction boom. Why might we expect such growth following the end of the Soviet-type economy? Is it a good sign for reform? Explain.

14. In 1993 and 1994, Russia ran current account and trade surpluses (which is to say that exports exceeded imports). Briefly explain whether this is desirable and whether it is what we would expect for a transition economy. (*Hint:* If the current account of Russia's balance of payments is in surplus, what is the probable status of the capital account and therefore of net investment into and out of Russia?)

15. In late 1995, interest rates on loans in the Moscow area were running 20 to 30 percent per month. Are these rates high in the Russian context? On what key measure does this depend? In general, have interest rates been rationing loanable funds in Russia? Explain briefly.

Suggestions for Further Reading

Chapter One

Barzel, Yoram, *Economic Analysis of Property Rights* (Cambridge: Cambridge University Press, 1989).

Cheung, Steven, "A Theory of Price Control," *Journal of Law and Economics,* April 1974, pp. 53–71.

Demsetz, Harold, "Toward a Theory of Property Rights," *American Economic Review,* May 1967, pp. 347–359.

Frey, Bruno S., "Decision Making via the Price System," in Morris Bornstein, ed., *Comparative Economic Systems: Models and Cases,* 7th ed. (Burr Ridge, IL: Irwin, 1994), chap. 6, pp. 92–114.

Furubotn, E. G., and Svetozar Pejovich, "Property Rights and the Behavior of a Firm in a Socialist State," *Zeitschrift für Nationalökonomie,* nos. 3–4, 1970, pp. 431–454.

Gordon, Scott, "The Economic Theory of a Common-Property Resource: The Fishery," *Journal of Political Economy,* April 1954, pp. 124–143.

Poznanski, K. Z., "Property Rights Perspective on Evolution of Communist-Type Economies," in K. Z. Poznanski, ed., *Constructing Capitalism: The Reemergence of Civil Society and Liberal Economy in the Soviet Union and Eastern Europe* (Boulder, CO: Westview, 1992), pp. 71–95.

Seneca, J. J., and M. K. Taussig, *Environmental Economics,* 3rd ed. (Englewood Cliffs, NJ: Prentice-Hall, 1984).

Tietenberg, Thomas, *Environmental and Natural Resource Economics* (New York: HarperCollins, 1992).

Umbeck, John A., *A Theory of Property Rights with Application to the California Gold Rush* (Ames, IA: Iowa State University Press, 1981).

Walker, M. A., ed., *Rent Control: A Popular Paradox* (Vancouver, B.C.: Fraser Institute, 1975).

Chapter Two

Berliner, Joseph, "The Informal Organization of the Soviet Firm," *Quarterly Journal of Economics,* August 1952, pp. 342–365.

Berliner, Joseph, *The Innovation Decision in Soviet Industry* (Cambridge, MA: MIT Press, 1976).

Birman, Igor, "From the Achieved Level," *Soviet Studies,* April 1978, pp. 153–172.

Bornstein, Morris, "The Soviet Centrally-Planned Economy," in Morris Bornstein, ed., *Comparative Economic Systems: Models and Cases,* 7th ed. (Burr Ridge, IL: Irwin, 1994), chap. 23, pp. 411–443.

Bornstein, Morris, and D. R. Fusfeld, eds., *The Soviet Economy: A Book of Readings,* 4th ed. (Homewood, IL: Irwin, 1974).

Brzezinski, Horst, *The Shadow Economy: An Assessment of Its Operation in Free Market, Socialist, and Developing Countries* (Boulder, CO: Westview, 1990).

Campbell, Robert, *The Soviet-Type Economies: Performance and Evolution*, 3rd ed. (Boston, MA: Houghton-Mifflin, 1974).
De Bardeleben, Joan, *The Environment and Marxism-Leninism* (Boulder, CO: Westview, 1985).
Kornai, Janos, *Economics of Shortage*, 2 vols. (Amsterdam: North-Holland, 1981).
Kornai, Janos, *The Socialist System* (Princeton, NJ: Princeton University Press, 1992).
Los, Maria, ed., *The Second Economy in Marxist States* (New York: St. Martin's Press, 1990).
Nove, Alec, "The Problem of 'Success Indicators' in Soviet Industry," *Economica*, February 1958, pp. 1–13.
Nove, Alec, *The Soviet Economic System*, 3rd ed. (London: Allen and Unwin, 1986).

Chapter Three

Abegglen, J. C., and W. V. Rapp, "Japanese Managerial Behavior and 'Excessive Competition,' " *The Developing Economies*, December 1970, pp. 427–444.
Akerlof, George, "The Market for 'Lemons': Quality Uncertainty and the Market Mechanism," *Quarterly Journal of Economics*, August 1970, pp. 488–500.
Becker, Gary, "A Theory of Competition Among Pressure Groups for Political Influence," *Quarterly Journal of Economics*, August 1983, pp. 371–400.
Benjamin, Daniel, "The Use of Collateral to Enforce Debt Contracts," *Economic Inquiry*, July 1978, pp. 333–359.
Buchanan, James, and Gordon Tullock, *The Calculus of Consent* (Ann Arbor: University of Michigan Press, 1962).
Lybeck, J. A., and Magnus Henrekson, eds., *Explaining the Growth of Government* (Amsterdam: North-Holland, 1988).
Mueller, Dennis, *Public Choice II* (Cambridge: Cambridge University Press, 1989).
Myrdal, Gunnar, *Beyond the Welfare State* (New Haven, CT: Yale University Press, 1960).
Stiglitz, J. E., and Arnold Heertje, *The Economic Role of the State* (Oxford: Basil Blackwell, 1989).
Tufte, E. R., *Political Control of the Economy* (Princeton, NJ: Princeton University Press, 1978).
U.S. Congress, Joint Economic Committee, *Industrial Policy, Economic Growth, and the Competitiveness of U.S. Industry* (Washington, D.C.: U.S. Government Printing Office, 1983).
West, Edwin, "Secular Cost Changes and the Size of Government: Towards a Generalized Theory," *Journal of Public Economics*, August 1991, pp. 363–381.

Chapter Four

Carneiro, Robert L., "A Theory of the Origin of the State," *Science*, August 21, 1970, pp. 733–738.
Childe, V. Gordon, *What Happened in History* (London: Harmondsworth, 1942).
Davis, Lance E., and Douglass North, "Institutional Change and American Economic Growth: A First Step Toward a Theory of Institutional Innovation," *Journal of Economic History*, March 1970, pp. 131–149.
Domar, Evsey, "The Causes of Slavery or Serfdom: An Hypothesis," *Journal of Economic History*, March 1970, pp. 18–32.
North, Douglass, *Institutions, Institutional Change, and Economic Performance* (Cambridge: Cambridge University Press, 1990).
North, Douglass, and Robert Paul Thomas, "The First Economic Revolution," *Economic History Review*, May 1977, pp. 229–241.

North, Douglass, and Robert Paul Thomas, *The Rise of the Western World* (Cambridge: Cambridge University Press, 1973).

Reed, Clyde, "Transactions Costs and Differential Growth in Seventeenth-Century Western Europe," *Journal of Economic History,* March 1973, pp. 177–190.

Tucker, Robert C., ed., *The Marx-Engels Reader* (New York: Norton, 1972). See as well the references to Marx and Engels in notes 1 and 15.

Wittfogel, Karl, *Oriental Despotism* (New Haven, CT: Yale University Press, 1957).

Chapter Five

Atkinson, Anthony, Lee Rainwater, and Timothy Smeeding, *Income Distribution in OECD Countries* (Paris: Organization for Economic Cooperation and Development, 1995).

Friedman, Milton, "The Role of Monetary Policy," *American Economic Review,* March 1968, pp. 1–17.

Fukuyama, Francis, "Capitalism and Democracy: The Missing Link," *Journal of Democracy,* July 1992, pp. 100–110.

Fukuyama, Francis, *The End of History and the Last Man* (New York: Free Press, 1992).

Gottschalk, Peter, "Changes in Inequality of Family Income in Seven Industrialized Countries," *American Economic Review,* May 1993, pp. 136–142.

Kornai, Janos, *Anti-Equilibrium* (Amsterdam: North-Holland, 1971), esp. part 3, pp. 221–343.

Lindbeck, Assar, and D. J. Snower, "Efficiency Wages versus Insiders and Outsiders," *European Economic Review,* February–March 1987, pp. 407–416.

Olsen, Mancur, Jr., *The Logic of Collective Action* (New York: Schocken, 1968).

Schumpeter, J. A., *Capitalism, Socialism and Democracy* (New York: Harper and Row, 1950).

Tucker, Robert C., ed., *The Marx-Engels Reader* (New York: Norton, 1972). See as well the other references in note 1.

Williamson, Jeffrey, *Inequality, Poverty, and History* (Oxford: Basil Blackwell, 1991).

Chapter Six

Aslund, Anders, *Gorbachev's Struggle for Economic Reform,* 2nd ed. (Ithaca, NY: Cornell University Press, 1991).

Goldman, Marshall, *What Went Wrong With Perestroika* (New York: Norton, 1991).

Linz, Susan, "Managerial Autonomy in Soviet Firms," *Soviet Studies,* April 1988, pp. 175–195.

Lippincott, Benjamin E., ed., *On the Economic Theory of Socialism* (New York: McGraw-Hill, 1964).

Lydall, Harold, *Yugoslav Socialism: Theory and Practice* (Oxford: Clarendon, 1984).

Pryce-Jones, David, *The Strange Death of the Soviet Empire* (New York: Holt, 1995).

Schroeder, Gertrude E., "Anatomy of Gorbachev's Economic Reform," *Soviet Economy,* July–September, 1987, pp. 219–241.

Shelton, Judy, *The Coming Soviet Crash: Gorbachev's Desperate Pursuit of Credit in Western Markets* (New York: Free Press, 1989).

Stephen, Frank H., *The Economic Analysis of Producers' Cooperatives* (London: Macmillan, 1984).

Tucker, Robert C., ed., *The Marx-Engels Reader* (New York: Norton, 1972). See as well the other references in note 1.

Vanek, Jaroslav, *The Participatory Economy: An Evolutionary Hypothesis and a Strategy for Development* (Ithaca, NY: Cornell University Press, 1971).

Weitzman, Martin, *The Share Economy: Conquering Stagflation* (Cambridge, MA: Harvard University Press, 1984).

Weitzman, Martin, "Soviet Postwar Economic Growth and Capital-Labor Substitution," *American Economic Review*, September 1970, pp. 676–692.

Yunker, James A., *Socialism Revised and Modernized: The Case for Pragmatic Market Socialism* (New York: Praeger, 1992).

Chapter Seven

As the transition to a market economy is an ongoing process, the best way to keep up with developments is through the media. I would note in particular the *Financial Times* of London, the *Wall Street Journal,* the *Economist, Challenge* magazine, *Business Week,* and *Fortune* as periodicals that often report on events in transition economies. Especially worth noting are the quarterly *Reports* and annual *Profiles* of virtually every transition economy by the *Economist Intelligence Unit,* which regularly give summary accounts of developments in these countries. In addition, several economics journals now devote a good deal (or even all) of their space to transition economies. These include the three major journals in comparative economics. The Association for Comparative Economic Studies publishes the *Journal of Comparative Economics* and *Comparative Economic Studies. Economic Systems* is published by Physica-Verlag for the East European Institute in Munich. Among other journals, I would note *Europe-Asia Studies* (formerly *Soviet Studies*); *China Quarterly; The Economics of Transition;* and *Post-Soviet Affairs* (formerly *The Soviet Economy*). Finally, M. E. Sharpe (Armonk, NY) publishes several translation journals relevant to transition, including *Problems of Economic Transition, Eastern European Economics,* and *Chinese Economic Studies.*

Akyüz, Yilmaz, Andràs Köves, Detlef Kotte, and László Szamuely, eds., *Privatization in the Transition Process: Recent Experiences in Eastern Europe* (New York: United Nations Conference on Trade and Development, 1994).

Blanchard, Olivier, Kenneth Froot, and Jeffrey Sachs, eds., *The Transition in Eastern Europe,* 2 vols. (Chicago: University of Chicago Press, 1994).

Bofinger, Peter, and Richard Portes, eds., *Economic Transformation: The Next Stage in Central Europe* (Washington, DC: Brookings, 1995).

Goldman, Marshall, *Lost Opportunity: Why Economic Reforms in Russia Have Not Worked* (New York: Norton, 1994).

Hardt, John P., and Richard F. Kaufman, eds., *East-Central European Economies in Transition* (Armonk, NY: M. E. Sharpe, 1995).

Islam, Shafiqul, and Michael Mandelbaum, eds., *Making Markets: Economic Transformation in Eastern Europe and the Post-Soviet States* (New York: Council on Foreign Relations, 1993).

Jackson, Marvin, and Wouter Biesbrouck, eds., *Marketization, Restructuring, and Competition in Transition Industries of Central and Eastern Europe* (Avebury, England: Aldershot, 1995).

Kornai, Janos, *The Road to a Free Economy* (New York: Norton, 1990).

Lipton, David, and Jeffrey Sachs, "Creating a Market Economy in Eastern Europe: The Case of Poland," *Brookings Papers on Economic Activity,* no. 1, 1990, pp. 75–147.

Mayer, Colin, and Xavier Vives, eds., *Financial Intermediation in the Construction of Europe* (Cambridge: Cambridge University Press, 1993).

Oi, Jean C., *Rural China Takes Off: Incentives for Rural Industrialization* (Berkeley, CA: University of California Press, 1996).

Roland, Gérard, "The Role of Political Constraints in Transition Strategies," *Economics of Transition,* no. 1, 1994, pp. 27–41.

Welfens, P. J. J., *Economic Aspects of German Unification* (Berlin: Springer-Verlag, 1995).

Index

About the Author

Richard L. Carson received an M.A. in journalism from the University of Minnesota and a Ph.D. in economics from Indiana University. He is presently professor of economics at Carleton University in Ottawa, Canada, where he teaches courses in comparative economic systems and economic theory. He has also published extensively in these areas, including articles in the *Canadian Journal of Economics,* the *American Economic Review, Comparative Economic Studies, Economic Systems,* the *Journal of Economics and Business,* and the *Eastern Economic Journal.*